1993

1879 and All That

Essays in the Theory and History of Psychology

Critical Assessments of Contemporary Psychology
Daniel N. Robinson, Series Editor

1879 and All That

Essays in the Theory and History of Psychology

MARY HENLE

COLUMBIA UNIVERSITY PRESS
New York 1986

LIBRARY OF CONGRESS CATALOGING-IN-PUBLICATION DATA

Henle, Mary, 1913–
1879 and all that.

(Critical assessments of contemporary psychology)
Bibliography: p.
Includes index.
1. Psychology—Philosophy—History. 2. Psychology—
Philosophy. I. Title. II. Series
BF38.H46 1986   150'.9   85-22432
ISBN 0-231-06170-6
ISBN 0-231-06171-4 (pbk.)

COLUMBIA UNIVERSITY PRESS
New York   Guildford, Surrey
Copyright © 1986 Columbia University Press
All rights reserved

Printed in the United States of America

This book is Smyth-sewn.

Book designed by Ken Venezio

Contents

Preface

This volume is, in part, a book of sermons. I hasten to add—since psychologists are probably not avid readers of sermons—that it has other uses as well. To these I will come presently.

As in the case of more usual sermons, my texts will seem reasonable to most readers, although not always easy to achieve. Out of consideration for the sermon-shy reader, they are not always stated explicitly in these essays, so I will venture to state here the major ones. One of my favorite texts, which will appear in different contexts in various essays, is that it is essential to know what one is talking about. I will analyze various approaches and issues in psychology, in which conceptual muddles result from careless terminology or, equally, careless terminology reflects conceptual muddles. A related theme is that to label a problem is not to solve it. Another text that will appear repeatedly in this volume is that it is necessary to analyze an author's assumptions, often to explicate them, in order to understand him. One cannot rely only on what the author himself says. Again, I will proceed by example. And I will emphasize the text that to understand an approach or an author, one must go to the sources themselves, not be satisfied with secondary sources. Another text of my sermons is that a historical approach is often useful, even when the psychologist is engaged in empirical work. Others have been there before, perhaps showing our problem in a broader framework. Here, too, the analysis of the underlying ideas is essential. Again, I will seek to illustrate the point that a problem-solving approach to the ideas of psychology and to their history is often a fruitful one and, indeed, an adventurous one.

Since the important thing is the text, not the particular manner in which it is illustrated, I will choose as my material instances which happen to have interested me. Another writer would doubtless use different material to illustrate the same points. For example, E. B. Titchener is no longer on the best-seller list, but he is used here to illustrate a problem-solving approach to an intellectual puzzle. The story of the disappearance of one of his famous elements becomes a detective story in which motive, means, and opportunity must be discovered before the problem is solved.

An attempt is made here to arrange these essays under the texts that have been mentioned. But it must be remembered that some of these papers take more than one of these (or other) themes as their text.

This volume is intended also for other uses. It provides supplementary reading for students who are studying the history of psychology, systems of psychology, current theoretical issues, and related courses. It is meant, as well, for all psychologists interested in the analysis of theory. Its aim is to illustrate, with material that figures in the courses mentioned and with contemporary material, the analysis of the ideas of historical and contemporary figures.

Since the book is meant for use in a variety of courses in psychology, its theory and history, it introduces some of the people of psychology. They are not, of course, chosen at random, but are psychologists who have been figures in my own life and who have strongly influenced my work, thus the ones with whom I am best acquainted. Another writer would, no doubt, choose other portraits from the history of psychology, but perhaps few would hold that the study of the history of the discipline should omit sketches of some of the great scientists in the field.

The selection of the portraits of psychologists here serves an additional function: it acquaints the reader with my theoretical orientation, that of Gestalt psychology. When embarking on theoretical adventures, the reader should know the point of view of the author, as well as that of the subject of investigation.

It should now be clear that the topics chosen for discussion are meant to be illustrative only; no attempt is made to cover completely—or to remain within the confines of—any particular course. The aim of the book is to provide models of analysis, and its hope is to cultivate in the reader the taste for close and critical reading and for looking to the implicit assumptions of our predecessors, as well as of current theoretical work in psychology.

The intention of the book, in short, is to take students beyond the passive reading of the history and theories of psychology simply to learn what significant figures said. It is meant to start them on the much more adventurous path of analysis. It would show that the same kind of analysis that enhances the understanding of historical material needs to be applied to our reading of contemporary theory.

I hope that my illustrious predecessors, W. C. Sellar and R. J. Yeatman, would not consider my contribution a criticism of their great book, *1066 and All That.* They ended it with the Peace of Versailles and concluded: "History came to a ." My thesis is that history has by no means come to an end, that the history of the ideas of psychology provides material for much needed analysis and thus for the understanding, not only of what has gone before, but also of the contemporary scene.

ACKNOWLEDGMENTS

I am indeed grateful to the following for permission to use previously published material:

"On the Distinction Between the Phenomenal and the Physical Object," in J. Nicholas, *Images, Perception, and Knowledge.* Copyright © 1977 D. Reidel, Dordrecht, Holland.

"Episodes in the History of Interactionism: On Knowing What One Is Talking About," *Revista de Historia de la Psicologia.* Copyright © 1985 University of Valencia, Spain.

"Gestalt Psychology and Gestalt Therapy," and "Kurt Lewin as Metatheorist," *Journal of the History of the Behavioral Sciences* (1978). "E. B. Titchener and the Case of the Missing Element," *JHBS* (1974). "Robert M. Ogden and Gestalt Psychology in America," *JHBS* (1984).

"On Places, Labels, and Problems," *Social Research* (1982), "Of the Scholler of Nature," *SR* (1971).

"Freud's Secret Cognitive Theories," *Annals of Theoretical Psychology* (1984). Copyright © 1984 Plenum Press, New York.

"Some Problems of Eclecticism," *Psychological Review* (1957). Copyright © 1957 American Psychological Association, Washington, D.C. "Fishing for Ideas," *American Psychologist* (1975). Copyright © 1975 American Psychological Association; letter in appendix reprinted by permission of B. F. Skinner. "On the Relation Between Logic and Thinking," *PR* (1962). Copyright © 1962 American Psychological Association. "One Man Against the Nazis—Wolfgang Köhler," *AP* (1978). Copyright © 1978 American Psychological Association. "An American Adventure," *Monitor* (January 1980). Copyright © 1980 American Psychological Association.

"On Controversy and Its Resolution," in Mary Henle, Julian Jaynes, and John J. Sullivan, *Historical Conceptions of Psychology*. Copyright © 1975 Springer Publishing Company, New York.

"The Influence of Gestalt Psychology in America," *Annals of the New York Academy of Sciences* (1977).

Review of R. L. Gregory, *The Intellgent Eye*, in *Science* January 29, 1971.

"The Snail Beneath the Shell," *Abraxas* (Winter 1971), and in Stanley Rosner and L. E. Abt, eds., *Essays in Creativity*. Copyright © 1974, North River Press.

"A Tribute to Max Wertheimer: Three Stories of Three Days." *Psychological Research* (1980). Copyright © 1980 Springer-Verlag, Heidelberg.

Introduction

If we are to strike out in new directions in psychology, it is necessary to see where we now stand. In anticipation of its inclusion in a series that will point to new ways of doing psychology, this collection of essays begins to take stock of our current conceptual tangles and, more important, to invite the reader to share in this endeavor. Its method is by example. Different instances might have been chosen for analysis. All those here included are occasions to ask the reader to find his own further examples and to apply the appropriate kinds of analysis to them.

Each problem, of course, demands its own appropriate treatment. Each problem analyzed helps to clear the ground for the next one. This volume, then, asks psychologists to think more clearly, not only about the material discussed here, but also about other issues that have been ignored, or taken for granted, or only superficially examined.

The plea for conceptual analysis is not a demand to stop experimentation and other empirical work in which contemporary psychology has distinguished itself. Rather, it is a demand to base that work more solidly on clear theoretical foundations. To see where the foundations must be strengthened, we probe first for weaknesses.

PART I. ON KNOWING WHAT ONE IS TALKING ABOUT

Science is a cooperative endeavor. To cooperate, we must understand each other, and to do that it is necessary to know what we ourselves are talking about. In psychology, the task of clarification begins, not with propositions, but with words. To propositions and systems of propositions we will return.

1. On the distinction between the phenomenal and the physical object. Where shall we start? It would be tempting to begin with those most characteristic terms of the psychological lexicon, stimulus and response. The distinction between distant and proximal stimuli was clarified for psychologists by K. Koffka in 1935. Fifty years later, we ignore the distinction and, indeed, cheerfully extend the meaning of stimulus to "stimulus object," "stimulus situation," even to "stimulus person" (and that even in cases in which no person is present, merely the simulation of a person, for example by the presentation of fictitious test scores).[1] The vagueness of the term "response" has not diminished after years of discussion.

We therefore start our first analysis with the seemingly still simpler, more innocuous term "object." Beneath our careless use of this everyday term in psychology lies concealed a problem, indeed a philosophical position which is technically called naive realism. Are we prepared to adopt this position? If not, we must be careful how we use the term "object."

Psychologists are not philosophers, but they do, often inadvertently, make philosophical assumptions, and it is important to be clear about them. The discussion here is, of course, by no means the first one of naive realism, but it is written for psychologists in the context of psychological theory. Its consequences for a theory of perception are shown.

A version of this paper was first presented at a conference on images, perception, and knowledge at a philosophy of science workshop at the University of Western Ontario. When I was giving the paper, I had the impression that some members of the conference felt that I was taking something away from them by my insistence on the distinction between the phenomenal and the physical object. But what? Not objectivity, certainly, as the paper shows. Instead, this very distinction also contributes to a clarification of the problem of subjectivity/objectivity. And it frees us to think about perception.

2. Episodes in the history of interactionism. The distinction between the phenomenal and the physical object has consequences far beyond what some might consider the esoteric problems of perception. In this essay, the analysis is extended from objects to the terms "person" and "environment." Here the analysis is carried on in the context of a popular contemporary system of ideas. Because the advocates of this position have not made clear—either to themselves or to their readers—what they mean by the major terms they use, the attempt is made to do it for them. With the best will in the world, it is found to be impossible to know whether psychological or physical persons and worlds are intended. And since we do not know the meanings of the terms, even in this primitive respect, it is shown that interaction between them becomes unintelligible and that behavior itself can therefore not be understood. The failure to develop concepts for the person and the environment—the failure even to see the need for such concepts—is again traced to the naive realism of the authors. We must consider a failure a system which cannot account for its subject matter (behavior) and whose major conception (interaction) becomes incomprehensible. And this failure is derived from not making clear the meanings of the terms in question. It is no trivial matter, particularly in science, not to know what one is talking about.

How is it possible, one may well ask, for well-known and respected writers to produce such an unfortunate conceptual muddle? In psychology we tend to use everyday language and to ignore the problems that language conceals. If the author gets trapped in the sheer ordinariness of common language, the task falls to the reader to unravel its meanings. What will just do for ordinary discourse is insufficient for the purposes of a conceptual psychology.

This essay also touches on the theme (further illustrated below) of the danger of using secondary sources. The criticisms by contemporary interactionists are probably directed against an (unnamed) source whose theses, properly read in their original formulations, do not make the errors for which they are criticized.

3. Gestalt psychology and gestalt therapy. New consequences of not knowing what one is talking about are seen in connection

with Fritz Perls' gestalt therapy. Perls claims that his perspective comes from Gestalt psychology. Does it? To answer this question, a claim of ancestry is not enough. Rather it is necessary to undertake a systematic comparison of the two approaches.

What are the appropriate respects in which they may be compared? No answer can be given in advance. In this particular case, comparison is made difficult by the fact that the two approaches deal with different subject matters: Gestalt psychology is most highly developed in the fields of perception and the cognitive processes, while gestalt therapy is concerned with personality, neurosis, and psychotherapy. Still, possibilities of comparison exist, starting with intellectual traditions and philosophical assumptions and going on to more specific concepts. It is shown that if Perls claims any intellectual kinship between his own psychology and Gestalt psychology, that claim is unfounded.

The two approaches do have some terminology in common, and the next task of analysis is the comparison of these terms in the two contexts. Perls is shown to use the terms "Gestalt," "figure," "ground," "closure," and so on without any specific definitions. The terms are found to be so loosely used that they are devoid of any specific characteristics and lack any specific application. We are forced to guess what Perls means by these terms, and these guesses lead to no more than commonsense usages. Perls' uses of these terms are in sharp contrast to those of Gestalt psychology, which discusses and demonstrates the specific properties of the concepts in question. No borrowing of terms will constitute a relation between these two approaches.

It is not maintained that gestalt therapy *should* be Gestalt psychology, only that it should understand its terms and assumptions well enough to know where it stands.

If the previous essay foreshadowed the theme of the pitfalls of using secondary rather than primary sources, this one leaves us with the uneasy feeling that almost *no* sources were used in deriving gestalt therapy from Gestalt psychology. It is hard for me to see how one can depart so radically from the ancestry one claims if one has read (or remembered) the sources at all.

4. On places, labels, and problems. A final essay in this section shows additional ways in which one can deceive oneself into

thinking one knows what one is talking about. A later chapter will be concerned with the importance of the problem or the question for thinking and research. Here we see ways in which the problem itself may be concealed.

In one set of cases, a process is relocated, either in a physical space such as the brain or in a conceptual space such as a model, and we are left with the spurious feeling of understanding. But localization is only a first step, and the problem remains to be solved. In the case of placing the process in a model, it is possible to lose the problem entirely. The model needs to be examined to see whether the solution to be achieved is incorporated in it as an assumption.

A prevalent practice in psychology is to label a phenomenon or a problem, which is then considered to be understood. We speak, without thinking twice about it, of repression or of projection, and we think we know what we are talking about, even that we can explain something. But once we ask ourselves: what is this strange process? how can it occur? we realize that we have no more than a problem (or a problem area), something to be explained, not an explanation. Only if the problem is recognized as such is there any possibility of solving it and coming to an understanding of the processes involved. Examples are selected not only from psychoanalysis, but from other familiar terms of psychology, terms which turn out to be no more than labels which hide from us what we are talking about. The reader is invited to continue the search for problems beneath the terms we use. The examples given here are only a beginning. What problems lie beneath the terms "storage," "retrieval," "reinforcement," "empathy"? This brief chapter is an invitation to conceptual analysis throughout psychology.

PART II. ANALYSIS

Next the analysis proceeds to recent systems of psychology and to the relations between theories. The task becomes especially interesting when we must explicate an author's implicit assumptions in addition to considering what is explicitly asserted.

5. Freud's secret cognitive theories. Freud, as everybody knows, was concerned with problems of human personality and psycho-

pathology. It might seem strange to search his work for theories of perception and cognition, in which he was not really much interested. It would have seemed strange to me until one day I noticed, casually tossed off in another connection, an answer to the question of why we see objects outside of ourselves, not inside, although the processes responsible for perception occur inside the organism. Freud's answer was, of course, wrong, and the question was not even formulated. But I was familiar with it in other contexts and recognized it. Then, again quite by accident, I noticed—presented as something self-evident—a brief statement about creative thinking, again a theory almost certainly wrong, with which I was also familiar. It dawned on me that there were implicit cognitive theories in Freud, and a systematic search began. This paper is the result of that search. It shows a consistent, though implicit (or taken for granted), set of ideas about problems on which Freud might have done well to keep silent since he was not expert in these areas.

If a person of Freud's stature could make so many errors in fields of psychology he did not know, it seems likely that others have done the same thing. In any case, the paper shows that alongside (and beneath) a major body of theory there may lie implicit assumptions which demand explication for full understanding of the author. After this analysis, for example, I would be more than ever skeptical of attempts such as those to reconcile Freudian and, say, existential approaches. It is doubtful that any one of us can make fully explicit our implicit assumptions, but it is the task of the systematic psychologist, standing at a safe distance from his subject matter, to do this. There is clearly more theory in a major psychology than meets the eye. This analysis of Freud is again an example; much more work of this kind, with other authors, remains to be done.

6. Kurt Lewin as metatheorist. I always had trouble teaching Lewin. I appreciated him, I recognized his importance, I had done experimental work within the framework of his psychology. Somehow, my students did not share my enthusiasm. The worst moment came in a seminar mostly of economists, (who, I had always supposed, make up their own theories of motivation), who wanted

to know what psychologists had done in the area of motivation. I chose Lewin, presented him with enthusiasm, and was not allowed to finish. The economists continued to make up their own theories of motivation, and I realized that I had better do some thinking about what, exactly, Lewin was doing.

I was working at the time on the relation between logic and thinking. (See chapters 15 and 16.) It occurred to me that the relation between Lewin's formulations and the psychology of motivation and personality was in some way analogous to that between logic and thinking. Logic does not describe actual thinking, but it has at least a normative relation to it, perhaps a closer one, as I suggest below. And Lewin's theory does not describe actual personalities but certainly has a relation to them. I did not at that time know much about metatheory. But I soon learned that what I was groping for was the distinction between Lewin's metatheory and other authors' efforts toward a theory of motivation or personality.

The story has a happy ending. Lewin became easy to teach, and he made sense to my students, who shared my enthusiasm for him. I hope that the essay in this volume will make Lewin comprehensible and interesting to a larger audience.

7. Some problems of eclecticism. Attempts are here examined to avoid controversy in psychology by taking the best aspects of competing positions and combining them. This essay shows in specific contexts that such a combination can be achieved only at the expense of theory in the area of the controversy. The importance of scientific theory cannot be doubted even by the most dedicated advocates of eclecticism, who would probably agree that scientific progress is more important than a conservative harmony.

It will be noted that the examples analyzed here are taken mainly from the psychologies of the 1940s and 1950s. This is an appropriate period in which to examine eclecticism, not only because it was then popular and explicit, but also because the positions it attempted to reconcile were likewise vocal and explicit.

Today many assert that we have left behind the "Age of Schools"; some even maintain that we have achieved a paradigm or paradigms in psychology. In any case, conflict is today underplayed as compared with the earlier period. To expose today the problems of eclecticism would require much more explication of assumptions than in the essay here presented, to show that conflict still exists. Since this is probably a first venture into a neglected area, the older, more transparent examples are retained.

That eclecticism remains on the psychological scene is suggested by such names as "cognitive behaviorism" and "existential psychoanalysis." They indicate that problems of analysis of the kind undertaken here are still with us.

8. On controversy and its resolution. The problems of controversy are taken up from a different point of view in this essay. This time the nature of controversy is addressed: controversy is seen to be rooted in the nature of cognitive processes, rather than as an intrusion of irrelevant emotion into the scientific process, as some writers have maintained. It is true that passion plays a role in good scientific work, but it is passion for the work, not merely the passion of egoism, as the critics of controversy hold.

Consequences of controversy are reviewed; while these consequences are not all positive, controversy is seen, on the whole, as good for psychology. Finally, methods of resolving controversy are discussed. In psychology, controversies have mainly been superseded rather than resolved. True resolution of conflict, by recognizing the conflicting claims and setting them within a broader context, may be premature in psychology today.

PART III. ON PRIMARY SOURCES

The next set of problems taken up in this volume concerns the use of secondary sources rather than primary ones. Secondary sources are often used even where primary ones are easily accessible, and they are responsible for needless errors. "I have now read at least seventy-five percent of the sources I use in my book," a well-known psychologist told me about his third edition. What about the other 25 percent? Perhaps the reader will initially share the reactions of a group in an institute in the history of psychology in which I once taught. I discussed with them the pitfalls of reliance on secondary sources, and they were flabbergasted. How can we know enough if you take away our secondary sources? they seemed to say. There is no single answer to this question. Psychology is a vast field and nobody today can master all of it. There needs to be a division of labor. In history of psychology, where the question arose, the subject matter is indeed intimidating. But not all courses in this field need start with Aristotle; if one has not read him, it is better to start elsewhere. Since one is likely to teach the course again, there is time to increase one's scope. In any case, one does not gain in knowledge if what one knows is wrong.

9. A whisper from a ghost. This essay, which was originally written for a Festschrift for Professor B. F. Riess, indicates, first of all, that the problems arising out of the use of secondary sources are not new. Its main intention is to consider well-known and respected writers as secondary sources. In a number of instances, the secondary source is compared with the original; the material chosen is neither esoteric nor ambiguous, but concerns major theories or clear statements by the primary sources in question—all of whom were writing in English. The differences between the primary and secondary sources are large; in some cases, the one simply contradicts the other. In some cases, the problem is doubtless one of misunderstanding; in others, it is possibly a matter of showing one's hero in the best possible light; in still others, a matter of sheer carelessness.

I have chosen only the best secondary sources for these comparisons. If one cannot trust them, it seems to me better to do one's own reading.

10. The influence of Gestalt psychology in America. Although this paper addresses other issues as well, it is included here because a good deal of attention is devoted to misunderstandings of Gestalt psychology found in textbooks of perception. These secondary sources misrepresent Gestalt positions presumably largely because of misunderstandings and selective omission of sources. In one case, for example, the criticism is of Köhler. The last cited publication of Köhler's dates from 1944, although a number of other publications over the next twenty-five years attempt to

correct the specific misunderstandings here exhibited. In most of these cases, the issues seem settled for the authors without any notice of repeated and convincing answers to criticisms.

In the particular case of psychophysical isomorphism, misunderstandings show a curious uniformity among authors. Many writers apply the concept to color (to which it does not apply). I have not read a single account that does not use the color green as an example. Can it be that the authors are reading each other rather than the sources?[2] In any case, it would be impossible to make the statements quoted here if one had read and understood the primary sources. Again, it is shown that these secondary sources are not to be trusted. If one wants to understand Gestalt psychology—just as with the psychologies considered in the previous chapter—it is best to read the Gestalt psychologists themselves. Indeed, I know of no other way.

Aside from the problem of secondary sources, this chapter reviews briefly the history of Gestalt psychology, its reception in America, and possible contributions it can make to a psychology of the future (if only it is understood correctly).

11. Review of R. L. Gregory, *The Intelligent Eye*. In this review we see in a single context the consequences of the use of secondary sources. A number of criticisms of Gregory's theory are made. The difficulties derive in large part from his failure to understand issues raised by Gestalt psychologists; these are the now-familiar misunderstandings which must have arisen from the use of secondary sources. Nobody who has read and understood the primary sources could maintain that Gestalt psychology sees organizing principles as inherited; and other problems arise from a failure to understand issues explicitly discussed by these psychologists. Indeed, Gregory's theory, which he sees as deriving from Helmholtz's, is an example of just the kind of theory criticized by Köhler in his first general polemical article, "On Unnoticed Sensations and Errors of Judgment" (1913). Another issue, now familiar to the reader, arises in connection with Gregory's book: the problem of naive realism reemerges (although not here referred to by name) in the interchangeable use of physiological (physical) and phenomenal terms.

It is interesting to note that this review is now more relevant to

the perceptual scene than when it was written. Unconscious inferences are coming back into fashion in perceptual theory.

PART IV. ON HISTORY AS PROBLEM SOLVING

In the preceding section and the one on knowing what one is
talking about, illustrations are provided of how *not* to do historical and theoretical work in psychology. Part IV offers an example
of one way of doing such work. It sees history as problem solving,
in this case as detective work.

Learning the history of psychology is too often a matter of learning what the textbooks say. In part III we have seen that the
textbooks are not always to be relied upon; it often takes a considerable amount of knowledge and sophistication to know which
textbooks are reliable in which areas. In the following essay we
see a much more active and interesting way of learning history;
we take as our model the detective solving a case.

12. E. B. Titchener and the case of the missing element. Titchener's original system contained the traditional three classes of
elements: sensations, images, and feelings. Then feelings suddenly disappeared. In the case of disappearances, it is standard
practice to establish the time the missing person was last seen,
and in this case, too, various sources are used to determine the
approximate time of the disappearance. The question "Who dun-
nit?" never arose in Titchener's laboratory; it was always Titchener himself. But the question of motive is examined in some
detail, and means and opportunity are established. With these
questions answered, the Case of the Missing Element is considered
closed.

Titchener is not today a household word, and he was not chosen
for his standing in recent lists of most frequently cited psychologists. But he was a powerful influence on the psychology of his
time, and his influence on contemporary psychology remains,
although it is not always recognized. Still, another example of
this approach to history might have been chosen. Indeed, the
essay on Freud's secret cognitive theories might have been placed
in this section, since it, too, is a piece of detective work: it in-

volves the sifting through of many clues and the explication of the implicit to identify the cognitive theories.

The case of Titchener and the missing element appealed to me because it is a classic detective story, it is a self-contained story, at the same time being central to the theory, and because it was possible to cover the entire relevant psychological literature in this case. In looking for cases in which to display his own badge, the reader might wish to seek out problems showing some of these characteristics. There are many unsolved problems in the history of psychology, and for me solving them is the most enjoyable and fruitful way of learning and writing history.

A notable example of detective work by a psychologist in a very different scholarly context is Freud's essay on "The Moses of Michelangelo."

PART V. HISTORICAL/SYSTEMATIC APPROACHES TO AN EMPIRICAL PROBLEM: THINKING

Some years ago psychologists believed that their knowledge was outdated every seven years. I have not seen a recent figure, but it would be less today. Isn't there something wrong with knowledge that is outdated every few years?

And is it true that we are advancing so rapidly in our science? If we look back farther than seven years, we find that earlier scholars knew some of the same things we do, even held some of the same theories we do. Our theories may not sound so original, but they may be more sophisticated if we consider what our predecessors had to say about problems with which we are at present concerned. Their outlook was broader than ours, even though they did not know how to control variables as we do. Even for laboratory work, we may find that a look backward is a step forward.

This thesis is illustrated in the problem area of thinking, but other areas of experimental psychology would benefit equally by a look at their history.

13. Fishing for ideas. In this essay, the essential criticisms of associationistic theories of creativity are taken from *Gulliver's*

Travels and applied, with some amplifications, to contemporary theories of the same phenomenon. The theory can be seen more clearly in its earlier, bolder version, stripped of the questionable ad hoc assumptions of later forms; but the major criticisms apply equally to earlier and later associationistic and behavioristic theories.

One interesting point is that associationistic and related theories (like so many others) do not die under criticism, but persist. Some of the considerations in the chapter on controversy and its resolution may be consulted on this matter.

Professor B. F. Skinner commented on this article when it appeared in the *American Psychologist*.[3] He correctly draws the parallel between the role of chance in associationistic theories of creativity and its role in the Darwinian theory of evolution.[4] He suggests that if I applied my criticism of association theory, with its reliance on chance, to Darwin's theory of evolution, I would have to reject the latter. This letter is included, along with my reply, because it extends the argument in interesting new directions. It raises, of course, the issue of the relation of theories of creativity to that of evolution, but also the problem of mechanism vs. vitalism, as well as the nature of evolutionary theory itself. In this connection, the issue is that of the role of chance: it may be that we have given chance too large a role in our thinking about evolution, just as I suggest that associationists have relied too much on chance to account for creative solutions.

14. The snail beneath the shell. "A well-packed question carries its answer on its back as a snail carries its shell," remarked James Stephens. The role of the question in problem solving is discussed here—an aspect ignored by the associationistic theories of the previous chapter, and largely neglected by psychologists in general. It is interesting to note that this paper could hardly have been written using contemporary psychological material. Instead, it has been necessary to seek material in writers in other fields, as well as in the ancients, to supplement the meager psychological material.

The posing of a good question is regarded as the most creative part of problem solving and of scientific work. Therefore, the properties of questions are discussed. The question sometimes begins vaguely, as a state of wonder or a feeling of uneasiness, and a process of differentiation is required before the question can be formulated. The conditions which favor the seeing of questions, as well as those which keep us from seeing them, are discussed.

Finally, some tentative suggestions are made that the processes of posing and solving problems have their analogues in the arts.[5]

15. On the relation between logic and thinking. An old tradition holds logic to be the science of thought, while more recent writers sharply separate the two disciplines. The change in point of view seems to be independent of any new discoveries about the nature of reasoning. The later writers have focused on observed errors in reasoning, facts of which their predecessors were equally aware. But the earlier tradition saw errors as evidence of disturbances of the true laws of thought, while the later view tends to reject such laws, seeing the laws of logic as irrelevant to actual thinking.

Here is a case in which a discontinuity in the history of a problem opens up an area for empirical investigation. Although there had been previous studies of the relation of logic to thinking, these considered only the performance of subjects presented with syllogisms to solve; no attempt was made to uncover the actual thinking processes of individuals. The present study departs from previous ones by attempting to discover the premises, both explicit and implicit, from which subjects actually reasoned—as distinct from those the investigator intended. The question became: If we know these premises, do errors indicate departures from logic? or are other processes involved? Although error was frequent in this research (as in previous ones), it was found that it did not necessarily indicate faulty reasoning. Some of the processes which might account for error are explored.

It will be noticed that the research reported here relies on qualitative data, self-reports by subjects who try to explain how they solved a problem. This seems to me to be an appropriate way to investigate a new problem or—as in the present case—a problem whose previous investigation seems inadequate. From such exploratory research it is possible to proceed to quantitative investigation; and a considerable literature has since grown up on the problems here given a new start.

16. Of the Scholler of Nature. This paper pushes the controversy over the relation between logic and thinking back to the time of Ramus (1555) and continues the investigation of the problem. For at least 300 years, the syllogism was regarded as the law of reason. One area in which this position became important was in the controversy over translation of scholarly works from the Latin into the vernacular. If ordinary people can reason logically, it was held, why should they not read scholarly books in their own language?

The question of whether the laws of the syllogism are rarely or frequently transgressed is further studied in this chapter. Again, every effort was made to determine the premises from which subjects actually reasoned (not those which the investigator understood). It was found that it is not enough to know the premises. In advance of inquiry, we cannot even be sure what task is undertaken by a subject. Problems which were presented to elicit deductive inferences were found in many cases to elicit inductions. This surprising finding opens up a number of other problems, and discussion shows further ramifications of the original question of the relation of logic and thinking. The methodological lesson of this and the preceding essay is clear. If you want to know whether a subject is reasoning logically, you need to know first what he is doing. Even after decades of research on this problem, cognitive exploration of the thinking of individuals is still necessary. The application of this methodological lesson, that one must know specifically what one's subjects are doing and understanding, is not, of course, restricted to work with the categorical syllogism.

PART. VI. PEOPLE

Since it is hoped that, among other uses, this volume will find its way into courses on the history of psychology, some of the great figures of psychology's recent history are introduced. There are, of course, many ways of teaching the history of psychology, but probably few such courses omit the people who made decisive contributions to that history.

Chosen for this volume are incidents in the lives of Wolfgang Köhler, Max Wertheimer, and Kurt Koffka. These great Gestalt psychologists were known to me and were important influences on my work. In a sense, then, the essays in this part introduce not only the subjects of the essays; by their selection, they tell the reader from where my orientation derives. If you want to combat or discount my point of view, it is best to know what it is. Or if you find it interesting, again know what it is. I have tried to be objective in my analyses of contemporary and recent trends in psychology; but it is difficult to write without a point of view. Different problems would be seen, different criticisms made by a writer with a different outlook on psychology. To show the need for explication of points of view has been one of the objectives of this volume; and I would be less than consistent if I did not state clearly that mine is that of Gestalt psychology.

17. One man against the Nazis—Wolfgang Köhler. This is the story of Wolfgang Köhler's courageous struggle against the Nazi authorities to try to save the Psychological Institute of the University of Berlin.

18. An American adventure. This small piece is a lighthearted account of an incident during Köhler's first visit to America. It shows another side of a complex character.

19. A tribute to Max Wertheimer: Three stories of three days. This paper was presented in observance of the centennial of Max Wertheimer's birth, April 15, 1880. It takes the form of three fables and is, perhaps, a story for Max Wertheimer as much as one about him. The first fable is Wertheimer's own, the search of a man for the meaning of freedom. Following the pattern of this fable, the next one sketches the story of Wertheimer's own lifelong search to clarify the nature of productive thinking. It draws upon his major works on this subject. Finally, in a third fable, I survey the current scene and conclude that we have still to achieve the under-

standing of productive thinking to which Wertheimer devoted so much of his scientific life.

20. Robert M. Ogden and Gestalt psychology in America. This essay tells the story of how three of the major Gestalt psychologists came to America and of the important role of Robert M. Ogden of Cornell University in bringing about these events. These psychologists were previously known to many American psychologists through their published work and through visits of Americans to Germany. Indeed, it was during Ogden's visit to Würzburg in the summer of 1909 that his friendship with Kurt Koffka began, a friendship that led to most of the events related here. In 1924, Ogden invited Koffka to spend the academic year at Cornell; the next term Wolfgang Köhler arrived at Clark University. Ogden succeeded in bringing Köhler to Cornell for a number of weeks in 1929 and was instrumental in finding a position there for Kurt Lewin in 1933–35.

The story derives largely from the Ogden-Koffka correspondence. It shows something of the characters and a good deal of the interests of the two men.

In conclusion, may I repeat: It is hoped that the next chapters will be supplied by the reader himself. Whether they are formal written chapters or simply a new attitude toward one's reading, new demands on one's thinking, is a matter for each reader to decide. Psychology has been generous in providing concepts and theories for explication and analysis; there is much systematic work to be done. The sequel to this volume lies in the minds of its readers.

1879 and All That

Essays in the Theory and History of Psychology

Part I

On Knowing What One Is Talking About

Chapter 1

On the Distinction Between the Phenomenal and the Physical Object

My assignment is to discuss the distinction between the phenomenal and the physical object. The failure to make this distinction is the doctrine of naive realism, a position that is as persistent as it is wrong. I shall start with Bertrand Russell's statement of the case against naive realism: "Naive realism leads to physics, and physics, if true, shows that naive realism is false. Therefore naive realism, if true, is false; therefore it is false" (1940:15).

By this remark I assume that Russell means that the identification of the perceptual world with the physical world led to the investigation of this physical world. The apparent objectivity of percepts invited scientific study of the world of objects. But then optics showed that the physical object is lost in the chain of events that leads to the perception of an object. From the physical object, whose existence nobody challenges, are reflected light beams of varying frequencies and intensities; these reach the eye from different directions. The important point is that the light beams are independent of one another. Thus an array of independent beams reaches the eye. While the phenomenal object is a unity, the corresponding optic array is an arrangement of independent beams. This discovery meant that it is impossible to identify the physical with the phenomenal object—that would be to identify an arrangement with a unity, an aggregate with an organization.

Some of the light beams, as we know, stimulate receptors in the retina, and from here on up to the cerebral cortex, interactions take place which produce the unity, the organization, corresponding to the phenomenal object. But the percept is the end product of a series of events which only *starts* with the physical object.

Now it must be admitted that in private life each of us is a naive realist—until the identification of phenomenal and physical object is called into question, as in a discussion such as this one. And yet this sturdy philosophy begs important questions of perception—most conspicuously the problem of organization, as I have just indicated. Thus it would seem to be tenable only if one takes perception for granted, as we do in everyday life. Then there is nothing against naive realism—except physics. And since our naive physics is no more sophisticated than our naive philosophy, it does not constitute a formidable objection.

Many behaviorists, especially but not exclusively the earlier behaviorists, likewise hold implicitly to a doctrine of naive realism because they take perception for granted. But for behaviorism this has the unfortunate consequence of creating an intolerable ambiguity in the definition of the key term *stimulus*. Does stimulus refer to physiological processes, for example in retinal cells—to proximal stimulation? More often it means the "stimulus object" that elicits a response; but is this object physical or phenomenal? It is impossible to tell if the two are not distinguished. But it is important to know because, regardless of the intentions of the psychologist, only if the phenomenal object is meant is it intelligible that it elicit a response.

There are other authors who do not take perception for granted—who are interested in the nature of perception—and who nevertheless fail to distinguish between phenomenal and physical object. This is the more interesting case, and I should like to look into it.

It seems to me that the motive behind naive realism in this more interesting case is the fear of subjectivity. If we make the distinction between the objects of our experience and physical objects, we acknowledge that physical objects are not directly accessible to us. Then we live each in our own world, knowing only our perceptions, cut off from the objective environment as well as from the world of others. How can we then make the observations necessary for the development of an objective science? How can we hope to confirm the observations of others if each of us is confined to his own phenomenal world? How can we understand other people? Have we not painted ourselves into the ridiculous corner of solipsism by the rejection of naive realism?

The question then comes down to that of whether the distinction between phenomenal and physical object leads to subjectivity. May I repeat that, whether we like it or not, physical and phenomenal objects *are* separated by a sequence of events in the physical world and in the nervous system in which the unified object is lost. And may I add that if the psychologist is confined to his phenomenal world, so, too, is the physicist. But the physicist, unconcerned with his epistemological predicament, proceeds to report perceptual data—pointer readings and the like—on the basis of which he constructs his science. Psychologists do not object that physics is subjective, even though it depends for its data on the phenomenal fields of observers in exactly the same way that psychology does. It would seem that, whether or not the phenomenal field is subjective, it does not prevent the development of science.

But is the phenomenal field subjective? It is time to examine some of the meanings of this elusive term. Köhler (1938:69–70; 1947:ch. 1) has pointed out that we need to distinguish between at least two meanings of subjectivity. All experiences are subjective in the sense that they depend upon processes in the physiological organism: perceptions, images, thoughts, emotions, etc., are equally subjective in this sense—and they are subjective in origin whether the physiological organism in question belongs to a physicist, a psychologist, or a layman. But it is misleading to leave the problem there. We need to recall the distinction between physical and phenomenal object—here specifically the distinction between the physiological (physical) organism and the phenomenal self. While all experiences are subjective in their *origin*, they are not all subjective in their reference. Some experiences are localized in the phenomenal self, others in objects outside this phenomenal self. My perception of that blue book, for example, depends on processes in my visual system and is in that sense subjective—in origin it is subjective. But the form and the blueness are located in the phenomenal book outside my phenomenal self and are, in that sense, objective. My interest in the contents of the volume, on the other hand, is located in my phenomenal self, and is thus subjective, although this same self is perceived as directed to events outside itself.

In short, the assertion that the distinction between physical and phenomenal object leads to subjectivity depends in part on that last refuge of naive realism, the confusion of the physical organism with the phenomenal self. Once we make the distinction, we see that neither the pointer readings of the physicist nor the behavioral observations of the psychologist are subjective; they are objective since they refer to phenomenal objects outside the (phenomenal) self.

It has, of course, to be conceded that the phenomenal field is private, even though it may contain objective as well as subjective facts. I cannot share your perceptual field; I cannot know your thoughts, and when I try to guess them, the mental contents involved are mine, not yours. The privateness of experience has been a source of embarrassment to psychologists. Various solutions have been proposed. Naive realism essentially denies that there is a problem. Methodological behaviorism advises us to confine our observations to "publicly observable behaviors of organisms." But it is obvious that, when intersubjective agreement is achieved, it is achieved by observers each of whom is reporting facts in his own private phenomenal field—the only facts accessible to him. Intersubjective agreement thus does not overcome the privacy of experience. Another solution has been in terms of increasing privacy of perception. I quote:

All observers can obtain exactly the same information about a tree if they all walk around it and get the same perspectives. Each observer gets a somewhat different set of perspectives of his own hands than any other observer gets, although there is much in common. But the perspective of one's own nose is absolutely unique and no one else can ever see it from that particular point of view. . . . The tree, the hand, the nose are increasingly private. (Gibson 1967:171)

In these examples, differences indeed exist between the perspectives of different observers and thus in the extent to which any-

one's particular description can be confirmed. These are differences in the likelihood of intersubjective agreement; but once
more, each observer remains confined to his own experience: the
phenomenal tree, hand, and nose are equally private.

In view of the inevitable privacy of experience, I prefer, with
Köhler, to make a virtue of necessity:

When the behaviorist says that the private "subjective" content of the
phenomenal world cannot interest a true scientist, this statement is
plainly contradicted by his own procedure. He actually proves that certain contents of the directly accessible world must, and can, be used as
reliable tools in his science. . . . [Perceptual] scenes are accessible to only
one person in each case? This may be true; but then, they are accessible to
at least one, while the independently existing objects in the sense of
physics, including the physical behavior of physical men and animals, are
directly accessible to *nobody*. (1966:86)

May I summarize to this point: to deny the distinction between
phenomenal and physical objects is to overlook the processes that
are responsible for perception. It is a position that arises either
from taking perception for granted or from fear of subjectivity.
Thus various meanings of subjectivity and objectivity were examined. Even the privacy of phenomenal experience is no obstacle to
the development of science; rather, the material directly accessible to the observer provides him with all the scientific data he can
obtain. There seems to be no scientific justification for failing to
distinguish between phenomenal and physical facts.

Now I would like to go farther and suggest that the identification of phenomenal and physical object actually impoverishes
our treatment of perception. A. J. Ayer has remarked:

A philosopher who thinks that he directly perceives physical objects does
not for that reason expect anything different to happen from what is
expected by one who believes that he directly perceives sense-data.
(1956:85)

For that last phrase we need, of course, to substitute a phrase like
"one who believes that he directly perceives the phenomenal
world." No philosopher directly perceives sense data. But even
though they might not expect anything different to happen, the

two philosophers are likely to discuss perception differently. If we believe that we perceive physical objects, we are likely to limit our treatment of perception as much as possible to the austere categories of physics. Then we will admit as "real" perceptual facts only such material as the physicist might use in his observations, or at any rate we are likely to favor such facts. The result will be that we will exclude Gestalt or Ehrenfels or tertiary qualities. (See Köhler 1937, 1938:78–79, 1947: ch. 6.)

Does the drooping willow look sad? Nonsense—it is only our sadness that we see projected onto the willow. Does a house look friendly? Nothing of the sort: it is our own good feeling that we see in the inanimate object. What does a house know about friendliness? Is a melody lively? a gait clumsy? a gesture menacing? Again, these are but the products of our own higher mental processes. If a meal looks inviting or a uniform forbidding—once more, these value experiences are something we ourselves add to the perceptual data.

But how does our sadness know to attach itself to the drooping willow and not to the floating dogwood? Why does our friendliness select one house rather than another as its object? Why is a melody lively even when our own state of mind is quite different? In all these instances we are overlooking the expressive characteristics of the percept itself and attributing them to properties of the self. And—within such a framework—we are ignoring the question of why a property of the self attaches itself to one particular percept and not to another. A friendly house may make us feel welcome, but it must first look friendly to do so. If the expressive character is in the percept, it is not necessary—and often not plausible—to add an explanation in terms of a projected state of mind. Rudolf Arnheim (1949) has gone far in showing the formal similarities between particular perceptions and the emotional and other characteristics they express. We perceive the sadness of the willow as truly as we perceive its yellow-green color and the shape of its flexible branches.

Once we start adding auxiliary assumptions to account for perceptual properties, we can go in a number of directions, all equally arbitrary with respect to particular percepts—unconscious inferences, influences of past experience, and so on. I would like to raise certain questions that apply to all such assumptions. How was the percept experienced the first time—before past experience or judgment or projection could act upon it? If a perception is seen as organized in a particular way the first time, without benefit of, say, past experience, why is experience needed at all to account for it? The same question has just been asked about the expressive characteristics of perception. Again, how is the experience itself (or the projection) aroused, if not by a percept already organized in a particular way? Once this organization exists, a perception can evoke all sorts of meanings and other influences of past experience; but it requires a particular organized percept to make contact with memory traces, themselves presumably after-effects of previous perceptual organizations. Again, *how* does judgment or experience or projection operate to transform our perceptions? Such questions are usually not raised, but they are crucial if these factors are to be given an explanatory role in perception. How do we know that such processes occur? By definition, we are not aware of unconscious inferences, and the other processes mentioned are likewise immune to observation. We assume their operation because the percept does not show the characteristics we expected it to show. To salvage our expectation, we thus posit an untestable process. This is not the way that science ordinarily proceeds: scientific observation usually takes precedence over the investigator's expectations. And, finally, what kind of theory requires the auxiliary assumptions of which I am speaking? I am suggesting that one kind is a theory impoverished by neglecting or minimizing those aspects of perception which do not figure in the physicist's observations. This is a sensation-based theory of perception.

And this brings us back to the distinction between phenomenal and physical object. If we distinguish clearly between the two, we are not forced to adopt these auxiliary assumptions. It is ironic to note that these assumptions are stated in terms of subjective influences, influences that refer to the self. Thus, by the failure to consider the phenomenal object in its own right, on its own terms, we are forced into subjectivity. This is the very trap which those who fail to distinguish between phenomenal and physical object seek to avoid.

Chapter 2

Episodes in the History of Interactionism: On Knowing What One Is Talking About

Interactionism has reemerged forcefully on the psychological scene, particularly in the last decade. I would like to examine some aspects of contemporary interactionism in comparison with its historical antecedents. I will not be concerned with statistical interactionism, which considers the question of how much of the variance in behavior derives from the person, how much from the environment, and how much from the interaction of person and environment. Rather, I will deal with the much more interesting conceptual questions.

Although the name was not used, interactionism probably first became important for scientific psychology with the work of Kurt Lewin in the 1930s. To the extent that they took cognizance of this work, current interactionists have criticized the earlier formulations.

Lewin's basic formula is $B = F(P,E)$: behavior is a function of the person and the environment. His theoretical work may be considered an explication of this formula: he is concerned with developing concepts for his three basic terms. Thus concepts for the person include structure and tension; for the environment the concepts of cognitive structure, valence, and force are developed. I will not review the detailed nature of these concepts; I will only say that in order to work them out, Lewin first employed the concepts of topology, then found that he needed to develop his own mathematics, which he called hodology.

Why do contemporary interactionists find fault with Lewin's formula? One prominent representative of the new development calls it a "unidirectional notion of interaction, persons and situations . . . treated as independent entities that combine to produce behavior." This critic continues: "Personal and environmental factors do not function as independent determinants, rather they determine each other."

Whoever is the appropriate target of this criticism, it is not Lewin, who states explicitly that $E = F(P)$. He adds:

The worlds in which the newborn, the one-year-old child, and the ten-year-old child live are different even in identical physical or social surroundings. This holds also for the same child when it is hungry or satiated, full of energy or fatigued. (1951:239)

Of course, the environment is not a function of the person alone, it is also a function of the physical facts present, a matter to which I will devote appropriate attention later. Thus $E = F(P, \alpha)$. In order to simplify the argument, I will omit consideration of the social and cognitive facts which also constitute the environment.

Nor is it correct to say that Lewin holds the person to be independent of the environment:

The state of the person depends upon his environment. . . . The state of the person after encouragement is different from that after discouragement . . . that in an area of sympathy or security from that in an area of tension . . . that in a democratic group atmosphere from that in an autocratic atmosphere. . . . The momentary intellectual ability of a child as measured by an intelligence test . . . is different in an atmosphere of good rapport with the examiner from what it is in one of poor rapport. (Ibid.)

Thus $P = F(E)$. Again, of course, the person is not a function of the environment alone. Lewin has given us no symbol for those more enduring or characteristic aspects of the person, but one might venture the formula $P = F(E, \psi)$.

Thus Lewin cannot be faulted for the unidirectional interactionism of which he is accused. His meaning is unmistakable: "The person and his environment . . . have to be viewed as vari-

ables which are mutually dependent upon each other" (*ibid.*).
The critic continues with another issue:

> Nor can "persons" be considered causes independent of their behavior. It
> is largely through their actions that people produce the environmental
> conditions that affect their behavior in a reciprocal fashion. The experi-
> ences generated by behavior also partly determine what a person becomes
> and can do which, in turn, affects subsequent behavior.

Once more, it is a misreading of Lewin to say that he omits
actions or the manner in which they change environmental conditions and affect the person. These are precisely the functions of
the motoric, which is represented as a boundary region between
the inner-personal regions and the environment. In Lewin's words:

> Two groups of facts stand in favor of such a representation.
>   1. Needs or other states of the inner-personal regions can influence the
> environment only by way of a bodily expression or a bodily action, that
> is, by way of a region which one can call the motor region. . . .
>   2. We find an intermediate region again when we consider the influ-
> ence in the opposite direction, namely psychological changes of the inner-
> personal region resulting from changes of the environment. This interme-
> diate region corresponds to the perceptual system. (1936:177–178)

It appears, then, that contemporary interactionism has not
arisen out of the shortcomings of the interactionism of the 1930s.
It seems likely that it arose independently, perhaps in ignorance
of the earlier work, first as an attempt to account for empirical
findings, then as a glimpse of a conceptual problem. I should like
to examine this new interactionism, concentrating on reciprocal interactionism, with frequent glances backward to Lewin's
conceptions.

Reciprocal interactionism is represented by the formula

P

B ⟷ E.

I would like to examine the meanings of its terms. For reasons of
simplicity, I will start with the term "environment."

The seemingly innocuous term "environment" has two meanings that are relevant for us. Lewin uses the expression "life space"
to include everything that exists psychologically for the individual at a given moment, everything that affects the behavior or
condition of the person at that time. It includes person and
environment. The environmental regions include "everything in
which, toward which, or away from which the person can perform locomotions" (1936:216)—that is, everything with respect to
which a person behaves. It is a *psychological* environment. It
includes, but is not limited to, the phenomenal world (1936:18).
In Lewin's example, "The little child playing in the garden behaves differently when he knows his mother is at home than when
he knows that she is out. One cannot assume that this fact is
continually in the child's consciousness" (1936:19).

Since the psychological environment includes the phenomenal
world, I will limit myself to this meaning to simplify discussion.
We recognize, however, that consciousness is insufficient as a criterion for what exists psychologically for the person (1936:18).

There is another meaning of the word "environment," what I
will call the physical world, roughly the environment studied by
the physicist. It is the world "out there," that exists independently of ourselves. This is what Lewin calls the "foreign hull" of
the life space or alien factors. The foreign hull consists of "facts
which are not subject to psychological laws but which influence
the state of the life space" (1936:216).

It is incorrect, of course, to equate the foreign hull with the
physical world. There are objective social and conceptual facts as
well which are not subject to psychological laws. A war is an
example in the social realm; it is not subject to psychological
laws, but it influences the life spaces of countless individuals. In
the conceptual realm, we may consider the logical properties of a
problem as belonging to the foreign hull; they depend on logical
relations, yet determine whether, and how, an individual will
solve a problem. If we limit our examples to perception, it will
suffice to equate alien factors to the physical world.

Thus we live in two environments, the physical and the psychological. Fortunately, the two usually show good correspondence:
perception is veridical. When the physical environment changes,

so usually does the life space. When I leave the house to go out-
doors, my phenomenal world changes along with my physical
surroundings. Where I see a bulky object before me, there is usually something corresponding in the physical world, whose presence could be detected by appropriate physical techniques. But
the two worlds are conceptually distinct, as we shall see directly.

In which environment do we behave? Behavior does not take
place in the physical environment, but rather in a psychological
environment. Koffka made the point vividly many years ago,
using as his example a German legend:

On a winter evening amidst a driving snowstorm a man on horseback
arrived at an inn, happy to have reached a shelter after hours of riding
over the snow-swept plain on which the blanket of snow had covered all
paths and landmarks. The landlord who came to the door viewed the
stranger with surprise and asked him whence he came. The man pointed
in the direction straight away from the inn, whereupon the landlord, in a
tone of awe and wonder, said: "Do you know that you have ridden across
the Lake of Constance?" At which the rider dropped stone dead at his feet.
(Koffka 1935:27–28)

Koffka makes clear that the man's behavior was a riding-over-a-
plain, not a riding-over-a-lake. "The fact that there was a frozen
lake and not ordinary solid ground did not affect his behaviour in
the slightest" (1935:28). His behavior would not have been different had he crossed a snow-covered plain. Indeed, when he discovered what he had done, he died of fright.

In the same way, Koffka asks: "Do we all live in the same town?
Yes, when we mean the geographical, no when we mean the be-
havioural 'in'" (ibid.).

Since we behave in a psychological environment, it is of the
greatest importance to use environment in its psychological meaning in discussing the interaction of person and environment. We
have seen that when Lewin uses the term "environment," he means
a psychological environment. What do contemporary interactionists mean? This is not so easy to ascertain. Let us consider
some random examples, which suggest conflicting meanings.

"Avoidance of subjectively real, but objectively unwarranted,
threats keeps behavior out of touch with existing conditions of
reinforcement." In this instance, whatever the intended status of

existing conditions of reinforcement, subjectively real threats must exist in a psychological environment. Again, "Physically aversive consequences increase responses when people believe these unpleasant outcomes signify correctness." Since there are no aversive consequences or unpleasant outcomes in the physical world, a psychological environment must again be intended despite the manner of expression. Still another example: "Composers . . . help to shape tastes by their creative efforts." Once more, tastes do not exist in the world of physics, so these composers must be acting in a psychological environment.

On the other hand, we find examples which suggest that reciprocal interactionists have in mind a physical environment. That today's interactionists frequently mean the foreign hull when they speak of environment is suggested by a recent article by Albert Bandura, a leading exponent of this position. Bandura's major thesis here is that "chance encounters play a prominent role in shaping the course of human lives" (1982:747). His examples include the chance visit of a young man to the Manson "family," an occurrence which deeply affected his subsequent life, the chance meeting of one's future spouse on the golf course or in a lecture hall, and so on. These events are clearly events in the foreign hull, which then influence the state of the life space.

I will limit myself to one other particularly telling example: "It is largely through their actions that people produce the environmental conditions that affect their behavior." What environment do people produce or change through their actions? It is clearly the physical environment, alien factors, not the psychological environment. This point is easy to see because Lewin himself was, for a time, caught in the same confusion between the two environments until Robert Leeper called it to his attention. (The same issue was raised independently by Ralph K. White and Karl Zener.)

What is the "environment" that can be influenced only by bodily expressions and bodily actions, and that can influence the needs and tension-systems of the person only through processes of perception? Obviously it is not the psychological environment. The development of a need within the person can cause a change in the valence of a remote region of the psychological environment—but not through any bodily action. . . .

Obviously, the environment Lewin is discussing . . . is the objective, geographical environment, or the foreign hull of the life space, and not the psychological environment. (Leeper 1943:116)

Leeper suggests that Lewin's argument might instead "be used for considering the motoric regions as a boundary zone between the whole life space and the *foreign hull of the life space*" (*ibid.*). Although Leeper did not advocate such a solution, Lewin (1943:iii) accepted both the criticism and the solution, thus eliminating his single confusion between the psychological and physical worlds.

If Lewin could temporarily fall into this confusion, it is easy to see how the same thing could happen to contemporary interactionists, who have been less concerned with the conceptual distinctions made by their predecessors. From the conflicting inferences that have to be drawn from the above examples of their use of the term "environment," it seems to me that present-day interactionists simply fail to distinguish between the phenomenal and physical worlds. They take the environment for granted, not considering its epistemological status.

This confusion of the phenomenal and physical worlds is called naive realism. It has been much discussed by philosophers and psychologists and is generally regarded as wrong. This is not the place for a full discussion of this position. It is perhaps enough to say that the phenomenal object is the outcome of a series of events which starts with the corresponding object in the physical world. But this physical object is lost in the process that results in perception. Independent light beams are reflected from it, and some of these reach the eye. These, I repeat, constitute an array of independent events. The unitary phenomenal object needs to be distinguished from the aggregate of independent physical events responsible for it. The phenomenal and physical worlds are by no means identical.

So far I have only discussed the meaning of "environment" in contemporary interactionism. My conclusion is that we cannot be certain what the term means until the authors escape from their naive realism.

I turn now to the meaning of "person." Lewin represents the person as "a differentiated region of the life space" (1936:216); thus it is a psychological concept. Is this also the case for present-day interactionists? Again it is hard to say. Physical characteristics seem to be included in the concept of person, for example: "People activate different environmental reactions, apart from their behavior, by their physical characteristics (e.g., size, physiognomy, race, sex, attractiveness) and socially conferred attributes, roles and status." Of course, it is not proper to call the characteristics mentioned physical; they are actually phenomenal attributes of the person, phenomenal size, perceived physiognomy, and the rest. If these are indeed meant as physical characteristics, or if the word "physical" is simply carelessly employed, we find a new application of the same naive realism that disturbed the description of the environment.

The person of today's interactionists includes expectations, for example expectations of success or failure, and perceptual and cognitive functions, among other things. It is interesting that, for Lewin, expectations do not belong to the person. Their representation includes regions of the psychological environment in the dimension of future time perspective (Lewin 1951:40). Nor does Lewin place perceptual and cognitive functions in the person; rather, they belong to the motoric, that boundary region between the psychological environment and its foreign hull.

Why the difference? It seems to me that we have returned to the problem of naive realism. Just as we must distinguish between the physical and the phenomenal object, so we must distinguish between the physical organism and the phenomenal self. (Cf. Köhler 1938:69–70; 1947: ch. 1.) All experiences depend on processes in the physical organism; they are thus subjective in origin. But they do not all refer to the phenomenal self; in that sense, in reference, they may be objective. It seems that contemporary interactionists have placed expectations in the person because they depend on processes in the physical organism. But they usually do not refer to the phenomenal self, or not exclusively to the phenomenal self; in reference they are objective. If, in writing this paper, I expect it to be completed by a particular date, that expectation belongs to me only in the sense that all my experiences do: in their dependence upon my nervous system. But functionally it refers to a relation between person and some goal region—that is, environmental region—in future time perspective. I expect to be in that particular goal region at that future time.

Cognitive functions, too, depend upon the nervous system of

the physical organism, but again that is no reason for placing them in the (phenomenal) self. Perception, rather, keeps the individual in touch with the nonpsychological world which must affect his psychological environment. That is why Lewin placed it in the motoric. If perception and other cognitive functions are placed in the person, it is from a confusion between physical organism and phenomenal self. I need not repeat the argument.

In the same way, other components of the person described by contemporary interactionists need to be examined.

In discussing the interactionists' use of person and environment, I have emphasized the issue of whether psychological or physical facts are meant. I believe that nobody will deny that it is important, especially in scholarly discourse, to know what we are talking about. But I also have another reason for this emphasis. All interactionists are concerned with the interaction of person and environment to produce behavior; the interest of the reciprocal interactionists is somewhat different, and I will return to this difference.

If there is to be any interaction, we need a common universe of discourse—a common medium—for the interacting events. Behavior cannot be derived from an interaction of the psychological person and an environment conceived in physical terms. We would be dealing with two universes of discourse, and that would be theoretically unintelligible. It is one of Lewin's great contributions to have brought person and environment into the same universe of discourse. This he did by conceiving the environment in psychological terms. Behavior, we have seen, is related to a psychological environment.

By obscuring the meanings of person and environment, so that it is impossible to know whether—or when—we are dealing with physical or with psychological facts, today's interactionists are undermining their whole enterprise. We cannot be sure that there is a single universe of discourse if we do not know to which universe the terms belong.

For the reciprocal interactionist, "behavior, other personal factors, and environmental factors all operate as interlocking determinants." This sentence is interesting because it makes behavior a personal factor. This meaning is later made explicit and is said to be for reasons of convenience. Thus the formula would become B,P ↔ E. What does it mean to make behavior a personal determinant? Again, I suspect, behavior is grouped with personal factors because it depends on processes in the physical organism. Thus we seem again to be faced with the problems of naive realism discussed earlier.

Lewin sees behavior as coordinated to a path in the environmental regions of the life space. This treatment makes behavior a relation between person and environment, as interactionism demands. Let us examine some examples of behavior given by reciprocal interactionists to see whether they, too, require relational treatment. Recall the statement cited earlier that "it is largely through their actions that people produce the environmental conditions that affect their behavior." This statement was used earlier to show that it made "environment" refer to the foreign hull of the life space, not to the environmental regions of the life space itself. Now we can see that it also places actions in the motoric. Some actions, for example social, vocational, and recreational skills, may indeed belong there. But many other specific examples of behavior are goal-directed activities, not just means by which we carry out these activities; thus they involve a relation between the person and a goal region in the psychological environment. "Issuing orders" would involve a relation between a person and some other person in the life space, presumably one in the power field of the actor. Fears and anxieties are usually directed to some object or state of affairs in the psychological environment, thus they demand relational treatment. Defensive and aggressive behaviors are related to a threat or obstacle, and their representation would have to show their relation to this environmental object. There is no point in multiplying examples. In all these cases, the origin of the behavior is, of course, the physical organism, but its reference is to an object in the psychological environment. Convenient or not, behavior needs to be distinguished from personal factors.

There is another consequence of lumping together behavior and personal factors. Traditionally, psychology has taken behavior (or behavior and experience) as its subject matter. The task has been to derive or explain or understand behavior. Koffka has used the example of anger, asserting that in the final solution it "must be intelligible as the intrinsically, not mechanically, necessary result of the interaction between a system and certain conditions of its environment" (1938:225). This formulation should please any interactionist; it applies to all behavior. But the problem gets lost if we write our formula B,P ↔ E. The older formulation of Lewin can encompass the interactions involved without losing sight of the problem. As we have seen, Lewin deals with the mutual influences of person and environment and distinguishes between behavior as motoric function and behavior as locomotion. The former relates the foreign hull to the life space, and the latter occurs in the psychological environment. And the problem remains the one that psychology has traditionally accepted: to account for behavior as a function of properties of the (psychological) person interacting with the psychological environment.

I have suggested that contemporary interactionism has first of all to clarify its terminology so that we can know what it is talking about. Then it needs to keep in sight and give special attention to the major problem of psychology. A third task remains, that of conceptualizing person and environment.

It seems to me that contemporary interactionism has failed to conceptualize its major variables. This is again, at least in part, a matter of naive realism. If, like the naive realist, we take the environment for granted, we do not develop concepts for it. If we take for granted that we experience the world as we do because that is how it is, there seems to be no reason for analysis. If we likewise take for granted what common sense means by person, not even distinguishing between organism and self, again one cannot see where concepts are needed beyond traits and other terms of our everyday vocabulary. And if behavior is no more than the man in the street means by it—issuing orders, behaving intelligently, acting aggressively, having an asthma attack—what more is there to say? The commonsense person behaves in a commonsense manner in the commonsense world.

To go beyond this commonsense view, perhaps we need to start with the formal properties of the systems constituting person and environment and only then fill in content. This is precisely the task that Kurt Lewin set for himself some fifty years or more ago.

We are frequently warned that those who do not know history are condemned to repeat it. It seems to me that the best thing that could happen to us in the part of psychology I have been discussing would be to be condemned to repeat our history. How long must we wait for this happy fate?

Chapter 3

Gestalt Psychology and Gestalt Therapy

The purpose of this paper is to try to set the historical record straight while the history in question is still in the making. It seeks to clarify the relations between gestalt therapy and Gestalt psychology, from which the therapy claims to derive.

In considering gestalt therapy, I will confine myself to the work of Fritz Perls, the finder, as he calls himself, of this therapy (Perls 1969/1971:16), with emphasis on his later books. Perls himself writes, in his introduction to the 1969 reprint of *Ego, Hunger and Aggression*, that much of the material in it is obsolete. About this first book of his he remarks in another place that he wrote it because he wanted to learn typewriting and was bored with exercises (1969/1972:39). About the next book, *Gestalt Therapy*, by Perls, Ralph E. Hefferline, and Paul Goodman (1951/n.d.), his editor states that Perls regarded it, too, as outdated (Perls 1973:ix). Perls' own comment is in reply to a student who finds its language too technical: "When did I write that book? In 1951. No, I am much more in favor now of making films and so on to bring this across, and I believe I have found a more simple language" (Perls 1969/1971:233). (In light of this statement, no objection can reasonably be made to the use of transcripts of films and of therapy

This paper was a presidential address to Division 24 at the meeting of the American Psychological Association, Chicago, September 1975.

sessions for an analysis of Perls' work.) My major sources will therefore be *Gestalt Therapy Verbatim*, *In and Out the Garbage Pail*, and *The Gestalt Approach and Eye Witness to Therapy*. *In and Out the Garbage Pail* might seem somewhat frivolous to the scholar, but Perls, in a conversation with himself, describes it as a serious scientific book (1969/1972:172), which means at the very least, I think, that he would not object to its use as a source in an analysis of his work. (It should be added that one side of the author questions the seriousness of his book.)

Now one more point about the limits of my topic. I will *not* be concerned with the merits of gestalt therapy as practice, but only with what Perls has written. And I will be concerned with it only insofar as it relates to Gestalt psychology. I will omit discussion of its relations to psychoanalysis, to existentialism, and to other systems of thought, although there is much to say about these too.

It seems fair at the outset to identify my own point of view, which is that of Gestalt psychology. I do not presume to represent my remarks as what Max Wertheimer, Wolfgang Köhler, or Kurt Koffka would have said about gestalt therapy. The only Gestalt psychologist who, to my knowledge, has written about this therapy is Rudolf Arnheim. His one-paragraph letter to *Contemporary Psychology*, of course, had no room for analysis (Arnheim 1974: 570). If the others have maintained silence, why do I now break it? I do so because there are today psychologists and students of psychology—I suspect there are many of them—who believe that gestalt therapy *is* Gestalt psychology, or, more moderately, that it is an extension of Gestalt psychology. I hope to disabuse them of this belief.

I was astonished to read the statement of Perls' biographer, Martin Shepard (1975:198), that traditional Gestaltists claim him. Certainly Arnheim does not claim him when he writes, "I can see Max Wertheimer fly into one of his magnificent rages, had he lived to see one of the more influential tracts of the therapeutic group in question dedicated to him as though he were the father of it all" (1974:570). Perls himself is at times clearer than his biographer about his relation to Gestalt psychology. "The academic Gestaltists of course never accepted me," he wrote. "I certainly was not a pure Gestaltist" (1969/1972:62). He admits not having read any of their textbooks, only some papers of Kurt Lewin, Wertheimer, and Köhler (*ibid.*). Nevertheless, he claims that his perspective comes "from a science which is neatly tucked away in our colleges; it comes from an approach called—Gestalt psychology" (1969/1972:61). He continues by saying that he admired a lot of the work of the Gestalt psychologists, "especially the early work of Kurt Lewin" (1969/1972:62).

First may I state the hard facts about his relation to Gestalt psychology. Perls tells us that he was Kurt Goldstein's assistant in Frankfurt in 1926 (1969/1972:4); he apparently also heard lectures by Adhémar Gelb (1969/1972:62). In this connection it may be pointed out that, while Goldstein did not view most of his differences with Gestalt psychology as "insurmountable discrepancies," he did not regard himself as a Gestalt psychologist but, rather, a holist or organismic psychologist.

And now the issues. Gestalt psychology arose in Germany around 1910 out of what was called the Crisis of Science. Not only science, but academic knowledge in general, was losing the confidence of more and more people, intellectuals included, because it could not deal with major human concerns, for example such problems as value or meaning, and, indeed, seemed uninterested in them. In psychology, in opposition to the traditional experimental psychology, there arose a speculative psychology whose goal was to understand rather than to explain. Let the experimental psychologists find causal laws in their narrow domain, so the argument went. The really central human issues must be dealt with outside the natural science tradition, in the tradition called *Geisteswissenschaft*—a word for which we have no contemporary English counterpart, although it is itself a translation of John Stuart Mill's expression, the mental and moral sciences.

Gestalt psychologists did not accept this split within their discipline. They believed that the shortcomings of the traditional psychology arose, not because it was scientific, but because it misconceived science. Scientific analysis, it was simply taken for granted at the time, was atomistic. The model of the traditional psychology was an atomistic, mechanistic conception of the physical sciences. Gestalt psychologists held that scientific analysis need not be atomistic. Using physical field theory as their model, they worked to develop a nonatomistic psychology within the tradition of natural science.

Here is a first issue: natural science vs. *Geisteswissenschaft*, explaining vs. understanding. Gestalt psychology is clearly an explanatory natural science. What about gestalt therapy?

Perls equally clearly supports an understanding psychology. Here are a few quotations:

In scientific explanation, you usually go around and around and never touch the heart of the matter. (1969/1971:16)

Aboutism is science, description, gossiping, avoidance of involvement, round and round the mulberry bush. (1969/1972:210)

If we explain, interpret, this might be a very interesting intellectual game, but it's a dummy activity, and a dummy activity is worse than doing nothing. If you do nothing, at least you *know* you do nothing. (1969/1971:70)

I reject any explanatoriness as being a means of intellectualizing and preventing understanding. (1969/1972:169)

This theme appears again and again in Perls' books.

It might be supposed that he is talking here about technique, about avoiding interpretations in therapy. He is, of course, *also* talking about technique, but some of these quotations go much farther. There are other indications of Perls' rejection of scientific psychology. He regards his approach as existential and asserts: "Existentialism wants to do away with concepts, and to work on the awareness principle, on phenomenology" (1969/1971:16). Again, his approach is described as "an ontic orientation where *Dasein*—the fact and means of our existence—manifests itself, understandable without explanatoriness; a way to see the world not through the bias of any concept" (1969/1972:61).

Science, of course, is conceptual.

In other connections, too, we see that Perls is operating outside the sphere of natural science. The structure of our lifescript, he says, is often called karma or fate (1973:120), by no means a scientific concept. Nor is satori (1970/1973:43), nor "mini-satori" (1973: 131). Hints of vitalism appear in his writing. For example, Perls

148, 569

identifies his "excitement" with Henri Bergson's *élan vital* (1970/ 1973:38). Again, he describes a tree whose roots grow in the direction of fertilizer and shift if the fertilizer is shifted; he comments: "We cannot possibly explain / By calling this 'mechanics'" (1969/ 1972:28). In this connection, it is interesting to recall a remark by Koffka, "I believe that the mechanist has no better friend than the vitalist" (1938:226). Perls, unable to account mechanistically for the phenomena of growth and regulation, resorts to vitalism. But science, as the Gestalt psychologists in particular have pointed out, need not be mechanistic; thus the failure of mechanism does not exclude a scientific approach.

In short, we find that Gestalt psychology is a natural science, while Perls—whether he knows it or not—stands in the tradition of *Geisteswissenschaft*. It would be interesting to know what science he has in mind when he modestly acknowledges, "The crazy Fritz Perls is becoming one of the heroes in the history of science, as someone called me at the convention, and it is happening in my lifetime" (1969/1972:265). Gestalt psychology is an explanatory science, while Perls chooses understanding psychology. The difference is so crucial that I could conclude at this point that there is no substantive relation between Gestalt psychology and gestalt therapy. Other important issues remain, however.

A related point is the anti-intellectualism that pervades gestalt therapy. "Intellect," says Perls, "is the whore of intelligence—the computer, the fitting game" (1969/1971:24). "It might sound a bit peculiar," he concedes, "that I disesteem thinking, making it just a part of role-playing" (1969/1971:37). "The intellect . . . [is] a drag on your life" 1969/1971:76). "Each time you use the question *why*, you diminish in stature. You bother yourself with false, unnecessary information" (*ibid*). I could multiply quotations. Gestalt psychologists, on the contrary, have the highest respect for disciplined thinking, one of whose finest achievements is science.

Let us now consider the mind-body problem. Gestalt psychology has formulated the hypothesis of psychophysical isomorphism, both as a position on the mind-body question and as a heuristic. Isomorphism starts from the prima facie dualism of mind and matter but hypothesizes that molar events in experience are structurally identical to the corresponding molar physiological events in the brain. This is a kind of parallelism, but more specific than mere parallelism; it is this specificity that has made isomorphism a powerful heuristic. Parallelism of any kind is, of course, a dualistic hypothesis.

How does Perls stand on this issue? He dismisses the mind-body dichotomy as a superstition (1969/1972:8) and comes out for monism: we do not *have* a body, he maintains, "we *are* a body, we *are* somebody" (1969/1971:6). "Thoughts and actions are made of the same stuff" (1973:14). Again, "If mental and physical activity are of the same order, we can observe both as manifestations of the same thing: man's being" (1973:15). On the whole, he seems to adopt a double aspect theory, though at times his formulation sounds idealistic:

Reality is nothing but
The sum of all awareness
As you experience here and now. (1969/1972:30)

"Philosophizing is a drag," Perls asserts (*ibid*). Of course it is if you do it so badly. But the present point is that, with regard to their positions on the relation of the mind and body, Gestalt psychology and gestalt therapy have nothing in common.

"*Figure/ground, unfinished situation and Gestalt* are the terms which we have borrowed from Gestalt psychology," say Perls, Hefferline, and Goodman (1951/n.d.:ix–x). It is time to examine the meanings of these terms in the two contexts.

For the meaning of *Gestalt*, I quote Köhler:

In the German language . . . the noun "*Gestalt*" has two meanings: besides the connotation of shape or form as an attribute of things, it has the meaning of a concrete entity *per se*, which has, or may have, a shape as one of its characteristics. Since Ehrenfels' time the emphasis has shifted from the Ehrenfels qualities to the facts of organization, and thus to the problem of specific entities in sensory fields. (1947:177–178)

Perls' use of the term *Gestalt* is much vaguer. His attitude toward it he describes as an article of faith (1969/1972:35). A gestalt is an essence, he says (1969/1972:63). Again, he describes it as "the irreducible phenomenon of all awareness" (1969/1972:30). Perls recognizes that a gestalt is a unit of experience, that "as soon as you break up a gestalt, it is not a gestalt any more" (1969/1971:16). But he does not go any farther into the description of its properties. Neither Perls' Gestalt Manifesto (1969/1972:243) nor his Gestalt Prayer has any relation to any known meaning of the word *Gestalt*.

A segregated entity possesses figural characteristics: shape and the substantiality of a thing by contrast with its background, which usually has no shape and is less compact. It owes its shape to the one-sided function of the contour, which ordinarily belongs to the figure, but not to the ground. There are other functional differences, too, between figure and ground. Although perceptual figures may be reversible under certain circumstances, this is not the rule.

Edgar Rubin's terms "figure" and "ground" were eagerly adopted by Perls. For example, "The dominant need of the organism, at any time, becomes the foreground figure, and the other needs recede, at least temporarily, into the background" (1973:8). It may be that needs possess the characteristics of shaped figures, but if so, this must be shown, not simply assumed. (More likely, it is the need-object organization that should be subjected to such analysis; the goal, as end, is comparable to the edge of a closed figure, as Köhler [1938:79] has pointed out.) Without any analysis, Perls seems simply to be using the distinction between figure and ground as equivalent to that between important and unimportant. While the figure *is* important in the perceptual field, it has its own specific properties that are lost in the equation. And why do you need figure-ground terminology to say that something is important?

"To change a habit involves pulling that habit out of the background again and investing energy . . . to disintegrate or to reorganize the habit" (1969/1972:66). This time Perls apparently means: focus attention on the activity usually performed automatically. I have no doubt that it is possible to conceptualize an activity sequence in Gestalt terms, but Perls has not done it—he has merely used the words. If his expression is equivalent to Rubin's distinction, this remains to be shown.

Perls asserts that ritual "makes the gestalt clearer, makes the figure stand out more sharply" (1973:29). The meaning is apparently once more that the special importance of something is being emphasized. I need not repeat my remarks about importance. But what is the figure that is made to stand out by a handshake or a toast? Perhaps the handshake emphasizes the beginning or the end of an encounter, but what is the structure of the encounter? The use of figure-ground terminology is no substitute for specifying the characteristics of a social event.

At one point Perls tells us that he is bogged down in his writing and remarks, "I would not be a Gestaltist if I could not enter the experience of being bogged down with confidence that some figure will emerge from the chaotic background" (1969/1972:37–38). What he means, it would seem, is that he is sure he will find something to say. Again, what is gained by speaking of figure? What is lost, I repeat, is the specific meaning of figure and ground. Incidentally, a chaotic background is hardly conducive to the segregation of a figure.

Perls finds it important that figure and background be easily interchangeable. "Otherwise we get a disturbance in the attention system—confusion, loss of being in touch, inability to concentrate and to get involved" (1969/1972:93). It has been pointed out earlier that in perception reversible figures are the exception. From the context it appears the Perls means that, for optimal functioning, there must be an alternation between what he calls coping and withdrawal, there must be flexibility of the personality, and the like; but what these have in common with figure and ground in the sense of Rubin and the Gestalt psychologists is never made clear.

In all these examples, and many others that might be discussed, it seems to me that the figure-ground terminology is used so loosely by Perls that it conceals problems rather than clarifies them.

Since Gestalt psychologists emphasize organization, let us turn to that problem. As Köhler puts it, organization "refers to the fact that sensory fields have in a way their own social psychology" (1947:120). That is, certain units or groups exist which are relatively segregated from their environment: certain parts of, say, the visual field belong together and are segregated from others.

Wertheimer investigated the factors that govern perceptual organization: similarity, proximity, good continuation, closure, etc.

Of Wertheimer's factors of organization, the only one in which Perls shows any interest is closure and lack of closure. The latter term he uses interchangeably with "unfinished situation"—a *technique*, not a *concept*, derived from Lewin. Let us consider some examples of unclosed gestalts as they are used in gestalt therapy.

"Our life is basically practically nothing but an infinite number of unfinished situations—incomplete gestalts." writes Perls. "No sooner have we finished one situation than another comes up" (1969/1971:15). The neurotic "individual somehow interrupts the ongoing processes of life and saddles himself with so many unfinished situations that he cannot satisfactorily get on with the process of living" (1973:23). These unfinished situations from the past compel him to repeat them in everyday life (1973:91). (Incidentally, Freud's repetition compulsion is here made a matter of unclosed gestalts without, so far as I can see, shedding any light on it.) If we find a certain plausibilty, along with a disdain for specific analysis, in the treatment of unsatisfied needs as unclosed gestalts, this plausibility is lost in further examples. In the case of one patient, Perls remarks that he was unable in one session to "achieve full closure, milk the symptom dry" (1969/1972: 139). War, with its frustrations, is apparently an incomplete gestalt; at any rate, peace is the possible closure (1969/1972:87).

Here is a final example of the many Perls provides: "We . . . have to fill in the holes in the personality to make the person whole and complete again" (1969/1971:2). I happen to believe that the phenomenal personality, like other percepts, can be conceptualized as an organized whole, though the theoretical problems involved are extraordinarily difficult and only the most primitive beginnings have been made—not, by the way, by gestalt therapists. Until we can say something specific about this organization, it does not add to our knowledge to say that "the neurotic man of our time" is an "incomplete, insipid personality with holes" (Perls 1969/1972:294).

As I have indicated, in some of these instances there is a certain vague plausibility about Perls' use of complete and incomplete situations, closed and unclosed gestalts. But vague plausibility is not enough for a theory of neurosis or therapy or personality—or of anything. It is necessary to be clear about the specific characteristics of the structure we are calling neurosis or personality, about the nature of the processes involved, and the nature of the closure demanded by that structure. Such questions are never found in the material I am considering, and we are left with a terminology so vague as to defy any specific use. A concept loosely applied to a perceived figure, to a neurotic personality, and to war does not shed any specific light on any of these phenomena. For a theory, we must also be able to say in what ways the perceived figure, the personality, and the war are different, not merely stretch the same term to include them all.

The following is a passage from Köhler on the extension of the concept of Gestalt:

The concept "Gestalt" may be applied far beyond the limits of sensory experience. According to the most general functional definition of the term, the processes of learning, of recall, of striving, of emotional attitude, of thinking, acting, and so forth, may have to be included. . . . By no means is it believed, however, that any of those larger problems can actually be solved by the application merely of general principles. On the contrary, whenever the principles seem to apply, the concrete task of research is only beginning; because we want to know in precisely what manner processes distribute and regulate themselves in all specific instances. (1947:178–179).

It is this crucial step—the working out of the Gestalt concept in connection with specific problems—that Perls has omitted.

He does have some things to say—at times, it seems, almost inadvertently—about how organization occurs, and it is interesting to compare these remarks with the formulations of the Gestalt psychologists. The conditions of organization suggest to the Gestalt psychologists what processes must be responsible for them. In accordance with the principle of isomorphism, the demonstrated relational properties of perception (and of other psychological phenomena which I will not discuss here) suggest corresponding physical interactions in the nervous system, particularly in the cerebral cortex. These interactions depend on the properties of the cortical events in relation to each other (Köhler 1940:55); and these properties, in turn, are ultimately largely a consequence of the nature of the stimulation that starts the chain of events leading to perception.

For Perls, interest, cathexis, motivation, or attention produces organization. This view appears in his first book (1947/1969:53) and is more explicit in *Gestalt Therapy*. We read, "The figure/ ground contrast . . . is . . . the work of spontaneous attention and mounting excitement" (Perls, Hefferline, and Goodman 1951/ n.d.:73). Again,"'Objects' of sight and hearing exist by interest, confrontation, discrimination, practical concern" (1951/n.d.: 372n). What would seem to be a motor theory of perception is, at times, assumed: "The eyes and fingers cooperate in drawing out- lines, so that the animal learns to see more shapes and to differen- tiate objects in his field. By outlining one differentiates experience into objects" (1951/n.d.:312). In another place Perls suggests that "we start with the impossible assumption that whatever we be- lieve we see in another person or in the world is nothing but a projection. Might be far out, but it's just unbelievable how much we project and how blind and deaf we are to what is really going on" (1969/1971:72). Although he does not hold with it completely, Perls seems to be saying that this assumption has something to it. The statement is less radical, but the meaning essentially un- changed, when he tells us that cathected objects become figure (1973:19). Once more, it is asserted that things—by which I as- sume he means phenomenal things—"come about, more or less, by man's need for security" (1970/1973:20).

It is difficult to discuss Perls' theory because we are not told on what the interest, attention, and cathexis are acting to produce percepts. It is certainly not on organized entities, since they do the organizing. Presumably, therefore, they are acting on sensory data. If this is the case, Perls' (partially implicit) theory is not only not Gestalt psychology; it is formally similar to the theories that Gestalt psychologists have criticized again and again, ever since Köhler's paper of 1913, "On Unnoticed Sensations and Errors of Judgment" (1913/1971). Indeed, Perls' theory, if it were spelled out, would seem to be very similar to those put forth by G. E. Müller and Eugenio Rignano in the 1920s, both of which were criticized by Köhler. About such theories it may be said that neither attention nor interest creates form; rather, a form must be perceived before it can be attended to or cathected. In both cases, the directional process presupposes the organization; the argument is thus circular. A similar problem arises if a motor theory is really meant: if visual organization comes from kinaesthesis, then that kinaesthetic organization remains to be explained. All the theory has succeeded in doing has been to push the problem into another sensory modality.

It is not necessary, so far as I can see, that a theory of therapy include a theory of perception. But if the author insists on such a theory, there are certain known pitfalls he would do well to avoid. If he believes that his theory is a Gestalt theory, he would be well advised to look into what the Gestalt psychologists have to say.

Gestalt psychology is most developed in perception and cognition, while gestalt therapy is concerned with personality, psychopathology, and psychotherapy. Comparison of approaches to such different areas is often difficult. Nevertheless, in the present case, additional issues invite comparison. As it happens, none of them is trivial.

Gestalt psychology has, from its inception, been interested in value. Challenging the widely held view of ethical relativism, the view that what is right and wrong changes with time and place, it has tried to understand values in terms of relations within happenings themselves. The value of an action is seen as depending on its appropriateness to the demands of the given situation. Thus, Gestalt psychologists have held that values are not arbitrarily attached to objects or actions, depending on subjective evaluation or on the individual's history of rewards and punishments. An analogy of Wertheimer's will perhaps be helpful:

Someone in adding makes seven plus seven equal fifteen. . . . And he says, I call it good because I love the number fifteen. . . . The determination of the fifteen is . . . in violation of that which is demanded by the structure of the objective situation. If I prefer the fifteen in this case . . . this is irrelevant to the fact that the fifteen is wrong. (1935:360–361)

What about Perls? In *Ego, Hunger and Aggression*, ethical relativism is simply taken for granted, and good and bad are derived from feelings of comfort and discomfort (1947/1969:59). The next book, Gestalt Therapy, describes two ingredients of moral evaluations: "(a) On the one hand, they are simply technical skills that one has learned, guesses as to what leads to success" and "(b) On the other hand, they are group-loyalties . . . : one acts in a certain way because it is the social expectation, including the expectation of one's formed personality" (Perls, Hefferline, and Goodman 1951/n.d.:424). Here values are obviously regarded as external to the events in question. They might just as well be reversed if the individual's personal history had been different or if he belonged to a different group.

The same relativism, more baldly and more cynically expressed, is to be found in Gestalt Therapy Verbatim: "The whole idea of good and bad, right and wrong, is always a matter of boundary, of which side of the fence I am on" (1969/1971:9). Perls distinguishes three kinds of philosophy: in addition to existentialism, which includes gestalt therapy, we have already encountered aboutism, encompassing science, gossiping, and other futile activities; and then there is shouldism or moralism, in which we find topdog and underdog engaged in self-torture games (1969/1971:16–18). Shoulds are internalized external controls, and they interfere with the healthy functioning of the organism (1969/1971:20).

It would be difficult to find a view of values farther from that of the Gestalt psychologists than Perls' view. The Gestalt psychologists have shown that "value-situations fall under the category of gestalt" (Köhler 1938:86). Perls has treated them without regard for this category, indeed without regard for values.

A word about truth. Apart from calling it one of the fitting games, Perls says that "by 'truth' I mean nothing but the assertion that a statement we make fits the observable reality" (1970/1973:13). This conception is precisely the one that Wertheimer has shown to be inadequate. For the same statement may, in one context, be true, in another false, in a third unintelligible. Nor does Wertheimer regard truth as a game: "Science is rooted in the will to truth. With the will to truth it stands or falls. Lower the standard even slightly and science becomes diseased at the core. Not only science, but man" (1934:135).

I have already mentioned the relation between mechanism and vitalism. Gestalt psychology has consistently rejected both. Machine theories of the nervous system have been its particular target: Gestalt psychology has emphasized free dynamics within the limits imposed by anatomical constraints. Perls, quite the contrary, refers to the organism as a machine (1969/1971:15), and to the "thinking system," as he calls it, as a computer (1970/1973:28–29).

I would now like to say a word about phenomenology as it figures in Gestalt psychology and in gestalt therapy. (I am using the term "phenomenology" as psychologists generally do, to refer to the unbiased description of the phenomenal world, not to refer to Edmund Husserl's theory of intentionality.) For Gestalt psychology, phenomenology is a first step, a propaedeutic to experimental research and to a science of functional relations that transcends phenomenology. Perls calls himself a phenomenologist (1969/1972:37); for him this method plays a different role than in Gestalt psychology. Phenomenology, he says, "is the primary and indispensable step towards knowing all there is to know" (1969/1972:69).

I have by no means exhausted my material. For example, Perls' misuse of the equilibrium concept might be discussed. His understanding of heredity and of evolution might be culled from his writings and contrasted with that of Gestalt psychology. His view of person perception, like that of object perception, could be shown to differ from that of the Gestalt psychologists. His mostly implicit conception of the thinking process might be examined, and so on.

From the material already discussed, it is not difficult to reach a conclusion. What Perls has done has been to take a few terms from Gestalt psychology, stretch their meaning beyond recognition, mix them with notions—often unclear and often incompatible—from the depth psychologies, existentialism, and common sense, and he has called the whole mixture gestalt therapy. His work has no substantive relation to scientific Gestalt psychology. To use his own language, Fritz Perls has done "his thing"; whatever it is, it is not Gestalt psychology.

Chapter 4

On Places, Labels, and Problems

"There is, in man, a remarkable tendency to be soothed and satisfied whenever a problem, instead of being solved, has merely been located somewhere," Wolfgang Köhler (1938:39) once remarked. I would add that we also tend to be tranquilized by finding a label for a phenomenon rather than solving a problem. I would like to examine some instances of these tendencies in contemporary psychology.

Köhler's remark was made in connection with Plato's treatment of values, which might be said to have been removed from the everyday world of experience and located in another, superior world, where the concept remains as little understood as before its relocation. As another example, Köhler refers to the early discoveries of cerebral localization of various mental functions:

When it had become obvious that such mental functions as speech, other movements, vision, hearing, and so on are connected with the activity of definite areas of the brain, there was as much satisfaction for a time as though the problems implied in those functions had been solved altogether. (Ibid.)

It is, of course, a great advance, he points out, to know the localization in the brain of these processes, but the functional problems remain. How, for example, is speech brought about in its neural location? The problem has been localized but not solved.

Today the same interest in localization of processes centers on lateralization. But if the left hemisphere has more to do with language, and the right with certain aspects of space perception, for example, that is interesting, but the psychological problems in these areas remain. Split-brain research may tell us a good deal about gross psychophysical correlation but not about how processes occur. *Where* is one thing, *how* another.

A common instance of localizing instead of solving or even seeing a problem is to be found in the now active investigation of deductive reasoning. Errors are common when subjects untrained in logic are asked to solve deductive problems; one frequent type of error is the illicit conversion. Subjects presented with the proposition "All A are B" often treat it as if it were "All B are A." What is to be done with this troublesome finding? Many investigators simply find a place for it. As a recent author puts it, "Conversion has been incorporated into most contemporary models of syllogistic reasoning" (Dickstein 1981:229). The following is a specific example of this tendency:

We claim here that in the comprehension of quantified relations between distinct categories, there is an automatic operation that treats inputs as symmetric, so that on hearing, for example, "All A are B," the listener automatically entertains the notion that all B are A. . . . The admittedly counterintuitive view taken here is that subjects actually reverse the subject and predicate terms in the utterance as part of the comprehension process and that this is no mere accident. (Revlin and Leirer 1980:447-448)

The authors (1980:449) add that, under certain conditions, storage of the encoded conversion is blocked; in the absence of blocking, the converted proposition is given priority over the unconverted one because it is generated later.[1] This conception of conversion is said to reflect "efforts towards symmetry," but since "symmetry" of subject and predicate ("a quasi-symmetric relation between the subject and predicate classes in a syllogism" [1980:448]) is nothing more than conversion, it changes nothing. The problem of conversion has been solved in advance by locating the "conversion operation" in the model.

Now, the problem of conversion is a very interesting one, not to be disposed of by giving it a place in a conceptual space. A number of authors have suggested that conversion is a function of the misunderstanding of the copula in the categorical syllogism. The copula seems to the naive problem solver to put subject and predicate on equal terms rather than to express a relation of class inclusion. Several attempts have been made to investigate this possibility but with conflicting results, an outcome that is perhaps not surprising in view of the differences in procedures and criteria employed. (Of these studies, the one that seems to me the clearest test of the hypothesis suggests that misunderstanding of the copula is indeed involved in conversion [Meyer 1980]—and other research suggests the same thing.)

The copula, then, does not necessarily suggest class inclusion to the subject untrained in logic. More than that, as I have indicated elsewhere (Henle 1978), it may in some cases actually mislead as to relations of superordination-subordination. In any case, the problem remains and will not be solved until it is taken out of its soothing location in a flowchart and examined.

"The unconscious" is a favorite dumping ground for what we do not know. Unknown instincts, motives, emotions, even inferences, are placed there with abandon to account for data which would otherwise be puzzling. In perception, unconscious inferences were—and still are—invoked to make data conform to a theory they apparently contradict. In the areas of personality, motivation, and psychopathology, the practice of locating functions in this territory beyond awareness is so common as to require no comment. In any case, I would like to save this dark area for the major concern of this paper, to which I now turn: the use of labels which effectively conceal problems.

Let us consider some putative unconscious processes that are so taken for granted that they have found a place in the demotic idiom. We think we know what we are talking about when we speak of repression of unbearable contents. But *how* can such a process take place? Freud drops some hints. One of them, too obscure for comment, is that in repression the death instinct is turned against the offending id impulse. More moderately, Freud suggests that the superego gives the ego the signal to repress and the ego carries out the repression. But what does the ego do? And how? By what processes can we exclude unwelcome material from consciousness? Is it, as Jung suggests, "a sort of half-conscious and half-hearted letting go of things, a dropping of hot cakes or a reviling of grapes which hang too high, or a looking the other way in order not to become conscious of one's desires"? (1938:91) Freud seems to have in mind some more drastic process, but of what it is he gives no inkling. Meantime, we continue to talk about repression, not only as if we understood it, but as if it had explanatory value.

The same kinds of problems arise in connection with projection—indeed in connection with all the defenses; again, the label has crept into our vocabulary and keeps us from seeing what interesting problems are involved. How can we fail to recognize a characteristic or impulse in ourselves but see it in another individual?[2] Psychoanalytic theory is not interested in such questions; but here the issues seem a bit less refractory than in the case of repression, and the beginnings of an analysis can be made. (For purposes of the analysis, it will be assumed that "classical" projection does indeed take place.)

How, then, might a perceived characteristic accomplish the change from being the possession of the perceiver to belonging to a perceived other? We are dealing with a problem of the perception of persons; the case is more complex than the ones usually studied since it involves simultaneously the perception of the self and that of another person.

This small step suggests that the problem as formulated above is misleading: how can we fail to recognize a characteristic in ourselves but see it in another individual? Can we be dealing with the same characteristic in the two cases? A quality will look different in the context of two different personalities. And this new statement perhaps gives us a clue. What has been labeled projection may involve at least two processes. It may, first, not be a matter of an inability to see a characteristic in ourselves but of reinterpreting what we do see. Hostility in oneself may be interpreted as forthrightness, honesty, enterprise, helpfulness, and the like. In the context of another person, this same hostility may be recognized for what it is. A second process (at least) is needed to produce the phenomena described as projection: the perceiver's special sensitivity to the characteristic in another individual. The quality must be there for projection to occur. We "do not project . . . into the blue, so to speak, where there is nothing of the sort already," says Freud (1922 18:226). It might be that some underlying tension or motivation in the perceiver is what unites the two processes suggested, making the person ready both to reinterpret an aspect of himself and to notice or exaggerate it in another individual.

The preceding discussion has not been an attempt to solve the problem of projection, which is certainly too complex for early solution. Rather, it has been an effort to remove the label and show the problem beneath.

Others have been dissatisfied with the way in which this problem of projection has been handled. I may perhaps be permitted a digression to show, in this connection, another way of getting rid of a problem—by denying that it exists.

The phenomenologist J. H. Van den Berg (1955) describes a patient whose phenomenal world has changed: the houses look old and tumbledown, the fields less colorful than before, the streets frighteningly empty. It is customary to say that it is the patient who has changed, not the world, and that the patient projects. How can this be? asks Van den Berg. How can "an abnormal state of mind, a psychical disturbance, i.e., something that is present *in* the patient and nowhere else, . . . move out of him and so closely attach itself to things . . . so become merged into things, that the patient sees the change as an unquestionable reality" (1955:16)? But there is no real mystery, he believes, only one we have created for ourselves. The problem is a pseudoproblem arising out of our Cartesian heritage of a dualism of mind and matter. "The relationship of man and world is so profound, that it is an error to separate them. . . . The world is our home, our habitat, the materialization of our subjectivity" (1955:32).

Van den Berg is thus denying the problem of projection by recourse to a metaphysical monism. But this way out does not help: however intimate the relation between the person and the world, we still consider some aspects of our experience as referring to ourselves, others as aspects of the phenomenal world. The patient sees houses as houses, not as himself; he distinguishes between his gloomy state of mind and the dilapidated condition of the dwellings he sees. So the problem remains of how our states of mind come to be reflected in our perceived world. It cannot be done away with by denying it, but perhaps analysis as a problem in perception and cognition will help to deal with it. Van den Berg's examples suggest that the analysis will have to be more complex than the simple case of the "projection" of hostility dealt with above. But seen in its proper problem area, projection in the extended sense here in question by no means eludes investigation.

One further example will be given of a defense described by psychoanalysis which conceals a problem. This is rationalization, the giving of acceptable and colorable reasons to explain actions, wishes, motives, attitudes, unacceptable to the ego. Rationalization, like projection, has crept into common usage;[3] it is accepted without any question as to how it can take place.

But is it not strange that we are able to believe what is acceptable about ourselves and to reject what is unacceptable? A century ago John Stuart Mill remarked:

We cannot believe a proposition only by wishing, or only by dreading, to believe it. The most violent inclinations to find a set of propositions true will not enable the weakest of mankind to believe them without a vestige of intellectual grounds—without any, even apparent, evidence. . . . it is a necessary condition to the triumph of the moral bias that it should first pervert the understanding. (1872: Book 5, ch. 1, sec. 3)

Mill's comments apply, it seems to me, to propositions about ourselves as well as to those about other objects and events.

The question, then, becomes: How is it possible for wish, for dread, or for bias to pervert the understanding? A simple beginning procedure is to analyze instances of rationalization for suggestions as to the processes involved in them. It is not easy, in the classics of psychoanalysis, to find analyzable examples of rationalization, partly because they are so embedded in case material as to be hard to extricate, partly, perhaps, because this defense is so taken for granted. Hartmann, using rationalization as an example, suggests that psychoanalysis may be seen as "a systematic study of self-deception and its motivations" (1964:335). Again, rationalization is often considered too superficial to merit much discussion.

Still, a few extractable instances may be found. Fenichel, for example, speaks of "rationalizing one's stubbornness as a 'fight for a good cause'" (1945:375); again, "a manic behavior may be rationalized or idealized as fulfilling some ideal purpose" (1945: 410). In both instances we find a process previously encountered in the discussion of projection: an item, here an action, is reinterpreted. Presumably most complex behavior permits a variety of interpretations, and the rationalizer has only to select one which puts his action in a good light.

In a very different tradition, G. W. Allport cites Emerson: "That which we call sin in others is experiment for us" (1937:172). Again, one meaning among several is selected for what may be dubious behavior. In my own collection of rationalizations, the same process is at work. An alcoholic, wanting to reform, switches from hard liquor to ale. Despite the fact that he consumes enormous quantities of ale, he can reason that he is no longer a drunkard, since a drunkard is one who drinks hard liquor. As another example, a lazy student reinterprets a high grade, not as indicating achievement, but as reflecting a not-very-admirable desire to enhance the ego.

Another process that could account for rationalization is a change in focus in one's view of a situation from the major determinants of the behavior in question to other aspects also present. Thus a smoker finds all sorts of reasons for not giving up the habit: she would get too fat, she would become disagreeable and her family would suffer, and the like, whereas the simple fact remains that she is unable to give up smoking. A man who does not want to marry finds undesirable qualities in every girl he meets, not focusing on the desirable ones. Or, as a nostalgic example from a simpler era, a woman who cannot tolerate change is quick to see the faults of each apartment she is shown.

Still another process that contributes to rationalization is the filling in of gaps in an incomplete (or incompletely understood) situation, for example, the adding of a premise, a process found to produce error in other kinds of thinking as well. Thus a driver justifies his none-too-courteous behavior: "Why should I yield the right of way? He wouldn't do it." Needless to say, our driver has no knowledge of what the other driver would do.

It is not appropriate, in the absence of adequate data, to push farther the analysis of rationalization. A few additional processes that might participate in this phenomenon may, however, be mentioned; they are derived from my collection of rationalizations. There is probably a vector in such cases, arising from the unacceptable motive or action, causing us *not* to look in a certain direction, not to push our understanding, not to undertake "the irksome labour of a rigorous induction," in Mill's words (1872: book 5, ch. 1, sec. 3). The motives responsible for the rationalization may influence the perception of relations; for example, the perception of means to an end, as research has shown in other connections. The motive or attitude may cause us to overlook differences, and so on. Once we lift up the label of rationalization, we see beneath it a host of problems in cognitive psychology.

It would be easy, in connection with the various depth psychologies, to continue to show problems underneath the labels employed.[4] I have chosen only the simplest examples. Instead of going farther in this direction, I will turn to a very different field, the familiar one of habit. What does habit mean psychologically? I can do no better than quote a little-known passage by Kurt Lewin, who is here concerned to show that he has not ruled out learning from his field theory, as some critics supposed:

There would be no significance, however, in dropping "habits" into the life space without applying to them the same analytical scrutiny that is applied to other processes represented by topological and vector concepts. Field theory demands a sufficiently analytical approach to *all* problems of psychology. If one uses such an approach, learning and habit take on a variety of forms, such as pattern of activities or change of such pattern, restraining forces against change, cognitive structure, fixation of valences, etc. (1943:iv)

The apparently innocuous label "habit," in other words, conceals a number of problems. Although a great deal of attention has been given to the question of how habits are formed, little interest has been shown in what habit *means* in various contexts.

Since Lewin's criticism of the use of the concept of habit was made some forty years ago, it seems appropriate to take a more current example from the same field. Modeling and observational learning have become extremely popular concepts in contemporary psychology. "Virtually all learning phenomena resulting from direct experience occur on a vicarious basis by observing other people's behavior and its consequences for them," says Bandura (1977:12). What is learned by watching a model? Children have been reported to imitate both the aggressive and prosocial bahavior of models. Here the relations involved are not very complex, and not much has to be learned that the child does not already know. It is not asking much of an observer to see that something can be achieved by aggressive or by cooperative behavior. Indeed, these are results which ten-year-olds not only give but can *predict*.

Where apparently more subtle concepts seem to be learned by observing a model, it is important to understand just *what* has been learned. For example, so-called divergent verbal responses have been found to be increased by observing a model, also the willingness to report hypotheses that the child would not ordinarily express publicly. What is learned in such cases? Certainly not creativity. Perhaps the child learns what is expected, or what is approved, under the given conditions—the great lesson of school, which children learn early and well. Surely the child does not learn divergent thinking (a concept which itself bears analysis, but which will not be considered here). What must have changed is the *product*, the performance, not the thinking *process*. It seems much more likely that we can imitate what we have understood than that we learn by imitating, by observing a model. In any case, it is essential to know *what* has been learned when we speak of observational learning. Bandura's examples suggest that he is most interested in what Lewin calls the learning of *paths* to goals. This is an important task of learning, but it does not cover "virtually all learning phenomena resulting from direct experience."

I cannot leave this discussion of the use of labels in place of solving problems without some attention to social psychology. I select the topic of similarity and interpersonal attraction. It is widely assumed that we like people who are similar to us better than those who are dissimilar, even though the empirical results have been obtained under highly artificial conditions. Thus the use of simulated others is standard methodology in this field; and similarity is usually taken as a matter of attitudes in common (often attitudes about which subjects are unlikely to have given any thought prior to the test) or scores on personality tests. So solid does the relation appear between similarity and attraction that I have seen similarity of attitudes used as an indirect measure of attraction.

What problem does this literature conceal? Quite simply, the problem of similarity. Even in the area of form perception, we know little enough about similarity, although the problem is under active investigation. For personalities, we simply have no concept of similarity, and the problem is not under investigation. One thing that is clear is that sharing more, rather than fewer, traits or other test items is not a suitable criterion for interpersonal similarity. We have already seen that a given trait functions differently in the context of different personalities. The centrality or importance of a trait can be expected to be a factor in its role in similarity, and a given trait may be of different importance in different personalities—a factor not considered, so far as I know, in this literature. For both reasons, the counting of traits in common is unlikely to give a measure of similarity. It even seems likely that traits (or other test items) are not the basis of similarity among individuals but rather *whole qualities* of personality, which have scarcely been discussed. It would appear that the label "interpersonal similarity" conceals not only the problem of the nature of similarity but also broader problems of the organization of personality itself.

I have by no means exhausted the topic of the use of labels which conceal problems (nor the earlier topic of the relocation of problems instead of solving them). But I have perhaps given enough examples to suggest that a useful occupation for psychologists might be to lift up the labels they use and to search for the problems underneath. Indeed, psychologists may not be the only social scientists who might find such an effort valuable.

The issues which have been considered here might seem to bear some relation to the logical fallacy of Begging the Question. In both cases, the question at issue is not even seen.[5]

Part II
Analysis

Chapter 5

Freud's Secret Cognitive Theories

Psychoanalysis, Freud wrote, " is accustomed to divine secret and concealed things from despised or unnoticed features, from the rubbish-heap, as it were, of our observations" (S.E. 13:222).[1] Again, he remarked, "You will be prepared . . . to work over many tons of ore which may contain but little of the valuable material you are in search of" (S.E. 20:219).

The same is true if one tries to dig out Freud's secret cognitive theories. In this respect—although by no means with respect to my assumptions—the exercise which I will undertake here may be considered a cognitive psychoanalysis of Freud. I am not sure whether the theories I will consider are theories Freud did not know he was presenting or theories he did not know were theories, or whether they are simply implicit theories. In any case, it is interesting to look at what he has to say—however obscurely—about the processes of perception, person perception, and other cognitive processes.

I think it would have been prudent for Freud—who was, after all, not much interested in these issues—in perception simply to accept the phenomenal world as given, without concerning himself with the nature of the processes involved. If he had to take a position, he might simply have accepted naive realism (which we will see that he did adopt inconsistently). This doctrine identifies the phenomenal with the physical object, and it is the view that, although it is incorrect, all of us adopt uncritically in our every-day relations with the world. In the same way, Freud might simply have accepted the fact that we perceive other people, their qualities, and their emotions, without asking what processes make it possible; similarly, he might have taken it for granted that we think, learn, forget, and so on.

It must be added that some cognitive processes are appropriately treated in commonsense terms: attention, for example (12:220), and judgment (12:221; 19:236–237). Indeed, Freud himself, speaking of people who reject portions of psychoanalysis for obscure reasons, recommends that one refrain from making judgments about matters outside the realm of one's own competence:

Some distinguished men, too, are included in this category. They, to be sure, are excused by the fact that their time and their interest belong to other things—to those things, namely, in mastering which they have achieved so much. But in that case would they not do better to suspend their judgement instead of taking sides so decisively? (22:138–139)

Too often Freud does not follow his own advice. It is interesting that a concept as important to him as that of projection is presented without any hint about how such a mysterious process might occur, and yet he has specific things to say about the nature of perception. (I should add that Freud's editors suggest that there may have been a paper on projection among the missing metapsychological papers. But judging from the prototheoretical level on which other central concepts are discussed, I would very much doubt that he would have considered the problem of how projection can occur.)

Why did Freud, knowingly or not, give us theories in the field of perception? I can suggest two answers, which may amount to the same thing. Freud, we know, was a student of Brücke, who was closely allied with the famous Helmholtz school of medicine (or, more properly, of physiology). This is the antivitalistic school which attempted to make physiology, and psychology along with it, subject to purely physical-chemical laws (see, for example, 4:xvi). Jones tells us that the young Freud wrote of Helmholtz: "He is one of my idols" (1953 1:41). Of Brücke he wrote: "Brücke . . . carried more weight with me than any one else in my whole life" (20:253).[2] Thus it is scarcely surprising that Freud should make some of the same errors that Helmholtz made.

What is surprising is that the *Standard Edition* of Freud's work contains not a single reference to Helmholtz in a scientific context with the exception of an obscure mention of Freud's defense of the Young-Helmholtz theory in a discussion with Charcot (3:13, 13 n. 2). Since Freud himself does not write about color vision, this reference is not relevant for the present paper.[3] It is easy to guess that Freud learned his Helmholtz from Brücke and from reading Helmholtz and that he simply accepted Helmholtz's theories as true.

The other answer to the question of why Freud offers theories of perception and other cognitive processes is that he never succeeded in freeing himself from the famous *Project for a Scientific Psychology* of 1895, although he seems to have forgotten it or, indeed, repudiated it. Thus, his editors tell us that "when in his old age he was presented with it afresh, he did his best to destroy it" (1:290). These same editors remark, correctly, I think, that the *Project* "contains within itself the nucleus of a great part of Freud's later psychological theories" (*ibid.*). Even if he would have liked to destroy the manuscript, he was unable to escape from the mode of thinking which clearly shows the influence of Brücke and of Helmholtz.

It would, of course, be a different matter if Helmholtz were the only authority in the field during Freud's formative years. But there were others, notably Hering. We know from Jones that Freud knew Hering, who offered him an assistantship in Prague (Jones 1953 1:222). Freud also knew at least some of Hering's work. Thus Freud's editors present Ernst Kris' suggestion that Hering may have influenced Freud in his views of the unconscious (14:205). Again, Hering is referred to in *Beyond the Pleasure Principle* in connection with his theory that the opposed processes of assimilation and dissimilation are always working in living matter; Freud invokes this theory in support of his own dualistic view of instinct (18:49). Since Freud thus knew at least some of Hering's thinking, we are probably safe in assuming that, in his views on perception, he is choosing the side of Helmholtz over the alternative of Hering.

Thus it is not surprising that Freud adopts a theory of perception based on sense data somehow worked over by higher mental processes—though if he had turned in the direction of Hering, his emphasis would have been more phenomenological. Here is an example made in passing, as something simply taken for granted: "In our efforts at making an intelligible pattern of the sense-impressions that are offered to us, we often fall into the strangest errors or even falsify the truth about the material before us" (5:499). Thus we start with sensory data, the products of stimulation, presumably of individual receptors, which must then be integrated (made into an intelligible pattern) by some higher mental process to produce the objects of our phenomenal world. Freud does not say much about what this higher mental process is; he speaks of interpretation (5:589), anticipatory ideas (5:575), expectation (6:112–113), and filling in gaps and introducing connections (22:21).

There were many other theories of the same formal type (sense data integrated by some higher process) at the turn of the century and in the first years of the twentieth century.[4] Of these, the most notable, perhaps, is that of Helmholtz, whose theory of perception is exactly comparable to the one just presented, except that his is worked out specifically, not something taken for granted. For example, in speaking of illusions, Helmholtz says: "It is . . . simply an illusion in the judgment of the material presented to the senses, resulting in a false idea of it" (1866/1962 3:4). That is, the judgment acts on sense data to give the perception. What is the nature of this judgment?

The psychic activities that lead us to infer that there in front of us at a certain place there is a certain object of a certain character, are generally not conscious activities, but unconscious ones. In their result they are equivalent to a *conclusion*, to the extent that the observed action on our senses enables us to form an idea as to the possible cause of this action; although, as a matter of fact, it is invariably simply the nervous stimulations that are perceived directly, that is, the actions, but never the external objects themselves. . . . These unconscious conclusions derived from sensation are equivalent in their consequences to the so-called *conclusions from analogy*. (Ibid.)[5]

I return to Freud and continue with a couple of other examples simply to show that the above instance is no passing abberation, but what he presumably thought—or took for granted—about perception. "Dreams interpret objective sensory stimuli just as illusions do" (5:589). Here Freud is talking about alarm clock dreams and the like, and the quotation is more confusing than the earlier one. The alarm is a phenomenal sound, which is then worked into the dream. It is the phenomenal sound that is interpreted, not the sensory data—and certainly not objective stimuli.[6]

Another example goes a little beyond our present problem but implies the same theory of perception: "Our thoughts originally arose from sensory images . . . : their first material and their preliminary stages were sense impressions, or, more properly, mnemic images of such impressions" (15:180–181).[7] Again we start with sense data, not with phenomenal objects, so again these data must somehow be worked over to give integrated, "intelligible" perceptions.

It is not irrelevant in this context to point out that this theory simply does not do justice to perception. Under ordinary conditions, neither raw sensory data nor the higher mental process invoked to integrate these data are to be found in experience; only the organized phenomenal scene is present. A process of interpretation or a conclusion not present to experience may be relegated to the unconscious; Freud would have had no more difficulty than Helmholtz had with such a solution. But its consequence would be to remove perception from the realm of the testable. Nor is any medium provided in these theories for the integration of sensory data, as William James already recognized in his criticism of the comparable "mind-stuff" theory (James 1890, 1:158), and as Gestalt psychologists have repeatedly pointed out. The nervous system provides the needed medium, in which excitations may form a unitary correlate of a unitary phenomenal object; given such a medium, it is unnecessary to resort to processes like interpretation or judgment to make sensory data intelligible. Again, although we interpret, anticipate, complete phenomenal objects, these processes hardly apply to raw sensory data which, as has been said, do not normally constitute our experience. The theory thus presupposes the organized perceptions it is meant to explain. (For further discussion of such theories, see Köhler 1913/1971.)

Before I continue, I may remark that Freud is not alone in presenting a theory of perception of which he had no need. Here is a quotation from Rorschach, who somehow felt that he needed a perceptual theory and took one from Bleuler. Bleuler, of course, was a psychiatrist, not a perceptionist; he did not know anything about perception either:

Perceptions arise from the fact that sensations, or groups of sensations, ecphorize [arouse] memory pictures of former groups of sensations within us. This produces in us a complex of memories of sensations, the elements of which, by virtue of their simultaneous occurrence in former experiences, have a particularly fine coherence and are differentiated from other groups of sensations. In perception, therefore, we have three processes; sensation, memory, and association. (Rorschach 1942:16–17)

This theory is of the same type as the one we have been considering, and equally incomprehensible.

To return to Freud, a good deal of the process of perception—presumably the working over of sensory data—can apparently go on unconsciously. Thus: "Excitatory material . . . from the *Pcpt.* system . . . is probably submitted to a fresh revision before it becomes a conscious sensation" (5:616). We are again reminded of Helmholtz's unconscious conclusions, although in Freud the participation of the unconscious seems to go much farther, working on the sensations themselves.

Before I leave Freud's views of the general nature of perception, I would like to add one phrase which suggests that, if he had really thought about it, he would not have been satisfied with the arbitrariness of his own formulations: "The dream is treated [by the *Pcs.*] just like any other perceptual content; it is met by the same anticipatory ideas, *in so far as its subject-matter allows*" (5:575). The emphasis is mine. It appears here that perception is not just a matter of the subjective interpretation of sensory data, but that the given material itself has something to say about it. Even though Freud, casually and perhaps unwittingly, adopts the prevailing theory, it may be that if he had really become interested in it, he would not have accepted its limitations.

The reader may be surprised, perhaps, that I do not mention the regrettable *Project* in my discussion of Freud's theories of perception. That is the one place in which he attempts explicitly to deal with perception. I omit it, not particularly because of his own repudiation of it, for which, so far as I know, the specific reasons are unknown, but out of respect for Freud. Just one example will suffice to show the kind of difficulty the *Project* makes for him: because perception is always ready for fresh excitations, whereas memory implies a more or less permanent alteration of the tissue, Freud invents one sort of neurone (the permeable neurones) to serve for perception and another, impermeable system of neurones as the vehicle of memory (1:229–300). But this still will not do. Consciousness exhibits qualitative differences, the sensory qualities, which are not part of the world of physics. Therefore Freud thinks he needs still another system of neurones to deal with quality, distinct from those which serve perception and memory. These latter are concerned only with the transference of quantity. The third set of neurones is receptive to the *period* of the excitations, period referring to the differences among sensory modalities. There is no direct link between the neurones responsible for quality and those serving perception; it must be by way of the neurones whose function is memory (1:311). While this conception is indeed reminiscent of Freud's later view of the interpretation of sensory data, it is based on a fictitious and erroneous conception of the nervous system, invented ad hoc for the purposes of the *Project*. I am not willing to treat it more seriously than Freud did in his later years.

I come to a more specific issue in perception:

But projection was not created for the purpose of defence; it also occurs where there is no conflict. The projection outwards of internal perceptions is a primitive mechanism, to which, for instance, our sense perceptions are subject, and which therefore normally plays a very large part in determining the form taken by our external world. Under conditions whose nature has not yet been sufficiently established, internal perceptions of emotional and thought processes can be projected outwards in the same way as sense perceptions; they are thus employed for building up the external world, though they should by rights remain part of the *internal* world. (13:64)

I will be concerned mainly with the first part of the quotation; the second part, which clarifies the first, perhaps deals with a different issue. Before discussing it, I will quote a second statement from a different work (the case of Schreber) of about the same period, which essentially repeats the quotation just given. I do so to indicate that Freud means what he is saying:

> [Projection] makes its appearance not only in paranoia but under other psychological conditions as well, and in fact it has a regular share assigned to it in our attitude towards the external world. For when we refer the causes of certain sensations to the external world, instead of looking for them (as we do in the case of others) inside ourselves, this normal proceeding, too, deserves to be called projection. (12:66)

(Here Freud postpones, but promises to take up on another occasion, the investigation of the process of projection. If he ever did so, it may be in one of the lost metapsychological papers referred to earlier.)

Freud does not even tell us what question he is answering in these two passages, but we can supply the question because others, including Helmholtz, have also foundered on it. Freud is asking why we see objects outside ourselves, even though the excitations responsible for perceptions depend on processes in our receptors and nervous systems, that is, on processes within ourselves. If the responsible processes are inside ourselves, why not the percepts, too?

Köhler (1929/1971) has dealt with this problem, calling it an old pseudoproblem. Let me repeat the major point in his argument, which rests on the distinction between the phenomenal world and the physical world. For the sake of simplicity, we may consider only the visual parts of our phenomenal world, although a complete discussion would consider other modalities as well. Perceptions depend, as we have said, on processes occurring in the physical organism of the perceiver.

The perceptual world exhibits everywhere the relation *outside of*, from which we started. My paper is outside of my pencil, my desk, my book, and so on. What about my hand—a part of myself? It, too, appears outside these other percepts, and it, too, is a phenomenal object. In general, the phenomenal body must be distinguished from the physical organism, on whose nervous system all these phenomenal processes depend.

Nobody is surprised that the phenomenal object "pencil" is outside the phenomenal thing "inkwell." But it is no more astonishing that the hand as a third phenomenal object appears *next to* the other two and that they, in turn, appear *outside of* the hand. (Köhler 1929/1971:130)

If we return to the physical processes in the organism and its nervous system, the same relation *outside of* must somehow be represented, but this question need not concern us here.

Now we need to take only one more step. Most scientists have no trouble in distinguishing between physical and phenomenal things—unless these things refer to their own body. But the same distinction applies here. When we localize phenomenal objects outside of ourselves, it is the phenomenal self to which we refer. When we say that all percepts depend on processes in ourselves, we are referring to a different self, the physical organism. As Köhler puts it, "Nobody has ever seen a phenomenal object localized relative to (outside of) his *physical* body" (1929/1971:132). External localization poses a problem only so long as we confuse the phenomenal body with the physical organism. If we are clear about that distinction, external localization follows in the same way that phenomenal objects are localized externally to each other.

Naive realism, we remember, is the phrase that refers to the identification of phenomenal and physical objects. I said at the beginning that, since Freud was not really interested in perception, he might have avoided all problems in this area by adopting the position of naive realism and taking perception for granted, as we all do in everyday life. There is much appropriate naive realism in Freud.[8] But when it came to external localization of perceptions, he took this position inconsistently: he correctly distinguished between physical and phenomenal things but failed to distinguish between the physical organism and the phenomenal body. Thus he is left with the old pseudoproblem and must resort to the pseudosolution of projection.

Incidentally, Köhler remarks that, after Mach and Avenarius, Hering in 1862 not only gave an essentially correct solution to this problem, but foresaw that his contemporaries would not understand his solution (1929/1971:125–126). Once again, since Freud insists on discussing the nature of perception, his choice of Helmholtz over Hering makes for this difficulty.

It is also worth noting that this old pseudoproblem was not just a passing error but remained a problem for Freud until the end of his life. A few disconnected notes dating from 1938 are published in the *Standard Edition*. On the last day for which such notes are recorded, August 22, 1938, we find the following elliptical paragraph:

Space may be the projection of the extension of the psychical apparatus. No other derivation is probable. Instead of Kant's *a priori* determinants of our psychical apparatus. . . . (23:300)

If the hints Freud drops about the nature of perception turn out to be essentially Helmholtzian theory, why does Freud not acknowledge Helmholtz? While the later Freud was, on the whole, mainly interested in the work of his own group and in his critics, the young Freud seems to me to be remarkably conscientious in reviewing literatures. My guess is, therefore, that, either from Brücke or from his reading, Freud learned his Helmholtz and took it as true or as representing the state of knowledge at the time. In referring to the law of inertia, after all, we do not usually include a page reference to Newton. I think that Freud is doing something entirely parallel in not citing Helmholtz.

Now we leave the Freud-Helmholtz connection and come to a problem with which Helmholtz, so far as I know, did not concern himself. It is the problem of how we perceive and understand other people, their emotions, motives, and qualities. How is it that we attribute to them emotions similar to our own? I can find in Freud, in addition to the unanalyzed theory of projection, only the familiar theories of inference by analogy and empathy. I will present these theories briefly, give a few examples of their use by Freud, and then equally briefly discuss the theories.

When we speak of understanding others on the basis either of inference or empathy, we do so because we recognize that each person's experiences are his own private possessions. Accessible to the observer are only behavioral and expressive changes in another person. One theory holds that we attribute psychological meaning to these changes by inference from our own experience.

Thus I see another person shaking his fist at someone; I recall that, when angry, I have shaken my fist, and I infer that he is angry. In the case of empathy, we are said to feel ourselves into the other person and so understand his emotion; we feel ourselves into the pride of his stance, for instance, just as we feel ourselves into the majesty of a palace, and so understand the one as the other. In the case of both theories, inference and empathy, understanding of others is indirect.

Now let us look at Freud's use of these theories. In my first example, he is discussing the necessity of inferring the existence of unconscious processes, which we cannot know directly:

It could be pointed out, incidentally, that this was only treating one's own mental life as one had always treated other people's. One did not hesitate to ascribe mental processes to other people, although one had no immediate consciousness of them and could only infer them from their words and actions. (20:32)[9]

Again:

It is as if I were obliged to compare everything I hear about other people with myself. . . . This cannot possibly be an individual peculiarity of my own: it must rather contain an indication of the way in which we understand "something other than ourself" in general. (6:24–25)

Now a couple of statements about the role of empathy in understanding others:

Empathy . . . plays the largest part in our understanding of what is inherently foreign to our ego in other people. (18:108)

A path leads from identification by way of imitation to empathy, that is, to the comprehension of the mechanism by means of which we are enabled to take up any attitude at all towards another mental life. (18:110 n. 2)[10]

Empathy, for Freud, plays a large role in the comic. The following passage indicates that he takes this concept directly from Lipps, "the father of the modern theory of empathy," as Koffka describes him (1940:213). Lipps applied this concept in the first place to aesthetic appreciation. Here is Freud's use of it in relation to the comic:

In "trying to understand" [a perceived movement] . . . in apperceiving this movement, I make a certain expenditure, and in this portion of the mental process I behave exactly as though I were putting myself in the place of the person I am observing. . . . I disregard the person whom I am observing and behave as though I myself wanted to reach the aim of the movement. These two possibilities in my imagination amount to a comparison between the observed movement and my own. (8:194)

In this instance, the effect is comic if the other person had made a greater expenditure than I thought I should need; hence the discharge by laughter. Freud continues:

The comic effect apparently depends, therefore, on the *difference* between the two cathectic expenditures—one's own and the other person's as estimated by "empathy." (8:195)

Let us look briefly, first at the inference theory, then at empathy as a theory of understanding others. Neither holds up under scrutiny.

Inference theory has been so well discussed, notably by Köhler (e.g., 1947) and by Asch (1952), that I will make only a few points. First of all, if we look for such inferences in our experience of others, we find no evidence for them: the most obvious thing about our perception, say of a sad or a happy person, is that it is direct and immediate. Thus we would have to resort to unconscious inferences, relegating the problem to the untestable. Further, as Asch remarks (1952:147), the theory holds that we have firsthand knowledge of ourselves but only secondhand knowledge of others. Nevertheless, we sometimes understand another person's state of mind and his situation better than he does himself, for all his firsthand knowledge.

Besides, young children, even babies, may show a high degree of social understanding; social understanding is obvious, as Köhler (1917/1925) observed long ago, in a group of chimpanzees. Yet we do not credit young children or apes with the ability to make the required inferences. How can we understand a person different from ourselves—as we must if social interaction is to occur? And if we look more specifically at the materials available for inference, we find further problems. Do I recognize that another person is afraid because he turns pale? But I *see* his pallor, whereas in my own case, during fear, I can only *feel* the coldness of parts of my body. I do not look in the mirror during strong emotion and note the changes in my appearance. For all these reasons, the inference theory cannot account for the major process in our perception of others (although inference may, of course, enter at certain points to enhance understanding).

With regard to empathy, Koffka's discussion is particularly pertinent (1935:326; 1940:213–220). The major point is that empathy, in any strict sense, begs the question. In order to initiate the empathic process, a perception of the emotion or the attitude of the other is necessary. How do I know whether to feel my friendliness or my hostility into the other person? He must first *look* friendly or hostile to activate my emotion. The activation of my emotion, in other words, presupposes my recognition of it—the perception of the other's emotion is prior to any empathic response to it. Further difficulties arise when we realize that the perceiver need not experience the same emotion as the observed person; one may, for example, want to help—rather than suffer—when one sees the suffering of another person.

I am aware that the meaning of the term *empathy* has been stretched considerably in contemporary usage. I quoted Freud's book on jokes precisely to show that he uses the term in the strict sense to which these objections clearly apply.

Because these indirect theories of the understanding of other people present such difficulties, I may mention that the Gestalt psychologists (Arnheim, e.g., 1949; Asch 1952; Köhler, e.g., 1921/1971, 1947) have looked, rather, to a direct relation between the whole properties of experiences and the actions that express them; these same whole properties are perceived by the observer who, therefore, understands the other's experience. The emotion shares certain formal properties with its behavioral expressions; the two are structurally similar. The uncertainty that we experience is expressed in speech and by actions that themselves lack decisiveness; it is hard to imagine a gentle feeling being expressed by harsh and aggressive gestures, and so on.

Such an alternative is not relevant to Freud, since it was not available during his formative years, the period from which, I suspect, his nonpsychoanalytic theories date. I will therefore not elaborate it. But what is relevant is that it takes only a little reflection to realize that the traditional theories do not account for the understanding of other people.

Since Freud's theories in this area are explicit, the task of the psychological sleuth is not explication, as it was in the case of the perceptual theories. Rather, the interesting question here is whether these theories illuminate what Freud tells us about his understanding of his patients.

Did Freud, in actual practice, rely on inference and empathy? I start with some descriptions of the first patient he treated with "Breuer's technique of investigation" (2:48), Frau Emmy von N.:

She . . . had finely-cut features, full of character. Her face bore a strained and painful expression. . . . Every two or three minutes she suddenly broke off, contorted her face into an expression of horror and disgust . . . and exclaimed, in a changed voice, charged with anxiety. (2:48–49)

Her features gradually relaxed and took on a peaceful appearance. (2:51)

She twitched all over and took on a look of fear and horror. (2:53)

. . . with an angry look on her face. (2:60)

She . . . made faces expressive of terror. (2:74)

I gradually came to be able to read from patients' faces whether they might not be concealing an essential part of their confessions. (2:79)

The furious look she cast at me convinced me that she was in open rebellion. (2:81)

She threw a reproachful glance at me. (2:84)

If Freud is making inferences about his patient's emotions, he does not tell us about them; indeed, any inferences seem to be based on the directly perceived expressions, as when he infers open rebellion from an angry look.

Many other instances lead one to believe that in actual practice

Freud did not rely on inference and empathy in the understanding of others:

One glance at her face, however, was enough to tell me that she [Dora] was not in earnest over her request. (7:120–121)

Warned through some slight impression or other, I told her one day that I did not believe these dreams, that I regarded them as false or hypocritical, and that she intended to deceive me just as she habitually deceived her father. I was right; after I had made this clear, this kind of dream ceased. (18:165)

Here is another example:

In this way I made the acquaintance of a . . . lady . . . friendly and simple in her nature. (16:248)

How did Freud know that this lady was friendly and simple? Certainly not by inference from her behavior in the analytic situation, which was most uncooperative after she had told her story. Indeed, after two sessions, "from resistance and from dread of the continuation of the analysis" (16:252), she announced that she felt well, and the treatment was terminated.

In another context:

No one who has seen a baby sinking back satiated from the breast and falling asleep with flushed cheeks and a blissful smile can escape the reflection that this picture persists as a prototype of the expression of sexual satisfaction in later life. (7:182)

That the infant is satiated may be inferred from its sinking back from the breast; but the blissful smile seems to be perceived directly before it can become the basis for reflection.

We may consider next Freud's discussion of jealousy, which is understood to depend directly on perceptual indications:

This strong motive [impulses to faithlessness] can then *make use of the perceptual material* which betrays unconscious impulses of the same kind in the partner. (18:224; my emphasis.)

These attacks [of paranoid jealousy] drew their material from *his observa-*

tion of minute indications, by which his wife's quite unconscious coque-
try, unnoticeable to any one else, had betrayed itself to him. She had
unintentionally touched the man sitting next her with her hand; she had
turned too much towards him, or she had smiled more pleasantly than
when alone with her husband. He was extraordinarily observant of all
these manifestations of her unconscious, and always knew how to interpret them correctly, so that he really was always in the right about it. . . .
His abnormality really reduced itself to this, that he watched his wife's
unconscious mind much more closely and then regarded it as far more
important than anyone else would have thought of doing. (18:225–226;
my emphasis.)

Here the man seems to *see* his wife's supposed faithlessness in her
gestures and her expressions; we are told nothing of inferences,
nothing of empathy. This interpretation seems to be supported by
a further statement in the same article:

They do not project . . . into the blue, so to speak, where there is nothing
of the sort already. (18:226)

Projection, it seems, must find a suitable target, and the only way
to do so is to perceive it.

    An especially interesting example is found in Freud's fine essay
on the *Moses* of Michelangelo. Speaking of his visits to the statue,
he remarks:

How often have I mounted the steep steps . . . and have essayed to support
the angry scorn of the hero's glance! Sometimes I have crept cautiously
out of the half-gloom of the interior as though I myself belonged to the
mob upon whom his eye is turned. (13:213)

In this instance, Freud understands the anger, scorn, and pain of
the hero, but these are not the emotions he feels. He identifies,
rather, with the crowd on whom the scorn is directed.

    In the case of understanding the emotions of others, Freud's
theories (inference, empathy, projection) are explicit. They are
not only palpably false, they are unnecessary for his purposes;
and I am suggesting that when he gets down to concrete human
situations, he quite properly disregards them.

Freud accepted the associationist tradition as a matter of course.

He need not have done so. The *facts* of free association, the *fact* that one item reminds us of another, do not require the *theory* of associationism. At least in the area of recall, an alternative was available in Freud's day, that proposed by Höffding. It was Höffding's argument that, given two associated items, the subsequent presentation of one of them cannot lead to the recall of the second by mere association. The newly presented item must first make contact with the trace corresponding to it (laid down by its original presentation). Since the new item, being new, was never associated with its trace, this contact, this selection of the right trace from among all those present in the nervous system, can only take place on the basis of similarity of process and trace. As Köhler expresses it:

Höffding argued that no association in the usual sense of the word could lead to any corresponding recall unless the way were prepared for this event by a selective effect of similarity. (1940:126)

Since the nature of associations and problems of recall and of ordinary forgetting were not Freud's concern, he quite simply espoused the prevailing view.[11]

In this area, I would like briefly to make two points: to show that Freud embraced associationism literally and mechanistically and to indicate a few interesting departures from this doctrine.

I will not include the unfortunate *Project* in this discussion of associationism, because there Freud was thinking in terms of associations mediated by specific neural paths, a view later repudiated. As his editors point out, he later "appears to turn his back on neurones and nerve-fibres" (1:395).[12] The discussion will therefore refer only to material subsequent to this change. Nevertheless, it will be seen, Freud continued to think in terms of associative paths. Here are some examples:

Under the pressure of the censorship, any sort of connection is good enough to serve as a substitute by allusion, and displacement is allowed from any element to any other. Replacement of internal associations (similarity, causal connection, etc.) by what are known as external ones (simultaneity in time, contiguity in space, similarity of sound) is quite specially striking and characteristic of the dream-work. (8:172)

Since, however, similarity and contiguity are the two essential principles of processes of association, it appears that the true explanation of all the folly of magical observances is the domination of the association of ideas. . . . The associative theory of magic merely explains the paths along which magic proceeds; it does not explain its true essence. (13:83)

The second stage of repression, *repression proper*, affects mental derivatives of the repressed representative, or such trains of thought as, originating elsewhere, have come into associative connection with it. (14:148)

In this case too an associative link between the disturbing and the disturbed intentions is present; but it does not lie in their content but is artificially constructed, often along extremely forced associative paths. (15:63)

In order to achieve this end it [the symptom-formation] will often make use of the most ingenious associative paths. (20:112)

There is much more material of this kind. I think there is no doubt that Freud is a strict associationist, like so many others of his day.[13] More interesting for Freud's implicit cognitive theories are his, possibly unwitting, departures from associationism.[14] My examples come from the *Interpretation of Dreams* and from the *New Introductory Lectures*. Here one catches glimpses of ideas that are almost organizational:

The dream is, as it were, differently centred from the dream thoughts—its content has different elements as its central point. (4:305)

A train of thought is referred to as a "complicated structure" with "foreground and background" (4:312). Again:

The dream-work is under some kind of necessity to combine all the sources which have acted as stimuli for the dream into a single unity in the dream itself. (4:179)

Another kind of departure from strict associationism is the idea that mental processes act under the influence of what Freud calls purposive ideas (e.g., 5:528). This is something quite different from a chain of associations, as the following quotation makes clear. Freud is speaking of parapraxes:

We must recognize the importance of the influence of sounds, the similarity of words and the familiar associations aroused by words. These facilitate slips of the tongue by pointing to the paths they can take. But if I have a path open to me, does that fact automatically decide that I shall take it? I need a motive in addition before I resolve in favour of it and furthermore a force to propel me along the path. (15:46)

This statement almost reminds one of Kurt Lewin's demonstration, in 1922, that syllables failed to call up their associates, with which they had been paired during 300 repetitions, when instructions were changed so that subjects were asked merely to read the syllables but not actively to try to recall. This finding, Koffka remarks, is "not derivable from the law of association as usually formulated" (1935:561).

Again it appears that if Freud had really thought about his associationism, instead of taking it for granted, he might have rejected it. Freud could not possibly have known what we know today about the nature of associations (cf. Köhler 1941; Asch, e.g., 1960). But since this was not his concern, one wishes that he had stayed with the facts instead of adopting a theory in which, after 1895, he was not really interested.

Associationism has a consequence, which is very clear in Freud, which Gestalt psychologists call *machine theory*. That is, order is derived, not from free dynamics, not from the interplay of interacting processes, but from constraints, such as histological constraints or associative paths. Freud equated the latter two, as has been pointed out, in the *Project*, but later saw order achieved by undefined associative paths. Other instances of mechanism may be indicated. Freud says explicitly:

Analysts are at bottom incorrigible mechanists and materialists,[15] even though they seek to avoid robbing the mind and spirit of their still unrecognized characteristics. (18:179)

The question of order is explicitly taken up in a later work:

[Order], like cleanliness applies solely to the works of man. But whereas cleanliness is not to be expected in nature, order, on the contrary, has been imitated from her. Man's observation of the great astronomical regularities not only furnished him with a model for introducing order into his life, but gave him the first points of departure for doing so. Order is a kind of compulsion to repeat which, when a regulation has been laid down once and for all, decides when, where and how a thing shall be done, so that in every similar circumstance one is spared hesitation and indecision. (21:93)

This account of order is hardly specific: it is difficult to say whether it falls under Freud's instinct theory (compulsion to repeat) or whether it is arbitrarily imposed (regulation laid down once and for all), or both. Whichever interpretation is meant, it is not the kind of order which accounts for the great astronomical regularities. These depend on the free interaction of bodies. It is necessary to distinguish between such regularities and the kinds of regulations that human beings devise.

Mechanistic thinking is seen, both in early and in late Freud, in the reflexological account of behavior. Here are two quotations:

All our psychical activity starts from stimuli . . . and ends in innervations. Accordingly, we shall ascribe a sensory and a motor end to the apparatus. . . . The psychical apparatus must be constructed like a reflex apparatus. (5:537–538)

In consequence of the pre-established connection between sense perception and muscular action, the ego has voluntary movement at its command. (23:145)

Freud's editors see in the infelicitous *Project* a possible forerunner of contemporary information theory:

It has been suggested latterly that the human nervous system may be regarded in its workings as similar to or even identical with an electronic computer—both of them machines for the reception, storage, processing and output of information. It has been plausibly pointed out that [in the *Project*] . . . we may see more than a hint or two at the hypotheses of information theory and cybernetics in their application to the nervous system. . . . It may be an alluring possibility to see [Freud] as a precursor of latter-day behaviourism. (1:292–293)

One may add to this suggestion the editors' own further remark:

The *Project*, in spite of being ostensibly a neurological document, contains within itself the nucleus of a great part of Freud's later psychological theories. . . . But in fact the *Project*, or rather its invisible ghost, haunts the whole series of Freud's theoretical writings to the very end. (1:290)

Thus Freud's editors see the mechanistic character here discussed, not only of the *Project*, but of the body of Freud's thinking.

It must be added that if Freud is a precursor of information theory and of behaviorism, he is one in the same sense that Descartes is.

Freud has little to say about the thinking process, and the hints he offers are often ambiguous. One thing that is clear is that, in part, he takes an associationistic view of thinking. Thought is referred to as the "weaver's masterpiece" in the *Interpretation of Dreams* (4:283). In the same work, Freud remarks:

Thinking must concern itself with the connecting paths between ideas, without being led astray by the *intensities* of those ideas. (5:602)

The associationistic view is extended to creative thinking:

The "creative" imagination, indeed, is quite incapable of *inventing* anything; it can only combine components that are strange to one another. (15:172)

This is a classic statement of an associationistic theory of creativity, a theory that is still found today. There is a good deal that might be said about such a theory (see Henle 1975), but I will merely point out that it robs creativity of its most distinctive achievement—novelty—and is, therefore, almost certainly wrong.

In another context, Freud again refers to creativity in a way that might seem to contradict the statement just quoted:

Accounts given us by some of the most highly productive men, such as Goethe and Helmholtz, show . . . that what is essential and new in their creations came to them without premeditation and as an almost ready-made whole. (5:613)

This passage sounds very different from the combining of unrelated components. But, in Freud's case, it most likely means simply that the process proceeds unconsciously; he regards thinking as probably originally unconscious (12:221).

A somewhat different view of the thinking process, not incompatible with associationism, is to be found in passages like the following:

Thinking is an experimental action carried out with small amounts of energy, in the same way as a general shifts small figures about on a map before setting his large bodies of troops in motion. (22:89)

This postponement due to thought . . . is to be regarded as an experimental action, a motor palpating, with small expenditure of discharge. (19:238)

Similar statements are to be found elsewhere in Freud's works (e.g., 12:221; 5:599–600; 23:199). What is the nature of this "exploratory thought-activity," this motor palpating? Possibly a clue is given in the ill-conceived *Project*, in which thought is described as "an aimless activity of memory" or of judging (1:331). If this conception is implied in later references to thinking, the process becomes a sort of implicit trial and error, a view not uncommon in behavioristic and other traditional accounts.

That thinking is conceived as functioning in the service of instinct is evident throughout Freud's writings. The ego develops out of the necessity of adapting the demands of the id to external reality. It is out of this necessity that the ego develops its function of reality testing. For example:

[The ego's] constructive function consists in interpolating, between the demand made by an instinct and the action that satisfies it, the activity of thought which, after taking its bearings in the present and assessing earlier experiences, endeavours by means of experimental actions to calculate the consequences of the course of action proposed. (23:199)

In this view, then, subjective demands are primary—indeed exclusive. And yet Freud occasionally glimpses an objective side to the matter, the demands of the material itself, to which thinking must do justice. Here are two examples of what is clearly a more adequate account of the thought processes than Freud's customary formulations:

But one cannot always carry out one's reasonable intentions [in exposition]. There is often something in the material itself which takes charge of one and diverts one from one's first intentions. Even such a trivial achievement as the arrangement of a familiar piece of material is not entirely subject to an author's own choice; it takes what line it likes and all one can do is to ask oneself after the event why it has happened in this way and no other. (16:379)

Unluckily an author's creative power does not always obey his will: the work proceeds as it can, and often presents itself to the author as something independent or even alien. (23:104)

In Freud we find emphasis on errors in thinking. He clearly has not much confidence in the rationality of human beings. For example:

It cannot be doubted that it is easier and more convenient to diverge from a line of thought we have embarked on than to keep to it, to jumble up things that are different rather than to contrast them—and, indeed, that it is *specially* convenient to admit as valid methods of inference that are rejected by logic and, lastly, to put words or thoughts together without regard to the condition that they ought also to make sense. (8:125)

Now it is inherent in human nature to have an inclination to consider a thing untrue if one does not like it, and after that it is easy to find arguments against it. (15:23)

It has not been possible to demonstrate in other connections that the human intellect has a particularly fine flair for the truth or that the human mind shows any special inclination for recognizing the truth. We have rather found, on the contrary, that our intellect very easily goes astray without any warning, and that nothing is more easily believed by us than what, without reference to the truth, comes to meet our wishful illusions. (23:129)

These statements, which recent research suggests can, indeed, be doubted (cf. Henle 1962),[16] are presented unanalyzed; therefore they will not be discussed here. The question is never asked: Where errors occur, *how* are they possible? Thus Freud cannot be said to have a theory of error in thinking; he merely makes assertions about it. If these assertions were correct, one might say that Freud is here treating cognitive processes at the commonsense level that is appropriate for a thinker whose interests lie elsewhere. But I doubt that they are correct.

Freud was, from the beginning, aware of the distinction between "normal" and motivated forgetting (e.g., 4:178). In the ill-advised *Project* he refers briefly to forgetting as gradual decay (1:382). Later, with Breuer, he describes forgetting as "the general effacement of impressions, the fading of memories . . . which wears away those ideas in particular that are no longer affectively operative" (2:9). In 1901, in the *Psychopathology of Everyday Life*, he remarks that "the basic determinants of the *normal* process of forgetting are unknown" (6:274); but by 1904 Freud has begun to think about how forgetting occurs:[17]

Normal forgetting takes place by way of condensation. In this way it becomes the basis for the formation of concepts. What is isolated is perceived clearly. (6:134, n. 2)

Condensation, it will be recalled, occurs in dreams and in parapraxes, on the basis of similarity:

A similarity of any sort between two elements of the unconscious material—a similarity between the things themselves or between their verbal presentations—is taken as an opportunity for creating a third, which is a composite or compromise idea. (6:58–59)

The idea that "normal" forgetting takes place on the basis of the similarity of the items in question is successively clarified. In 1905, Freud states:

Unique impressions offer difficulties to forgetting; those that are analogous in any way are forgotten by being condensed in regard to their points of resemblance. Confusion between analogous impressions is one of the preliminary stages of forgetting. (8:168 n. 1)

And in 1907:

I may perhaps put forward the following suggestions as regards the mechanism of forgetting in its proper sense. . . . The traces that have grown indifferent succumb unresistingly to the process of condensation. . . . It is highly probable that there is no question at all of there being any direct function of time in forgetting. (6:274, n. 2)

These observations are reminiscent of interference theories of forgetting put forth by experimental psychologists. Both retroactive and proactive inhibition depend on the similarity of the items in question; and within a series the harmful effects of similarity are even stronger. Particular items lose their individuality in a monotonous series—this is what Freud means by *concept;* items simply become "another one of the same kind."

The contrast between isolated (Freud's "unique impressions") and crowded items ("analogous impressions") was investigated by von Restorff in 1933. As Köhler summarizes: "Items which differ in kind from the monotonous remainder of the series are much better recalled than are items which belong to this homogeneous part" (1940:36). Gestalt psychologists, of course, went farther than Freud in pointing to similarity not only as a condition of forgetting, but as a condition of the interaction among members which is responsible for the forgetting.

It is tempting to speculate that Freud gave thought to the nature of forgetting, and so arrived at some remarkably pertinent hints about it, because (so far as I know) Helmholtz did not write about it. Thus Freud could not have regarded the matter as settled, as he seems to have done in the case of perception.

In conclusion, if we consider the cognitive theories, implicit and explicit, adopted by Freud, we find that, on the whole, they are the prevailing, traditional views of his time. This man, whose ideas on psychoanalysis were so radical that, for many years, they alienated him from the medical and academic communities, was an arch conservative when it came to cognition. On the other hand, when we see him at work with his patients, his practice no longer conforms to these traditional theories. And as soon as he begins to think about a process—when, for example, he is not overwhelmed by the doctrines of Helmholtz, of Lipps, of the associationists—we find hints of the originality that earned Freud his place in intellectual history.

Chapter 6

Kurt Lewin
as Metatheorist

When Erling Eng first discussed Kurt Lewin with me, at a Cheiron meeting some years ago, he started: "Why did Lewin fail?" I countered with the question: "Why did personality theory fail?" It seems to me that Lewin did *not* fail and that personality theory would be farther advanced today if its formulators had understood the nature of Lewin's contribution.

I will not consider Lewin as a social psychologist, but will limit my discussion to his work in the fields of motivation and personality. This work takes two directions: the experimental investigations by Lewin and his students and his own theoretical writings. The experimental work, begun at the Psychological Institute of the University of Berlin, was to some extent continued in America, but the empirical work associated with his name turned more and more to social issues. Apart from numerous important articles, Lewin's theoretical writings are to be found in two volumes, *Principles of Topological Psychology* (1936) and *The Conceptual Representation and the Measurement of Psychological Forces* (1938). The second volume is a natural continuation of the first.

The experimental work essentially opened up the field of human motivation to an experimental approach. It is impossible not to notice the difference, pre- and post-Lewin, between work on such problems as reward and punishment or success and failure.

Lewin brought life to a series of problems whose experimental treatment had previously been unbelievably artificial, trivial, and dull. I shall return to these researches.

In the textbooks Lewin is treated side by side with other theorists of personality. Hall and Lindzey, for example, in their *Theories of Personality* (1970), sandwich him between Henry Murray and Gordon Allport. (In their third edition [1978], Hall and Lindzey interpolate additional theories between Murray and Lewin.) What has he in common with the approaches of these authors? Or, since Eng (1978:230) refers to psychoanalysis as Lewin's silent competitor, in what respects are the competitors comparable?

Freud has accustomed us to detailed case histories, to a developmental approach to personality, with a description of typical crises that occur in the socialization of the individual. He speaks of the agencies that constitute the person and of conflicts and alliances among them; he describes various means by which these parts of the person manage to coexist, by subreption or otherwise. The major forces responsible for the phenomena of life are described, each with its own energy and each governed by its own principle, though ultimately subject to the repetition compulsion.

Since Freudian theory—or prototheory—has to a large extent set the pattern for personality theory in America, we may look at Lewin in terms of some of the same categories.

Case histories in Lewin? A person takes a train from Iowa City to Chicago. Another goes to the kitchen for a glass of water. A baby tries to reach a rattle a little distance away. These are typical of Lewin's examples. The following is about as far as he ever goes in describing the life situation of an individual—a woman who is annoyed because a thread is broken on the loom at which she is working in a large factory:

She has been married for three years. For a year and a half, her husband has been unemployed. The two-year-old child has been seriously ill, but today he seems somewhat better. She and her husband have been quarreling more and more recently. They had a quarrel this morning. Her husband's parents have suggested that she send the child to them in the country. The woman is undecided what to do about it. (Lewin 1936:22–23)

The cast of characters remains completely unknown to us. Although we know something of the immediate worries of this woman, we know scarcely more about her personality than we know about the traveler to Chicago. If we know her problems, we do not know how she copes with them or evades them, where she attributes responsibility. What kind of person is she and how did she get that way? What are her goals and values? We do not know.

In another case (1935:146ff.), an example from Tolstoy is presented in some detail, the elaborate fantasies of a boy awaiting punishment. But this episode is not used for any light it might throw on the boy's personality, rather as a characterization of the punishment situation.

Lewin is obviously not interested in problems of the content of personality. But how is it possible for a personality theorist not to be interested in the content of personality? It is *not* possible—and it thus becomes clear that Lewin was undertaking a different task. One writer describes Lewin's neglect of content as an "unfortunate oversight"—but no theorist, least of all Lewin, could inadvertently omit his major subject matter.

I would like to return to Lewin's traveler and place him in context. Here is the relevant paragraph: "Two persons are taking the train from Iowa City (I) to Chicago. One wants to go to Detroit (D), the second by way of New York to Europe (E). Do both go in the same direction? Is $d_{I,D} = d_{I,E}$?" (1938:30). Why should a personality theorist be interested in the question of whether two riders on the same train are going in the same direction?

Lewin, it seems to me, was developing a *metatheory*, not a theory of personality. That is, he was writing a *theory of personality theory*, trying to specify the requirements that a dynamic theory of personality must meet. It might be said that existing personality theories are based on implicit and incomplete and perhaps inconsistent metatheories, and not all on the same metatheory. Thus any S-R theory which makes drive a matter of strong stimuli would not meet Lewin's specific requirements. Stimuli are scalars (that is, they have magnitude only), and Lewin's metatheory employs a vector concept (vectors possess magnitude and direction). What Lewin was doing was writing an explicit and consistent metatheory of personality. He states explicitly that he is "not promulgating a new 'system' limited to a specific content, but rather . . . describing a 'tool', a set of concepts by means of which one can represent psychological reality" (1936:6). Psychological reality must include both person and environment, and in the same terms, in order to make the relations between them comprehensible. (This is something that contemporary interactionists—who may not even know that Lewin was there first— would do well to remember.) Lewin early realized that spatial as well as temporal concepts are needed in psychology, and he designated his central concept "life space." Behaviors were seen as locomotions in the life space, or else restructurings, a more general concept, but one which need not concern us here.

It early became apparent to Lewin that topology, a nonquantitative, non-Euclidian geometry, was "particularly fitted to the specific problems of psychology" (1936:vii). Topology is based on the whole-part relation, a basic relation for psychology, as seen first of all in the relation of the person to his environment. Euclidian geometry would not serve his purposes. For one thing, many of the locomotions in the life space are social or conceptual—as when a person gets a new job or solves a problem—rather than physical. Again, even with physical locomotions, the direction to the goal is not necessarily defined by the shortest distance between person and goal; in a detour, for example, the first step toward the goal often consists in turning one's back on that goal and going in the opposite direction. So Lewin looked elsewhere and used topology as his starting point.

If, as I suggest, Lewin was developing a metatheory, not a theory of personality, we can see that the title of his first collection of essays published in English, A Dynamic Theory of Personality, is a misnomer. The same must be said of Principles of Topological Psychology. The latter must be read as a setting forth of the general requirements of psychological theory, an exposition of the concepts of topology which are relevant to psychology, and their application to the person and the psychological environment. (A better, though still incomplete, title might have been Topological Representation of Psychological Concepts.) It should be noted that Lewin, doubtless tired of being misunderstood, was more careful about what he called his next book; to it he gave the rather forbidding title already mentioned, *The Conceptual Representation and the Measurement of Psychological Forces*. This book was probably not so much misunderstood as unread. (Parenthetically, the group that met annually with Lewin, the Topological Psychologists, was also misnamed. The more informal "Lewin Gesellschaft" was a more accurate designation.)

But topology was insufficient. Being nonquantitative, it could handle neither direction nor distance; both are essential for a vector psychology, essential specifically for the representation of psychological forces. Finding no suitable geometry, Lewin himself began to work out the characteristics of what he called hodological space. In this connection he began to develop concepts for direction and distance. How is direction to be defined in a space that knows no shortest distance between two points? When are the directions of two forces equal? Now we see the relevance of the example of the two travelers taking the train at Iowa City— an example with no possible relevance for a *theory* of personality. Opposite directions were also defined in terms of a concept of distance based on the whole-part relation; and many other related problems were worked out.

It should now be clear that Lewin was concerned with the conceptual properties and the representation of psychological forces and other concepts required for a theory of personality. This is different from developing a theory of personality. This difference accounts for Lewin's preference for momentary examples and his neglect of the content of the personality. On the other hand, to the extent that this metatheory is useful, it should clarify problems of personality theories regardless of their content.

Lewin was, and I believe still is, ahead of his time. Personality theories are still notably lacking in precision. They are not averse to dealing with conflict, for example, without specifying the directions of 'he opposing forces, their magnitude, and aspects of the topology of the situation which permit certain outcomes while precluding others—just the problems on which Lewin was working. Perhaps behavioristic theories have been more precise than, say, neo-Freudian theories, but they are based on an implicit metatheory entirely different from Lewin's. I have already indicated that drive is often reduced to a scalar, while the need for concepts for the psychological environment is concealed by that most ambiguous of terms, "stimulus." Lewin's metatheory will not find its testing ground in such theories. Only theories based on a vector concept will enable us to assess the usefulness of Lewin's formulations. At the same time, these formulations could do much to clarify personality theory. With Lewin as a standard, we would no longer be satisfied with the prototheoretical status of the discipline.

It must be noted that Lewin's contribution is not limited to his metatheory. A metatheory can be tested by its consistency, its usefulness in clarifying and advancing theory, and perhaps by other criteria; but it cannot be tested experimentally. The fact remains that Lewin was extraordinarily ingenious in experimentation in the areas of motivation and personality. These experiments, many of which are closely related, must derive from theory (more precisely, from hypotheses themselves derived from theory). Although it is not the main thrust of his work, there must be some sense in which Lewin has provided us with a "dynamic theory of personality."

Beginning with Zeigarnik's work, a number of the experimental studies concern the effects of interruption of tasks. It is assumed that when an experimental subject accepts a task, a system under tension is set up in him. The tension is normally released by completion of the task. If completion is not permitted, the unresolved tension is manifested in such effects as enhanced recall or resumption.

Underlying these statements, an equilibrium theory may be recognized, that is, the assumption of a tendency toward resolution of tension. This is a theoretical statement, a statement about how motives actually behave. It is not a statement about requirements of motivational theory. Such an assumption was by no means exclusive to Lewin, but was made by practically every personality theorist writing at the time. Today it is being questioned, without actually being discarded; nor has an adequate substitute been thought out. (It may also be remarked that Lewin's is not a pure equilibrium theory, in the sense of a tendency toward minimal tension; rather, he thought in terms of a tendency to equalization of tension in surrounding systems [1938:98].)

Regardless of the merits of equilibrium theory, it enabled Lewin to do experimental work. In light of the tendency toward resolution (or equalization) of tension, it may be predicted, for example, that if resolution is not achieved through completion of the task, an unfinished task will, after sufficient time, behave no differently from a completed task. Zeigarnik showed this to be the case. Furthermore, the speed of resolution of tension will depend upon the properties of the medium in which the tension system exists. Lewin assumed that levels of unreality—fantasy, for example—are more fluid than levels of reality; thus changes are easier to achieve in fantasy than in reality: there one can do more as one pleases. This is again a theoretical assumption, not a metatheoretical one. It tells us something about differences between fantasy and reality, not about the requirements of theory, and accordingly it may be tested experimentally. Indeed, research showed not only that resolution of tension is faster on a level of lesser than on a level of greater reality, but also that substitution (which involves communication between tension systems—another theoretical statement) is easier on such a level.

Another very fruitful set of theoretical assumptions concerns level of aspiration. It led to a very interesting line of investigation which transformed both the previous conceptions and the experimental treatment of success and failure.

Thus, Lewin must be regarded as a theorist, an experimentalist, and a metatheorist in the areas of motivation and personality. What seems to have been overlooked is that his most systematic efforts lie in the latter direction.

More than thirty years after his death, Lewin's major legacy, it seems to me, remains to be appreciated and put to use. Personality theorists have tried to fit his work into their own pattern, rather than pay close attention to what he was doing and why. He is recognized as a great psychologist, but the nature of his greatness seems not to be clearly understood. It is to be hoped that the day will come when Lewin will again be discussed, not in the setting of the history of the social sciences, but in that of the contemporary psychology of personality. Kurt Lewin has become a historical figure too soon.

Chapter 7

Some Problems
of Eclecticism

Some ten years ago Woodworth (1948:254), commenting on the situation in psychology as a whole, wrote: "Some may lean toward one school and some toward another, but on the whole the psychologists of the present time are proceeding on their way in the middle of the road." He suggested that "if we could assemble all these psychologists [all the psychologists in the world] in a convention hall and ask the members of each school to stand and show themselves, a very large proportion of the entire group would remain seated" (1948:254–255).

A similar position was taken by Boring at about the same time:

During the 1930's the *isms* pretty well dropped out of psychology. . . . The only reason for mentioning these four schools in this book is that the student hears about *behaviorism* and *Gestalt psychology* and has a right to be told what they are and that they are no longer important as schools. What was good in all the schools is now simply part of psychology. (1948:11)

The eclectics, rising above the conflict of schools, hold that psychologists today are in happy agreement. It is their position that no real issues exist among the various points of view in psychology. For it is only on the basis of such a belief that one is able to select from each approach, combining the theoretical contributions of all. As Woodworth presents the middle-of-the-road position: "Every school is good, though no one is good enough. . . .

One points to one alluring prospect, another to another. . . . Their negative pronouncements we can discount while we accept their positive contributions to psychology as a whole" (1948:255).

If eclecticism is as prevalent in contemporary psychology as the above statements suggest, it becomes important to examine its consequences for theory. It is the hypothesis of the present paper that the eclectics have, to a large extent, succeeded in reconciling differences only by obscuring theoretical issues. An alternative to this kind of eclecticism will be proposed.

We may begin with an examination of specific instances of eclectic reconciliation of differences. Examples of two kinds of eclecticism will be discussed, one having to do with reconciliations of positions which refer to the entire field of psychology— the attempt to resolve conflicts among "schools" or general points of view—and a more circumscribed eclecticism relating to particular psychological problems.

As an instance of the first kind, Woodworth writes:[1]

A broadly defined functional psychology starts with the question "What man *does*" and proceeds to the questions "How?" and "Why?" . . . So broadly defined . . . functional psychology scarcely deserves the name of a school because it would include so many psychologists who have not professed themselves. Now the question is whether our middle-of-the-roaders are not after all members of this broadly conceived functional school. . . . But if the middle-of-the-roaders are really functionalists, the question is then whether the same would not be true of all the schools. Are they not all functionalists at heart? (*Ibid.*)

Commenting on such a functionalism, Boring wrote in 1950: "Woodworth believed that psychologists were more in agreement than their quarrels indicated, and he sought a system to which all could subscribe. He very nearly succeeded" (1950:565).

It is not likely to be denied that psychology today has a functionalist flavor. The interest in the adaptive value of psychological processes is everywhere apparent. Nor can there be much disagreement with a functionalism defined in terms of these three questions of Woodworth's. But it tells us very little about a psychologist to say that he is a functionalist in this sense. What we need to know are the kinds of answers which a particular psychology gives to these questions. These are the issues in contemporary psychology, and here it is that disagreements arise. What, for example, is the relation of reinforcement, or of repetition, to learning? How does the learning process proceed? What is the nature of the fundamental human motives? How does the group exert its influence on the individual? It is the answers to such questions as these that divide psychologists. It would seem that Woodworth has succeeded in bringing all together only by obscuring such issues. If all are functionalists today, we still have the problem of examining the differences among the several varieties of functionalism.

The point may be made more specifically in connection with the same author's theory of the conditions of transfer of training, the doctrine of identical components (Woodworth 1938), reformulated by Woodworth and Schlosberg (1954) as a theory of "common factors." It is put forward to resolve the differences between those who hold that transfer is a function of the identical elements in two learning tasks, and those who maintain that it is a matter of the application of common principles or other whole properties to the two activities. Woodworth's view is that anything concrete can be transferred—thus both identical elements and principles—since "any idea that can be recalled, or any attitude that can be reinstated is concrete enough to qualify. Perhaps anything that can be learned can be transferred" (1938: 207).[2] Again, "What is successfully transferred is usually something you can put your finger on—a principle, a good emotional attitude, a technique" (Woodworth and Marquis 1947:582).

The controversy about the conditions of transfer is settled, in other words, by saying that *something* is carried over from one activity to the other. It is true that this is a formulation which covers most of the cases. But it lacks an advantage of both of the theories it displaces, namely the attempt to state the specific conditions of transfer. It would seem that the differences are resolved only at the expense of any specific theory in the area of the controversy. The theory covers all the cases only by telling us nothing specific about any of them.

To return to the more general kind of eclecticism, there exist today a number of efforts to reconcile the various significant theoretical positions in psychology. A number of authors have attempted to resolve the differences between behavior theory and psychoanalysis, Gestalt psychology and psychoanalysis, behavior theory and Gestalt theory.[3] Several examples of this trend in contemporary psychology will be examined.

The problems seen above in Woodworth's formulations exist also in Abt's statements about basic agreements between psychoanalysis and Gestalt psychology with respect to the structure and development of the personality:

Freud's multiple-structured self is not essentially different conceptually from Lewin's division of the person into regions. The dynamic and economic interchanges that are postulated as occurring with respect to the id, ego and superego in psychoanalysis find parallel expression in Lewin's system of barriers and the classes of movements across them. (Abt 1950: 38–39)

If Abt means that Lewin's *metatheory* is compatible with Freud's *theory* of personality structure, a case could be (but has not been) made for this position. But to equate Lewin's division of the personality into regions with Freud's topographical analysis of the person is to lose all the specific psychological insights of the latter and much of the metatheoretical contribution of the former. Lewin's inner-personal regions, if translated into Freudian terms, would undoubtedly fail to distinguish between id, ego, and superego; his motor-perceptual region includes some but not all of the functions of the Freudian ego.[4] Lewin is, indeed, largely unconcerned with the specific content of the personality, with the distinction between conscious and unconscious motivation, and with the historical development of the person; it is impossible to discuss Freud's topographical divisions apart from such considerations. Again, Lewin has not discussed the content and nature of the forces responsible for behavior; thus the parallel with Freud's statements about dynamics can be maintained only if one turns one's attention away from the specifics of Freud's successive instinct theories. It is indeed possible to find parallels between Lewin's statements about the tendency of systems under tension to seek discharge and Freud's formulations about the pleasure principle; but to equate the two is to lose the specific character of both the pleasure and reality principles and to neglect Freud's theories about behavior which is independent of the pleasure principle (Freud 1920).

A further illustration will be given of the tendency prevailing in contemporary psychology to reconcile the ideas of Freud and Lewin. Another author writes: "It is the thesis of this paper that a synthesis of the ideas of Lewin and Freud provides a basis for the beginnings of an integrated system of psychological theory" (Bronfenbrenner 1951:206). More specifically, "We have already noted the structural parallelism between Freud's divisions of the personality and Lewin's psychical systems" (Bronfenbrenner 1951: 222). This writer, it is true, limits the parallelism, remarking, "Freud has provided the living clay for the Lewinian scaffolding" (1951: 228).[5] Still, closer examination suggests that essential differences between the "living clay" and the "scaffolding" have been neglected. For example, "One of these [defense mechanisms], projection, becomes the equivalent for Lewin's unreality" (1951:222). While there are, of course, important components of unreality in projections, the two concepts are by no means equivalent, if only because not all events on a level of unreality (for example, dreams, fantasies, vague hopes and wishes) can be described as projections, at least as Freud uses the term. Again, to put the Freudian unconscious "directly into Lewinian language" by saying that "there are sub-systems within the region of the self which are not in communication with each other" (1951:225) is to slip over the specific nature of unconscious processes in Freudian theory. Furthermore, if this is meant as an equation, it fails to do justice to the very important communications which do exist between conscious and unconscious systems. The point may be illustrated by the dream, which draws upon the person's waking experiences (e.g., experiences of the "dream day") and which is recalled by the waking individual.

Another instance of a premature reconciliation of Gestalt psychology and psychoanalysis may be taken from the work of Witkin et al.[6] These authors point out:

Although psychoanalytic theory, in its conception of primary and secondary processes, recognizes the relation between intellectual functioning and personality, it has not really been concerned with the nature of secondary processes. . . . Gestalt psychology, in contrast, has offered a well-developed theory of cognition, in which the role of the nature of reality in determining perceptual and thought processes has been emphasized. But . . . Gestalt theory has on the other hand neglected the role of personal factors in perception. By showing that a perceptual act cannot be understood without reference to *both* personal factors *and* the nature of reality, studies such as ours help to bridge the gap between Gestalt and psychoanalytic theory, and provide a basis for bringing together the main aspects of both into a single comprehensive theory of human psychological functioning. (1954:481)

If, as I believe, the authors are correct in saying that "there is still lacking in psychoanalytic theory any specific account of cognition or of the nature of secondary process" (*ibid.*), and that Gestalt psychology has neglected personal factors in perception— these are precisely the reasons why studies such as theirs do *not* help to bridge the gap between the two theories. The gap can be bridged only by a true reconciliation of existing differences; and since these two approaches have been concerned, as the authors point out, with such different areas of psychology, it is difficult even to know where the essential differences lie. A systematic analysis of the assumptions of both psychologies, one concerned with implicit as well as explicit assumptions, would undoubtedly reveal both important differences and surprising compatibilities of the theories. But in the absence of such an analysis we cannot, without glossing over real differences, say that a particular finding helps to bring the two theories together. To do so, it would need to be shown (a) that the results demand a theory which reconciles actual differences between the two approaches; or (b) if the two psychologies are in agreement in the area in question (which would require demonstration), that the findings can be handled in terms which are compatible with both.

To say, in other words, that both personal factors and reality factors determine a perceptual effect is to pose a problem. It is to point out that we need a human psychology which will include both kinds of factors; but it is not to say that such a psychology will be compatible with Gestalt psychology or with psychoanalysis or both. To me it seems more likely that a finding which cannot be handled adequately within the framework of either of these existing systems will demand, not a reconciliation of the two admittedly incomplete theories, but rather a new theory. This point will be discussed below.

A final example, which will show again how eclectic reconciliation of differences may be achieved at the expense of a specific theory in the area of the controversy, may be taken from Welch. This author has offered some fundamental propositions which he believed should be acceptable both to Gestalt psychology and to contemporary behaviorism. For example, "Perceiving is the result of a stimulus compound producing effects upon the sense organs which establish brain traces similar to or in otherwise related to brain traces formerly established" (1948:181). Surely everyone will agree that present percepts are related to traces of past ones; where dispute exists it concerns the specific effects of past experience on perception. Welch has succeeded in reconciling the differences by omitting the specific area of controversy. Again, we are told:

In interacting with its environment, the organism changes in many ways. . . . [Among other changes] it may learn. Learning is the effect of a stimulus compound or stimulus compounds upon the nervous system of the organism and the responses which these evoke, that makes possible the establishment of new responses, as a result of such experiences. (1948:187)

Many psychologists may, indeed, accept this as a rough definition of learning. But when one leaves this level of generality and raises the question of how this process is to be envisaged, this happy harmony disappears. Hilgard points out: "There are no laws of learning which can be taught with confidence" (1956:457). Likewise no one questions the fact that "behavior of any type is the result of the interaction of the organism and its environment" (Welch 1948:176). But what is the nature of this interaction? What are the roles of organism and environment? Here are questions on which different writers have taken divergent positions. (See Henle 1957.) While no one will disagree that memorizing and generalizing (Welch 1948:181, 182) occur, and while Welch's definitions might provoke little controversy as rough identifications of the phenomena in question, different theories exist about the nature of these processes.

It will be clear from the above discussion that the existence of facts which all psychologists accept is irrelevant to the problem of eclecticism. Likewise the circumstance that some developments in psychology have called attention to facts ignored by others has no bearing on the issue. The important questions are: How are these facts understood? and, What is their place in the overall theoretical system? Even where agreement exists as to the facts, differences are current with respect to these questions.

In all the examples considered here, it would appear that differences have been reconciled and controversy eliminated at the price of obscuring the issues with which research is concerned in contemporary psychology.

Boring (1929), years ago, pointed out the productive role of controversy in scientific research. Not only does the eclectic lose prematurely the advantages of controversy, he may to some extent give up the advantages of theory as well. The above discussion contains the suggestion that the eclectic at times renounces specific theory in the area of a controversy in order to reconcile differences. This statement will be qualified below. But now attention must be drawn to a consequence of the intimate relation between fact and theory.

There is a certain amount of fact that can be discovered in the absence of any theory. For example, time errors forced themselves to the attention of psychologists who were concerned with quite different problems. For the most part, however, problems for investigation arise out of the theories one holds. New facts are discovered in the course of research designed to test one's hypotheses. To the extent, therefore, that the eclectic gives up specific theory in the area of a controversy, he is handicapped in the discovery of new facts.

Closer examination will, however, often show implicit theories which may contradict the eclectic's avowed intention by placing him in a position on one side or the other of the (now only implicit) controversy. Woodworth, for example, deals with transfer in terms of *carrying over* something from one learning situation to another rather than in terms of *application* of what has been learned to the training tasks as well as to the new ones. That is, transfer is seen as occurring because knowledge acquired in the original training is carried over to the new activity; the new tasks, to the extent to which they are similar to the learned ones, are considered already partially learned. The alternative is ignored that what is learned is not tasks but principles or other whole properties; thus the training activity may merely provide examples of the use of the principle which can be applied equally to the new situation. Woodworth's theory is thus close to a theory of identical elements in this respect, opposing one derived from the study of learning by understanding (Katona 1940: ch. 5) and, indeed, unable to deal with many cases of such learning.[7] This consequence is particularly impressive since, as will be illustrated immediately below, Woodworth is by no means opposed to learning by understanding; it is another instance of the confusions which eclecticism breeds.

In another place Woodworth calls attention to the following controversy:

Among present-day theories of learning those which emphasize reenforcement or the law of effect minimize the perceptual factor, often stigmatizing it as "mentalistic" and impossible to conceive in physical terms, while those which emphasize perceptual learning are apt to deny any direct importance to the factor of reenforcement. (1947:119)

In attempting to show that there is "no obvious incompatibility" of these two factors, he makes (explicit) assumptions about learning as a cognitive process[8] which would be likely to be unacceptable to many S-R theorists, and (both implicit and explicit) empiristic assumptions about perception[9] which many cognitive theorists might find equally unacceptable (assumptions, incidentally, which are not necessarily consistent with those about the learning process).[10]

Several questions suggest themselves with respect to the theory implicit in eclectic solutions. A question worth examining is whether there is a tendency for such implicit theory to be too heavily weighted in the direction of traditional theory. As the above examples show, this need not always be the case; but it seems plausible to think that when theory is not explicit, and thus not examined, it draws upon doctrines prevailing both in psychology and in the culture in general rather than upon the newer and less widely accepted theoretical currents. In a similar connection Köhler has pointed to a certain conservatism in eclecticism:

It has been said with approval that psychology now tends to be eclectic. Again, we have been told that in psychology we had better stay in the middle of the road. I cannot agree with these prescriptions because, if they were followed, psychologists would have to look first of all backward. In an eclectic attitude, they would be too much concerned with ideas which are already available; and, in attempting to find the middle of the road in psychology, they would have to give too much attention to the tracks along which others have moved before them. Such attitudes could perhaps be recommended if, in research, security were an important issue. Actually there is no place for it in this field. In research, we have to look forward, and to take risks. (1953:136)

Another question which arises in connection with the theory underlying eclectic solutions is the following: Since such theory is often implicit, and thus unexpressed and unexamined, is it adequate to lead to the discovery of new facts? For example, since the idea of "carrying over" (i.e., as opposed to that of "application") is only implicit in Woodworth's theory of identical components, it seems unlikely that it would be subjected to test. Or again, the implicit elementarism in Welch's statement about learning (see note 10) is unlikely to be tested since the author's main focus is on other aspects of the statement.

Also worth looking into in connection with the theory implicit in eclectic solutions are the questions of its adequacy for ordering the facts and its susceptibility to proof or disproof. For example, to say that "something" is transferred is too unspecific a statement of the conditions of transfer to test empirically. Any finding of transfer seems to confirm it, and there is no result which could disprove it. Again, it has been suggested above that the theory implicit in a given eclecticism is not always internally consistent. This is a question which deserves examination in connection with particular eclectic psychologies.

We may summarize the discussion so far by saying that eclectics have to a large extent succeeded in resolving conflicts in psychology by ignoring differences and obscuring the issues. Some reasons for dissatisfaction with such solutions have been indicated.[11] Is there no alternative? It seems to me that reconciliations can be reached in psychology only by focusing on the existing differences, examining them, and carrying on research to settle issues. If this is eclecticism, it is eclecticism after the fact rather than the prevailing eclecticism before the fact. And it is clear that it will not be a matter of reconciling existing theories. Since competing theories on any particular issue in psychology today—or competing psychological systems—each tend to be plausible and to be supported by evidence, it is unlikely that any one will win a clear victory over the others. Yet none can offer a fully satisfactory explanation—or else the controversy would not exist. Controversies do not exist in science with regard to processes which are fully understood. Thus the task seems to be one of arriving at new, more comprehensive theories of the processes in question.

An example should make this clear. It seems safe to say that theories of forgetting arising out of experimental psychology have found no adequate place for repression. Nor have the psychoanalysts succeeded (or tried) to bring repression into relation with a general theory of memory and forgetting. Can the two kinds of theory be brought together? It seems to me that the most fruitful starting place is not the attempt to reconcile existing theories. Actually, useful theories of repression do not exist. (See Bruner 1956 for a similar point, more generally stated.) It is hardly sufficient to say:

Repression proceeds from the ego when the latter—it may be at the behest of the superego—refuses to associate itself with an instinctual cathexis which has been aroused in the id. The ego is able by means of repression to keep the idea which is the vehicle of the reprehensible impulse from becoming conscious. (Freud 1926 20:91)

This statement contains no hypothesis about the processes involved, about how repression can possibly be brought about. Thus there seems to be no point in attempting to reconcile the theories of experimental psychology and psychoanalysis on repression; neither has an effective theory in this area. What we need is to look into the processes themselves, in the light of what we know about forgetting in general (cf. Henle 1955). Can affective processes act, for example, to produce a failure of the Höffding function—i.e., that selective interaction between present process and memory trace which is the basis of recognition and the first step in the process of recall? (Cf. Köhler 1940:126ff.) Under what conditions can emotional and motivational processes introduce interferences? Answers to such questions might lead not only to a hypothesis about the nature of repression, but might also introduce considerable modification into our present theories of the nature of forgetting in general.

The eclectics are, of course, right in maintaining that where a genuine controversy exists in psychology, and where evidence seems to support both sides, there is likely to be some truth to both positions. But they solve their problem too soon. Existing theories cannot be made more comprehensive by adding divergent ones together. They can be broadened to include all the relevant evidence only by looking more deeply into the phenomena with which they are concerned; and this means arriving at new theories.

At this point the parallel between productive solutions of theoretical problems and of personal problems becomes striking. In connection with the reconciliation of opposites within the personality, C. G. Jung points out that conflicts are never resolved on their own level. They are outgrown. Only on a higher level can you see both sides.

SUMMARY

Examples have been presented to show that eclectics tend to resolve conflicts in psychology by glossing over real differences and obscuring the issues. Such solutions achieve harmony at the price of specific theory in the area of the controversy, and thus sacrifice fruitfulness in the discovery of new facts. Closer examination often reveals implicit theories underlying such solutions, but unexpressed and unexamined theory can hardly be expected to equal explicit hypotheses either in fruitfulness or in adequacy in dealing with known facts.

It is here suggested that differences need to be resolved in psychology not by denying them and attempting to combine existing theories, but by focusing on the differences and using them to get a better view of the relevant phenomena. We will achieve more comprehensive theories not by combining existing ones but by understanding better the processes in question.

Chapter 8

On Controversy
and Its Resolution

We seem in psychology to be a little ashamed of our controversies. Or—what amounts to the same thing—we smile indulgently at the foibles of our elders. We attribute controversy to the Age of Schools, and we make it altogether clear that we are well past that age. The instinct controversy has recently been described as "one of the dirtiest of our controversial wash" (Krantz and Allen 1967:336). The Baldwin-Titchener controversy—some 40 pages of it—we say concerned nothing more than a tenth of a second in reaction time. What contemporary editor would have allotted 141 pages to the Wundt-Stumpf controversy on tonal distance? And who is interested in these disputes today? Psychology does not have a very good record in resolving its controversies; rather, we lose interest in them.

My theme will be that we need not be ashamed of our controversies or dismiss them as trivial. Controversy is not only useful, but probably unavoidable, since it arises out of essential properties of our cognitive functioning. Further, controversies have

A number of friends have read and criticized an earlier draft of this paper. I am grateful to Dr. Rudolf Arnheim for forcing me to clarify my thinking at crucial points and to Dr. John Sullivan and Dr. Theta Wolf for many helpful and interesting suggestions.

made positive contributions, and resolution—in one way or another—is sometimes possible.

Why are controversies in such bad repute? It seems that we dislike them because we see in them the intrusion of emotion in the rational structure of our science. We read, for example: "If science were a totally rational enterprise, controversy would, in all likelihood, not exist" (ibid.). Again: "What is it that creates scientific controversy? Ego-involvement. Ego-bias" (Boring 1954: 639). Also: "When two incompatible egoisms come together, they account for the wasted time of scientific warfare, for the dethronement of reason by rationalization" (Boring 1955:105). Elsewhere, Boring is still more explicit:

Egoism and the need for prestige . . . tend to close the mind in controversy, a phenomenon which is illustrated in any thoroughgoing scientific quarrel. . . . Not distinct from egoism is the need for self-consistency. Every quarrel shows that too. When a man takes up a position, his pride prevents retraction. . . . Sometimes it is not respectable to be right if you have to change your mind out loud. (1942:612)

Let me begin my defense of controversies by pointing out that they have not, as a rule, been insignificant. The issue between Baldwin and Titchener was that of functionalism vs. structuralism. It was a controversy over the legitimate problems of psychology and the legitimate conditions of collecting psychological data. To speak of the controversy as if it were over a minor difference in reaction time is to rob it of its context and meaning. But when torn out of context, most scientific work sounds trivial. What does it matter, for example, if an eclipse arrives a little late? So do jets, and nobody minds very much. To the astronomer, of course, seeing the event in its scientific context, it would make a tremendous difference.[1]

But the main issue is undoubtedly that of the role of passion in controversy. Aside from the presence of personal attack, why do we see in controversy the operation of factors less than ideally rational? For the effects attributed to emotion, I will draw considerably on Boring, the psychologist who has been most interested in the analysis of controversy.[2]

1. It has usually been true in psychological controversy that

neither side has changed its position. Boring comments: "Controversy is more than discussion. It involves emotion: and passion, while of itself irrelevant to scientific procedure, enters to prejudice reason and to fix the debaters more firmly in their opinions" (1929:119). Again, he remarks: "Plainly there is a perseverative tendency in scientific thinking" (1929:113). He quotes a remark of Max Planck: "New scientific truth does not triumph by convincing its opponents and making them see the light, but rather because its opponents eventually die" (Boring 1954:640).

One of the most striking forms such a perseverative tendency takes is seen in the use of the ad hoc hypothesis to deal with contradictory evidence. As an example from the history of psychology, we may consider the famous constancy hypothesis. When many perceptual phenomena did not behave as they ought to have behaved from this point of view—the illusions, constancies, contrast, perceived movement, and so on—nothing was easier than to add assumptions, untested and untestable, about the effects of unconscious inferences, errors of judgment, and the like. What could be better evidence for ego involvement in one's theoretical position than such frantic efforts to save it?

2. Controversy, it is said, blinds us to alternatives so that we can see neither the point of our opponent nor the relevance of his arguments, or even of his data.

Thus, controversies in psychology have tended not to be settled by factual evidence. Krantz (1969) has shown this clearly in the case of the Baldwin-Titchener controversy, where there was little argument about what the facts were. As a matter of fact, both participants were pretty well aware of the facts before the controversy began. (See Titchener's review article of 1895.) As another example, the same seems to be true in the case of the long controversy over continuity in learning.

3. Another curious and apparently nonrational characteristic of controversies is that they may seem to die out, only to reappear in connection with a different problem. Thus the controversy over reaction times had died out by 1900 (Krantz 1969:12), but the structuralists and the functionalists had by no means lost interest in refuting each other's positions. Instead, they found new problems, new arenas for their debates. It is easy to blame emotion for

the refusal of certain debates to die out: passion would seem to motivate the search for new points of attack.

4. As Boring sees it, some personal need—enthusiasm, loyalty, egoism—"gets the work done, but it may also blind you to the defects and shortcomings of the work itself. . . . The truth of objectivity may be left for others to perceive, or even reserved for posterity" (1954:645).

5. Participants in controversy are frequently accused of still another apparently emotional indiscretion. In Boring's words:

Social attitudes also constrain thought. Here we have the influence of the schools, the need for men to stand together. The in-group magnify their agreements and rise to repel, or at least to depreciate, the out-group. . . . Wundt's students confirmed the tridimensional theory of feeling; others did not. Würzburg never found images for thought; Cornell did. Is feeling a sensation or not? Laboratory atmosphere largely determined what would be found in answer to that question. (1942:612)

While other such effects can be gleaned from the literature, these should suffice. It can certainly not be denied that such phenomena may be observed in our psychological controversies. Must we conclude that—whatever the motivational advantages of emotion, of commitment, of intense interest, for scientific work—controversy does no more than reveal the scientist in his entirely human capacity for passion?

It will be suggested here that all these phenomena are characteristic of cognitive processes in general, and especially so when we are dealing with organizations of any complexity. The relevant facts are so well known that extended discussion is unnecessary.

1. What Boring calls a perseverative tendency in scientific thinking—what I would prefer to call perseverance—is necessary for all problem solving. In the case of problems of any complexity, most scientific problems certainly included, failure is assured if the thinker abandons his approach in the face of every obstacle. "Hold to your strategy, vary your tactics," advises Humphrey:

The strategy of thought, its general aims, must be carried through, in spite of all difficulties, with all the persistence one can summon. The tactics must be altered to suit the particular difficulties that arise during the process of solution. (1948:62)

Wertheimer, describing his talks with Einstein about the thinking that culminated in the theory of relativity, quotes his subject as saying: "During all those years there was a feeling of direction, of going straight toward something concrete" (1959:228 n. 7). Examples are familiar: Newton, it is reported, came to discover the law of gravitation by always thinking about it. Gauss worked for four years to prove a theorem (Humphrey 1948:129). Poincaré offers numerous instances of his prolonged efforts to solve particular problems (1952).[3]

Perseverance in a wrong direction, of course, leads to foolish processes or to error. Einstellung is a well-known phenomenon in certain kinds of problem solving. Similarly, in the case of systems of thought, perseverance in a nonessential direction may be unproductive: the most familiar example in American psychology is Titchener's structuralism, which Heidbreder describes as a "gallant and enlightening failure." (1933:151).[4]

But coherent thinking requires persistence in a given direction. Such persistence leads, at times, to failure, but it is essential for cognitive achievement.

2. The fact that it is often impossible to see the relevance of an opponent's arguments, or even of his data, may be derived from one of the most basic phenomena of all cognitive processes: a given item appears different in different contexts. First demonstrated in the case of perception, where an item may not even retain its identity in a new configuration, as Ternus has shown, the statement may be exemplified everywhere in thinking and in understanding. At the most commonplace level, a word has different meanings in different sentences. At a somewhat more complex level, the meaning of a statement will depend upon the author to whom it is attributed, and thus upon the context of ideas in which it is set (Asch 1948). Wertheimer has given compelling instances in which "a thing may be true in the piecemeal sense, and false, indeed a lie, as a part in its whole" (1934:137).

For purely cognitive reasons, then, it is scarcely surprising that a fact in the context of Titchener's system would have different significance from the same fact in the context of Baldwin's thinking. That the facts of the case did not change the mind of either participant in this controversy is testimony, not to the emotional character of controversy, but to the powerful role of context in endowing facts with meaning.

Once more it must be added that the effects of context may, on occasion, lead to error. Functional fixedness, as one example, is an expression for the fact that an object that could be used to solve a particular problem—that could be relevant in a particular context—is not seen as relevant because of its known relevance to some other context.

Because of the power of context in determining the meaning of items, contexts themselves are usually difficult to change. New items, immediately interpreted in the light of a body of ideas, lose much of their potential ability to threaten those ideas. When the organization in question has the complexity of a theoretical system, reorganization is, of course, exceedingly difficult. In commenting on Einstein's achievement in reorganizing physical thinking, Wertheimer remarks:

> In appraising these transformations we must not forget that they took place in view of a gigantic given system. Every step had to be taken against a very strong gestalt—the traditional structure of physics, which fitted an enormous number of facts, apparently so flawless, so clear that any local change was bound to meet with the resistance of the whole strong and well-articulated structure. This was probably the reason why it took so long a time—seven years—until the crucial advance was made. (1959:232)

Given the difficulty of achieving reorganizations of complex systems, one can understand the tendency to use ad hoc hypotheses to patch up a system rather than attempt to achieve a new theoretical framework. Nor is this necessarily irrational where the apparently contradictory facts are neither central nor overwhelming in number. The necessity for perseverance in thinking has been pointed out above.[5]

But to return to the main point: facts do—and ordinarily must—find their meaning in context. If we failed to interpret facts, we could not explain them or even think about them. We would be in the position of Thurber's man who "doesn't know anything except facts," and we would obviously not be solving scientific problems.

3. It was pointed out that controversies often seem to die out, only to reappear in a new connection. In other words, the controversy has been transposed. Transposition first became known in perception, and it has wide relevance to thinking processes as well. Organized bodies of knowledge, which may be challenged at a number of points, are, of course, particularly conducive to such transposition.

4. That we are often unable to see the defects of our own work as clearly as we see those in the work of an opponent is most likely largely a matter of the difficulty of achieving reorganizations of already organized material.

5. The influences attributed to schools seem to be even more simply explainable. That different findings are obtained in different laboratories is a matter of the conditions set up, the tasks presented, the instructions to subjects and to experimenters, and the like. One special case will be considered below.

I have been suggesting that we do not need to look to emotional factors to account for the phenomena of controversy, but that we are dealing with basic characteristics of cognitive processes. The same factors—the role of context and the rest—that enable us to have any coherent view of the world, or any theoretical framework, are the ones that make it difficult for us to resolve our controversies. Is this to say that passion does not enter into controversy? By no means. Wundt did insult Stumpf (Boring 1929), and Titchener's term "polite invective" might at times be applied to both participants in the Baldwin-Titchener exchange.[6] Certainly, passion and commitment figure in controversies; but, apart from name-calling, they doubtless function by way of processes of the kind described here.

This is another chapter that cannot be treated here; but I would like to indicate a direction by quoting a passage from John Stuart Mill.[7] Here intellectual and "moral" sources of erroneous opinions are discussed; the latter, for Mill, consist of indifference to the attainment of truth and of bias:

But the moral causes of opinions, though with most persons the most powerful of all, are but remote causes: they do not act directly, but by means of the intellectual causes; to which they bear the same relation that the circumstances called, in the theory of medicine, *predisposing* causes, bear to *exciting* causes. Indifference to truth cannot, in and by itself, produce erroneous belief; it operates by preventing the mind from collecting the proper evidences, or from applying to them the test of a legitimate and rigid induction; by which omission it is exposed un-protected to the influence of any species of apparent evidence which offers itself spontaneously, or which is elicited by that smaller quantity of trouble which the mind may be willing to take. As little is Bias a direct source of wrong conclusions. We cannot believe a proposition only by wishing, or only by dreading, to believe it. The most violent inclination to find a set of propositions true, will not enable the weakest of mankind to believe them without a vestige of intellectual grounds—without any, even apparent, evidence. It acts indirectly, by placing the intellectual grounds of belief in an incomplete or distorted shape before his eyes. It makes him shrink from the irksome labour of a rigorous induction, when he has a misgiving that its results may be disagreeable; and in such exami-nation as he does institute, it makes him exert that which *is* in a certain measure voluntary, his attention, unfairly, giving a larger share of it to the evidence which seems favourable to the desired conclusion, a smaller to that which seems unfavourable. It operates, too, by making him look out eagerly for reasons, or apparent reasons, to support opinions which are conformable, or resist those which are repugnant, to his interests or feelings. . . . But though the opinions of the generality of mankind, when not dependent on mere habit and inculcation, have their root much more in the inclinations than in the intellect, it is a necessary condition to the triumph of the moral bias that it should first pervert the understanding. Every erroneous inference, though originating in moral causes, involves the intellectual operation of admitting insufficient evidence as sufficient; and whoever was on his guard against all kinds of inconclusive evidence which can be mistaken for conclusive, would be in no danger of being led into error even by the strongest bias. . . . If the sophistry of the intellect could be rendered impossible, that of the feelings, having no instrument to work with, would be powerless. (1872: Book 5, ch. 1, sec. 3)

To return parenthetically to the role of passion in scientific work, Boring points to its motivating effects: "Out of egoism are derived the drive and enthusiasm that lead men to undertake research, to keep at it, to publish the results, to keep promoting the knowledge and use of these results" (1954:640). With T. S. Kuhn (1962), I prefer to view normal science as puzzle solving, with the demands of the problem itself and the curiosity of the scientist supplying the motivating forces. This is not to minimize the role of passion in scientific work. But passion for what? For the work, I am suggesting, not merely the passion of egoism.

If one considers controversy to be irrational to a high degree, this has certain consequences for its resolution. Thus Boring recommends that we cultivate both judiciousness and effective prejudices (1929:121)—judiciousness with a view to reducing fruitless controversy, and effective prejudices with a view to getting the work done. He holds out the hope that, if we do not outlive our outmoded views, at least science will (1954:641). And Krantz and Allen consider that "to accomplish . . . confluence of views, some form of persuasion must occur" (1967:337).

If one holds controversy to be a consequence of normal modes of cognitive functioning, the problem of its resolution changes. But since, as I have mentioned, psychology has not been notably successful in resolving its controversies, let us first look briefly at some effects of controversy even in the absence of resolution.

My references will largely be to recent controversies. It should be noted that these are not controversies in the grand style of the nineteenth century. We do not find a critique, a reply, a rejoinder, an *Antikritik*, a *Schlusswort*, and still another *Schlusswort*. Rather, we are fortunate to find a critique and a rejoinder. But the changes, I suspect, are changes in editorial policy, not in the dynamics of controversy.

1. Controversy leads to research undertaken in the hope of settling the issue. We have seen that controversies in psychology have tended not to be settled by factual evidence. "But facts are facts," as William James put it, "and if we only get enough of them they are sure to combine. New ground will from year to year be broken, and theoretic results will grow" (1890 1:193).

2. Since controversy arises where existing research leaves questions of interpretation, it may lead to an improvement of techniques and of research designs.

Köhler makes this effect of controversy explicit in a reference to Postman's criticism of his work on the nature of associations:

The experiments, I will candidly say, are perhaps not yet entirely conclusive. But I am grateful to Postman; his arguments tell me exactly what further tests must now be done in order to reach a clear decision. At times, work in psychology does become a lively affair. (1969:132)

Another controversy which seems to have led to improved research design and procedures is the one over learning and awareness; still another example is the long controversy over subliminal perception.

3. Controversy may lead to a clarification of issues. This may take the form of a clarification of the implicit assumptions of one's opponents. For example, Krantz and Allen point out that "McDougall forced a clarification of the underlying assumptions of radical behaviorism" (1967:336). Many similar examples could be given.

Köhler once remarked that it is the responsibility of each scientific generation to make explicit the implicit assumptions of its forebears. Controversy enables us to do this within a generation—at least for uncommitted outsiders, if any exist.

4. Some positive effects of controversies, quite independent of their resolution, have been indicated. It must now be added that the criticism which is essential to controversy may lead to changes that are not necessarily advances:

(a) A hardening of position. Titchener in 1898 saw functionalism as having a great future; of course, by this he meant that its future was assured to the extent to which it could be taken over by his own experimental psychology (1898:465). In later years his position hardened—in part, no doubt, as a result of his continuing debate with the functionalists. (This is, however, not an unmixed effect of controversy. In part his position hardened because, as he systematically set forth his ideas about science, it became clear that functionalism in no way fit.) At any rate, in the *Systematic Psychology* he wrote: "Functional psychology . . . is a parasite, and the parasite of an organism doomed to extinction" (1929:254). The image no longer suggests a great future, indeed no future at all.

(b) A restricting of position. In a minor controversy in which I was once involved, the opponents first described what they called "pure phenomenological psychology" as concerned with nonconceptualized experience; under criticism, they seemed to add a condition not previously discernible: "ppp" deals with experience that is conceptualizable but not conceptualized (Brody and Oppenheim 1967:332). That this is a restriction, not simply a clarification, is seen from the circumstance that it would exclude mystical experience which, before the criticism, was the most plausible material on which they could draw for their conception of "ppp."

(c)   A position becoming more extreme under criticism. Krantz and Allen have indicated that this was one effect of attacks on early behaviorism by McDougall and others (1967:336). Similarly, most of us have seen ourselves pushed under attack into extreme positions we didn't really hold.

Still, controversies are sometimes resolved. How?

1. Resolution may be the result of mutual decision that new methods should be used to settle issues. The decision may not be explicit at the time; and it may be made by those who inherit a controversy rather than by those who initiated it.

A number of early scientific controversies disappeared when scientists agreed to decide them by empirical evidence rather than by authority. In the controversy on the comets of 1618, for example, one of the arguments brought against Galileo was a biblical story. He took the trouble to answer the argument, but this, of course, did not resolve the issue; it could be settled only later by the methods of empirical science. Again, Harvey had to contend mainly with the authority of the Galenists. Here is one of his replies:

Who will not see that the precepts he has received from his teachers are false; or who thinks it unseemly to give up accredited opinions; or who regards it as in some sort criminal to call in question doctrines that have descended through a long succession of ages, and carry the authority of the ancients—to all of these I reply: that the facts cognizable by the senses wait upon no opinions, and that the works of nature bow to no antiquity; for indeed there is nothing either more ancient or of higher authority than nature. (1649)

This controversy, too, disappeared when the higher authority of nature was generally recognized.

Likewise in modern times, controversies may drop out with the introduction of new methodology. Krantz and Allen (1967) have shown that the instinct controversy in psychology disappeared for this reason: an experimental methodology was being introduced for problems of social psychology. (Revival of interest in instinct in contemporary ethology had to await acceptable methodology for problems in this area.)

2. Occasionally a controversy can be resolved by showing that the alternatives as formulated are too narrow. Thus Köhler has

shown that both nativists and empiricists have seen their problem too narrowly. Both have neglected all those factors which the organism shares with the rest of nature—thus, factors independent of the heredity of the individual or the particular species, and likewise independent of the individual experience of any member of the species. Thus a perceptual phenomenon that is unlearned need not depend upon the existence of inherited mechanisms.

The dichotomy as formulated, in short, leaves out a very large part of the story:

It is three factors by which events in organisms . . . are generally determined. First, the invariant principles and forces of general dynamics, secondly, anatomical constraints which evolution has established, and thirdly, learning. . . . Why so much talk about inheritance, and so much about learning—but hardly ever a word about invariant dynamics? It is this invariant dynamics, however constrained by histological devices, which keeps organisms and their nervous systems going. (Köhler 1969: 89–90)

Here is a case, I think, in which it does not matter whether nativists continue to oppose empiricists. The controversy has been superseded: once it is seen that three factors are involved, not two, the controversy loses its meaning. If we do not realize that this controversy has been bypassed, so much the worse for us. The next generation will find it out.

3. In still other ways, a controversy may be shown to be a pseudocontroversy. Arnheim has suggested, for example, that the controversy over imageless thought arose because the Würzburg psychologists did not know what to look for in examining their consciousness for images. The experienced content did not correspond to their notion of an image (Arnheim 1969:102). They thought of images as replicas of objects, ignoring the essential abstractness of images.

If Arnheim is right, the imageless thought controversy disappears. It then becomes a pseudocontroversy arising because the two sides were talking about different things, but using the same name for them.[8]

4. A controversy may be resolved by formulating a more inclusive theory which will in some sense incorporate the com-

peting positions. For example, Mary Calkins (1906) attempted to resolve the conflict between structuralism and functionalism by finding for both a place within a broader context: her own self-psychology. But in order to do this, she had first to ask: What is essential about each approach—that is, specifically what is the problem of reconciliation?

As to structuralism, the essential thing, she thought, is not its atomistic unit, whose inadequacies the functionalists had already pointed out. If this were the essential thing, there would be no point to the reconciliation. Rather, it is the method of structuralism which is to be retained: the analysis into irreducible elements and the classification of experiences. Within the new context, the structural task is the analysis of consciousness regarded as experience of a self (Calkins 1906:70).

What about functionalism? Again Calkins went to what she regarded as essential—here, too, a type of psychological analysis. This she viewed as embodying two conceptions: "first, and fundamentally, the conception of consciousness in terms of the relations to environment which it involves; second, the conception of consciousness in terms of the significance or value of these relations" (1906:72). The first of these conceptions may be made to coincide with self-psychology; the second may be subsumed under it. In short, "Functional psychology, rightly conceived, is a form of self-psychology" (1906:75).

Today we are not much interested in this solution by Calkins, but the reason does not lie in any inadequacy of the solution. Rather, we no longer experience the conflict: we are no longer interested in structural problems in the Titchenerian sense; and, on the other hand, functionalism never became a developed system of psychology, but has persisted as a flavor, an interest of contemporary psychological theories. As a matter of fact, Calkins herself lost interest in this solution as she came more and more to "question the significance and the adequacy, and deprecate the abstractness" of structural psychology (see Calkins 1930:40).

It should be noted that Calkins took *two* steps, not one, to resolve the controversy. First she decided *what* was to be reconciled; then she placed the apparently conflicting material within a larger framework. There have been many recent attempts to resolve controversy; one reason for their failure has been the omission of the first step. And, more serious, we have tended to try to resolve the controversy while staying within a framework not sufficiently broad to encompass what is of value in each point of view.[9]

Anatol Rapoport (1967) has suggested a similar method as a means of escape from paradox. (He is concerned only with step 2; but since he is dealing with clear-cut logical problems, this makes no difficulty.) Apparently insoluble problems, he shows, can sometimes be solved by broadening the logical framework in which they are presented.

This procedure, it seems to me, applies not only to the resolution of theoretical conflict and to escape from certain kinds of paradox, but much more generally to the resolution of conflict. We may restate this method of solution in more formal and more general terms. Given conflicting demands | a | and | b |, resolution is possible only when a configuration is found—say, abc—which includes both. Solution is possible in the larger context because the components alter their character within the configuration. The | a | is not the same item as the a in abc, and may thus not be in conflict with the b of abc. Furthermore, our focus is no longer on | a | but on the configuration.

Once more, particular items look different when seen within a broader context: the conflicting claims look different, and the conflict may therefore sometimes be resolved. The same influence of context which has been seen to make the resolution of controversy difficult can be used for just that purpose. Perpetuation of controversy, as well as its resolution, may be seen as Gestalt problems.

In summary, most of the methods of resolution of controversy listed above may be seen to be means of superseding the controversy rather than resolving it. To free a science of a pseudocontroversy is a positive achievement. True resolution has been discussed in terms of setting conflicting positions within a broader framework; but this method has rarely been used in psychology. Indeed, if it is envisaged, as Calkins envisaged it, as a means of reconciling general theories, it seems today to be premature. Meantime, rather than look away from controversy, we may recall its productive consequences:

Heated argument is to be avoided. But to set opposing points of view into plastic relief is our obligation.

Goethe's maxim (Curtius 1964:122) seems to be good advice to contemporary psychology.

Part III

On Primary Sources

Chapter 9

A Whisper
from a Ghost

In the course of one of his Travels, Gulliver was in the enviable position of being able to call up and converse with figures long dead. I quote:

Having a Desire to see those Ancients, who were most renowned for Wit and Learning, I set apart one Day on purpose. I proposed that *Homer* and *Aristotle* might appear at the Head of all their Commentators. . . . I had a Whisper from a Ghost, who shall be nameless, that these Commentators always kept in the most distant Quarters from their Principals in the lower World, through a Consciousness of Shame and Guilt, because they had so horribly misrepresented the Meaning of those Authors to Posterity. . . . *Aristotle* was out of all Patience with the Account I gave him of *Scotus* and *Ramus*, as I presented them to him; and he asked them whether the rest of the Tribe were as great Dunces as themselves.

It may be added parenthetically that these were no ordinary Dunces; the logic of Ramus was influential for more than a hundred years, until the Port-Royalists took over.

In psychology, we have only a few generations of authors to misrepresent to posterity, but we have done so with a thorough-

I am grateful to the Cornell University Libraries for permission to use unpublished letters of E. B. Titchener. E. B. Titchener Papers, Accession #14/23/545, Department of Manuscripts and University Archives, Cornell University Libraries.

ness that could have impressed Gulliver. I would like to illustrate the point with some examples of the treatment of a few major figures in the recent history of psychology. My account will be limited to figures whose work is available in English, so that the primary sources would be as easy for American readers to obtain as secondary ones. On the whole, I will avoid naming my secondary sources, since the problem with which I am concerned is widespread; I am interested in a trend, not in individuals. Only widely used secondary sources will be considered.

I will, however, mention by name the most famous writer of our contemporary secondary sources, E. G. Boring, whose histories have long been considered standard. Boring, it will be recalled, was a student and then a junior colleague of E. B. Titchener until 1918. As published and unpublished correspondence shows, he remained in touch with Titchener until the latter's death. He might thus be expected to be an authoritative source on Titchener, although he candidly admits that "Titchener alive did not always confirm the author's [Boring's] interpretation of his views" (Boring 1933:33). I will confine myself to three instances which suggest that Titchener had reason to have misgivings about Boring's interpretations of his views.

In Boring's discussion of the subject matter of Titchenerian psychology, one finds the sentence: "No wonder Titchener could conclude (posthumously, 1929) that introspective psychology deals solely with sensory materials" (1933:19). Titchener was certainly an impressive personality, but posthumous conclusions are too much to expect even of so towering a figure.[1] As early as 1914 (the year of Boring's doctorate at Cornell), Titchener publicly expressed the wish that he could deal solely with sensory materials. Feelings stood in the way of such a simplification, and Titchener wrote: "I only wish that I could see my way clear to" the "reduction of affection to organic sensation" (1914:12–13 n.32). It is hard to believe that Boring was ignorant of this paper. He could easily have known that Titchener was actively engaged in the effort to reduce feelings to sensory data some ten years before the publication of the posthumous book. He did know that Nafe's research of 1924, by identifying "affective pressures," settled the matter for Titchener (Boring 1933:18).[2] Indeed, Titchener wrote to Boring about how to observe these affective pressures (Boring 1937:476). But even apart from these considerations, if Boring had paid a little attention to the dates by which the posthumously published chapters were written, he would not have had to ascribe to Titchener conclusions from beyond the grave. If we cannot trust Boring on a matter of simple chronology, we need to be wary in connection with substantive matters.[3]

I come to one of these: Boring's discussion of the context theory of meaning, Titchener's theory that meaning is carried by a context of images and sensations that cluster around a sensory or imaginal core. This discussion appears in an article of 1942, but since Boring allowed it to be reprinted in a collection of his papers published in 1963, it seems safe to conclude that he did not later take serious issue with it. I will quote a single sentence, though there are other things in the passage in question that would perhaps not have appealed to Titchener. "If the core is a face, then a name may be sufficient context" (1963:104). The interesting thing about this passage is not that Boring adopts a context theory, but that he says he does, but doesn't get it right. A perceived face is no mere bundle of sensory data; it has meaning. It is not a sensory core but a meaningful percept. In connection with what is perhaps Titchener's most famous theory, Boring is committing the stimulus error—for Titchener, the worst error a psychologist can commit.[4]

One final example: In a paper presented to the American Psychological Association in 1967, Boring speaks of "Titchener's . . . shift toward behaviorism even before behaviorism began" (1969: 21). It is the "facts of nature" and "the inexorable Zeitgeist" that nudge Titchener into a kind of behaviorism in 1910 (1969:30). What is the basis for this new interpretation?

Titchener's "behaviorism," to be found in the *Text-book*, apparently consists in his bringing meaning "under the scrutiny of psychology" (Boring 1969:26), and in the recognition that meaning need not be carried consciously, from which Boring concludes that "context is carried unconsciously" (1969:29). What Titchener actually says in the passage under consideration (1910:369) is that "meaning may be carried in purely physiological terms." He rejects what he calls the invention of "an unconscious mind to give coherence and continuity to the conscious" (1910:40). If we do so, he warns, "we voluntarily leave the sphere of fact for the sphere of fiction." Thus it cannot be correct to speak of the "forces that were pressing Titchener toward the acceptance of unconscious psychological processes" (Boring 1969:32). What he is speaking of is physiological processes, and there is no change in his position in this regard. His first book, *An Outline of Psychology* (1896), presents the position of psychophysical parallelism, which is maintained in the *Text-book*.

These passages seem to me not only *not* to show a drift by Titchener toward behaviorism, but also to misinterpret behaviorism. Surely behaviorism is something other than the recognition of physiological processes with no conscious counterpart. Furthermore, not being conscious seems to be equated by Boring with "the unconscious"; but the early behaviorists were certainly no more friendly to this concept as it was then (and is now) used than they were to a context theory of meaning. With regard to the involvement of meaning in Titchener's alleged behaviorism, it may be noted that it was not until the 1950s that the behaviorists became seriously interested in problems of meaning.

It is interesting to consider some of the things Titchener was saying about behaviorism in the years after he himself was said by Boring to have become a behaviorist. His reply to Watson's so-called Behavioristic Manifesto of 1913 was given before the American Philosophical Society on April 3, 1914, and published that year. In this paper, in which we see Titchener at his polemical best, he remarks: "Watson is asking us, in effect, to exchange a science for a technology. . . . Watson's behaviorism can never replace psychology because the one is technological, the other scientific" (1914:14).

Ten years later, in a letter to Watson himself, Titchener says:

It is quite true that the logic of the behaviorists is muddled; both Roback and I myself have pointed this out in print. The strength of the movement lies not in its fundamental logic but in its laboratory performance. (Cited by Larson and Sullivan 1965:348)[5]

Boring suggests that the shift to behaviorism in Titchener's thinking "occurred without his knowledge of what was happening to his own thought" (1969:31). Even apart from the evidence reviewed, I find it hard to admit so large a discrepancy between what he thought and what he thought he thought in a man of Titchener's logic, clarity, and consistency.

Let us now turn to the treatment of behaviorism in a secondary source. Here is a quotation from another distinguished historian of psychology in an article on John B. Watson. He cites a number of comments about Watson written during the 1950s:

> The most laudatory of all is from one who looks at Watson's work from the standpoint of logic and the history of science. Bergmann writes:

> Second only to Freud, though at a rather great distance, John B. Watson is, in my judgment, the most important figure in the history of psychological thought during the first half of the century . . . . although the attention he receives now, in the fifties, is perhaps not as great as it was in the twenties and thirties. . . . Among psychologists the sound core of Watson's contribution has been widely accepted; his errors and mistakes have been forgotten. . . . Watson is not only an experimental *psychologist* . . . he is also . . . a systematic thinker . . . a *methodologist*. In this latter area he made his major contribution.[6]

What did Bergmann really say? For the full text, the reader is referred to the *Psychological Review* of 1956; here it will suffice to supply a bit of the context of this correct quotation.

As an experimental psychologist, Bergmann describes Watson as "fairly distinguished no doubt but without transcendent distinction." He sees Watson also as a social philosopher, a metaphysician, and a methodologist. How is he regarded in these roles? This is what Bergmann says:

> His social philosophy is, in my opinion, deplorable. His metaphysics is silly. . . . His metaphysics . . . has a core both true and important. The trouble there was that Watson, unsubtle and, I fear, also very ignorant in philosophical matters, did not know how to state the true and commonsensical core without at the same time asserting a lot of patent nonsense. (1956:266)

Watson's greatness must therefore lie in his role as a methodologist. Bergmann continues:

> As I see him, Watson is above all a completer and a consummator—the

greatest, though not chronologically the last, of the Functionalists. . . .
The one methodological contribution of Watson which is specifically his
own is merely a footnote—though, I insist, a most important one—to the
methodological ideas of the Functionalists. (1956:267–268)

This footnote which, according to Bergmann, has earned Watson
such a high place in the history of the psychology of this century
is the thesis of methodological behaviorism.

This somewhat expanded account of the quotation from Bergmann gives an entirely different impression of his view of Watson
from the quotation as previously presented. Indeed, if the contribution of a mere footnote to functionalism places Watson second
only to Freud, one wonders about the security of Freud's own
position in the history of our science.

I have a trunkful of misinterpretations of Gestalt psychology by
highly regarded writers, some of which I have discussed elsewhere
(Henle 1977). Instead of them, for my final example, I will turn to
one of the most widely used sources in theories of personality, and
I will look in it for the treatment of Kurt Lewin, contenting myself with one or two issues.

In the text I have selected, difficulties arise from the beginning:
"The separation of the person from the rest of the universe is
accomplished by drawing an enclosed figure. The boundary of the
figure defines the limits of the entity known as the person."

What is wrong with this apparently straightforward statement?
Only that it contains an outdated conception of the motoric,
Lewin's term for the perceptual and motor regions. It is true that
Lewin's revision of this concept appears in a rather out-of-the-way
place, in his foreword to a monograph by Robert Leeper (1943);
Lewin himself never had the opportunity to incorporate it into a
book of his own. But since Leeper's monograph appears in the
bibliography of our text, the authors might be assumed to be
familiar with this important change. And important it is: it makes
of the motoric a functional rather than a phenomenal concept
and thus removes an inconsistency from Lewin's theory.

Here is another statement from the same source that reveals a
serious difficulty: "The hollow man was replenished with psychological needs, intentions, hopes, and aspirations. The robot was
transformed into a living human being. The crass and dreary ma-

terialism of behaviorism was replaced by a more humanistic picture of people." This is all very nice, but it has nothing to do with Lewin. What are these needs that fill the hollow man? The authors themselves admit that Lewin gives no list. What are these fine hopes and aspirations? What is the specific nature of this humanistic picture? It is quite clear that Lewin does not tell us. Indeed, his neglect of the contents of personality suggests that Lewin was not interested in developing a theory of personality. He was, it seems to me, doing something different, working out a metatheory—but that is a matter that is not relevant for our present purposes. (See Henle 1978.) It *is* relevant to expect those who discuss Lewin in the context of personality theory to notice his neglect of content. It should not be dismissed as "an unfortunate oversight," as one author did; it should be used as a clue to what Lewin was really doing. It could help us to appreciate his contribution.

I could continue indefinitely with these and additional secondary sources, with their additional distortions. The point seems clear: if we want to know what somebody said, it seems wiser to read the original than to trust to what somebody else said he said.

If Gulliver could see Commentators as a Tribe of Dunces, what would he call those whose erudition rests upon the Commentaries of these Dunces?

Chapter 10

The Influence of Gestalt Psychology in America

In America, Gestalt psychology has always been a minority movement. A brief look at its history, both here and in Germany where it originated, will help us to understand why. It is well known that it began around 1910, when Wertheimer made his fateful stopover in Frankfurt to test his hypotheses about stroboscopic movement. Like the man who came to dinner, he remained for a number of years. Here he found Köhler and Koffka, and the three of them collaborated in what was to become Gestalt psychology.

The publication launching the new movement was Wertheimer's paper on the perception of movement (1912b). Koffka left for Giessen in 1911, and work, particularly in perception, was soon coming out of his laboratory. In 1913 Köhler was appointed director of the Anthropoid Station of the Prussian Academy of Sciences on the island of Tenerife; because of World War I, he was unable to return to Germany until 1920. By 1914 a few significant titles had been added to the literature of Gestalt psychology. But then Wertheimer and Koffka were engaged in war work. Only Köhler, in the isolation of Spanish Africa, was able to continue his psychological research.

Köhler, in 1920, became acting director, and soon afterward director, of the Psychological Institute of the University of Berlin. Wertheimer was already there, as was Kurt Lewin, whose work bears a significant relationship to Gestalt psychology. From that time until the coming of the Nazis to power, Gestalt psychology flourished. Graduate students were coming to the institute from a number of countries; the *Psychologische Forschung*, the journal of the Gestalt psychologists, was founded, and work was progressing in many directions.

In 1922 Koffka introduced Gestalt psychology to America with his paper "Perception, an Introduction to the Gestalt-Theorie." Two years later he came to the United States, settling in 1927 at Smith College, Northampton, Massachusetts.

Wertheimer moved his family out of Germany before Hitler came to power: he was quick to realize what was happening. Köhler remained for some two years of courageous struggle with the Nazi authorities, who harassed his students, dismissed his assistants, made appointments to the institute without consulting him.

By the end of World War II, the first generation of young Gestalt psychologists was essentially wiped out. For example, von Lauenstein was lost in the war, von Restorff died in Germany, Duncker in America, to name Köhler's last assistants in Germany. The others were scattered. A few migrated to America, England, the Scandinavian countries, Israel; Zeigarnik returned to the Soviet Union. Some went into practical work. For example, Paul Koseleff, one of the Nazis' first targets at the institute, became a psychoanalyst in Denmark; I recently learned that Krolik, whose perceptual experiments are among the most beautiful I know, became a school psychologist; Erich Goldmeier, who did excellent work on similarity and on memory change, practiced medicine in America. Others found positions in school, not university, teaching.

Could a second generation be started in the United States? Koffka, it will be recalled, was a professor at Smith College, an undergraduate institution; nevertheless, he gave one Ph.D., to Molly Harrower. Köhler went to Swarthmore, another undergraduate college in Swarthmore, Pennsylvania. And when Wertheimer arrived at the New School for Social Research, it was not yet giving degrees; only at the very end of his life were a few graduate students working with him for the Ph.D.

But it was not only the lack of graduate students that stood in

the way of a new generation of Gestalt psychologists. Behaviorism
was and—however modified—has remained the dominant psychology in America. Köhler relates an amusing anecdote:

In 1925, soon after my first arrival in this country, I had a curious experience. When once talking with a graduate student of psychology who was,
of course, a behaviorist, I remarked that McDougall's psychology of striving seemed to me to be associated with certain philosophical theses which
I found it hard to accept; but that he might nevertheless be right in
insisting that, as a matter of simple observation, people do this or that in
order to reach certain goals. Did not the student himself sometimes go to
a post office in order to buy stamps? And did he not just now prepare
himself for certain examinations to be held next Thursday? The answer
was prompt: "I never do such things," said the student. There is nothing
like a solid scientific conviction. (1953:124–125)

Even when, years later, behaviorists became interested in cognitive problems, it was still a cognitive behaviorism; and the differences that distinguished Gestalt psychology from behaviorism
remained. New developments were more closely related to behaviorism than to Gestalt psychology. As one example, the use of
computer models of thinking still involves machine theory, no
matter how sophisticated the machine. Machine theories of neural functioning have consistently been criticized by Gestalt psychologists.

Thus, the Gestalt immigrants found themselves in an intellectual atmosphere dominated by behaviorism and its relatives; they
were mainly without graduate students; and several of them died
too soon to have much influence on the psychology of their new
country. It is scarcely surprising that a new generation of Gestalt
psychologists did not grow up in America.

And it was hardly likely that Gestalt psychology would be understood, even when it was listened to politely or with respect.
Misunderstandings may be seen as both cause and effect of the less
than overwhelming influence that Gestalt psychology had in
America. I would like to discuss a few of these.

The interesting thing about these misunderstandings is that,
except for the first I will mention (which I have only recently
begun to take as something other than a bad joke), they are not
new. Gestalt psychologists have repeatedly spoken to these issues,

but without effect. This problem of the persistence of misunderstandings is one that I hope will interest some future historian of ideas and one that the cognitive psychologist should not neglect.

1. The most grotesque current misunderstanding of Gestalt psychology is the notion that it has some relation to gestalt therapy. I will not discuss this distortion of history and of ideas, but will merely state that there is nothing in common between these two developments. (See Henle 1978.)

2. Gestalt psychologists, because of their opposition to certain empiristic hypotheses, have repeatedly been called nativists: for example, by Piaget in the 1930s, by Boring in the 1940s, by Allport and Tolman in the 1950s, by the Mandlers in the 1960s. Here is a quotation from R. L. Gregory in 1970: "To the Gestalt writers, these Organising Principles were innate, inherited" (1970:20). Another perceptionist, writing in 1975, remarks: "By and large, the Gestalt psychologists were nativists" (Rock 1975:20). Considering the Gestalt psychologists' answer to the question of why units are perceived as units, Rock says:

First, regarding the perception of the natural environment, evolutionary change has guaranteed that the brain will operate on the basis of laws that work, that is, that generally yield veridical perception. . . . Proximity and similarity evolved as laws of neural organization because of the nature of the environment in which animals evolved. In some other environment, different laws of organization would have evolved. (1975:280)

This last quotation is particularly interesting because it spells out exactly the *opposite* of what Gestalt psychologists say about evolution and thus about nativism. In the 1920s, Köhler (1929) had already made his position clear. He left no room for doubt, in 1950, about what he thought evolution can do and what it can*not* do (Köhler 1950), and his last book, *The Task of Gestalt Psychology* (1969), contains perhaps the clearest statement of all. Gestalt psychologists are not nativists. I have no hope of being understood where the others were not, but I feel the obligation once more to state the position.

Nativism refers, of course, to explanations in terms of inherited mechanisms; we may consider, in particular, inherited features of the nervous system, though other parts of the anatomy are, of course, relevant. The nervous system exhibits certain histological structures because the organism is equipped with particular chromosomes—products of evolution. Thus, a nativistic explanation, say of perceptual facts, makes these facts the contribution of evolution.

In his examination of this theory, Köhler shows that evolutionary theory does *not* permit such an explanation. Although we most often think of evolution as a theory of change or of variance, it contains, as an essential part, a principle of invariance. If organisms develop from inorganic nature, they must have something in common with this nature; factors that apply to inanimate nature apply also to the organisms that develop from it. The alternative is vitalism or emergent evolution, which scientists have for the most part rejected.

What is it that organisms share with inorganic nature? General principles (like conservation of energy), forces, elementary processes such as electric currents. Thus electric currents occur in the brains of organisms as well as in streaks of lightning. Since they are found throughout nature, they must be independent of the genetic equipment of any species or any individual. Surely, nobody would maintain that electric or chemical processes corresponding to perception are inherited. As Köhler puts it, the principle of invariance states that "no essentially new kind of action appears in living systems" (1950:292). It is only constraints that are contributed by evolution—in our case, anatomical structures in the nervous system and elsewhere that exclude certain possibilities of action. But actions themselves owe nothing to evolution. "Any action in any organism involves the operation of factors which are entirely independent of evolution," writes Köhler (1950:293). A nativistic interpretation can therefore not account for the facts of perception.

I started with a quotation that attributes to Gestalt psychologists the view that the laws of neural organization are a product of evolution. But evolution cannot possibly be responsible for such laws, since actions as such are independent of evolution. It is precisely the Gestalt psychologists who have pointed this out.

There is another, perhaps surprising, consequence of this application of the principle of invariance in evolution to psychological problems. It forces us to reject certain empiristic interpretations as well. We do not learn to see, learn to think, learn to learn, nor are motives learned in the usual meanings of these expressions. For again, these are all forms of action. Thus, they involve the operation of factors that the organism shares with inanimate nature, with all species, and with all individuals— factors that must therefore be independent of the individual experiences of anybody.

This is, of course, *not* to deny a role to learning in all these cases. Each one exhibits important influences of experience. It is just that the *processes* themselves are no more learned than they are inherited.

To return to the main point, Gestalt psychologists are not nativists. They do not accept the nativism-empiricism dichotomy; there is a third class of factors, invariant dynamics, that applies to all of nature. In Köhler's words, "An enormous part of the business of living can never, as such, have been affected by the changes introduced during evolution" (1969:87). He continues: "Why so much talk about inheritance, and so much about learning—but hardly ever a word about invariant dynamics? It is this invariant dynamics, however constrained by histological devices, which keeps organisms and their nervous systems going" (1969:90).

I do not know why we find it so difficult to break out of the nativism-empiricism dichotomy. Are we unable to think in terms of trichotomies? If we are, we will continue to misinterpret Gestalt psychology and—more serious—our explanations will not do justice to our subject matter.

3. The criticism that Gestalt psychologists have neglected the role of past experience in psychological processes likewise has a long history, and, once again, clarifications of their position do not seem to help. We still find statements like the following:

A further feature of the theory was an almost complete denial of learning as important for perception. (Gregory 1973:52)

The Gestalt psychologists did not absolutely deny that past experience affects perception. (Epstein 1967:101)

As a matter of fact, the dialogue between the behaviorists and the Gestalt psychologists seems to have centered upon the relative importance of past experience and innate organizing properties of the brain. (Kaufman 1974:21)

That Gestalt psychologists reject certain kinds of empiristic explanations has just been indicated. That they do not confine the issue to nativism vs. empiricism has been sufficiently discussed. But that they deny an important role of past experience in perception, thinking, motivation, and so on is far from the case. The question they ask is: *How* does past experience operate in these connections, what role does it play? Space does not permit me to do more than refer you to the sources; consulting them would be a valuable exercise also for the critics I have been quoting.

4. Isomorphism has come in for its share of misunderstandings. This is the hypothesis that there is a structural similarity between percepts and corresponding brain events. Here is an example of a recent version of isomorphism by a critic of Gestalt psychology:

When viewing a circle, there was supposed to be a circular brain trace; for a sphere a spherical brain trace, and presumably for a house a corresponding house-shaped trace. . . .
There is far more to perception than the recognition of shape. How does the "isomorphism" idea cope with other perceptual features? Consider colour: are we supposed to believe that when we see a green traffic light, part of our brain turns green? (Gregory 1973:52–53)

This same author asserts that "Gestalt writers did tend to say that there are pictures inside the brain" (Gregory 1966:7), and elsewhere he asks: If pictures, why not melodies? Another writer refers to the "picture-in-the-head Gestalt school," adding:

This need not be a literal representation such that an actual recognizable picture of objects may be found in the brain if we know how to look for it. . . .
. . . Köhler . . . was the first to assert that there is a one-to-one topological correspondence between what goes on in experience and what goes on in the brain. This is like saying that there is a picture in the head which is in topological correspondence with the picture in the mind. (Kaufman 1974:7–8)

Gestalt psychologists do not know anything about pictures in the brain. Köhler, in particular, has taken pains to explicate the functional—not geometrical—meaning of isomorphism. One formulation of his is particularly relevant to the current interpretations I have quoted: "Certainly, the processes in our brain do not represent a geometrical picture of spatial visual experience" (1930:569). Let us take an example from the same source. What is the functional meaning of "between"? "In cases of dynamic self-distribution . . . a local process of the functional context is 'functionally between' two other processes whenever mutual influence of these two is mediated by an alteration of the third." He offers an analogy:

I tell Mr. A a story which is meant for Mr. F, whom for some reason I cannot address directly. Mr. A is in the same situation and hands the story down to Mr. B. Mr. B talks with C, C with D, D with E and, at last, E with F. Thus A, B, C, D, and E are "functionally between" me and F in this case of an influence. At the same time F may be nearer to me geometrically than D; for example, he may even be "geometrically between" me and D. Still, functionally, the opposite is true. (1930:568–569)

Other specific relations have likewise been analyzed.

Qualities, such as color, are not dealt with by isomorphism, which is a structural principle, since qualities do not possess structure. It is obvious that the brain does not turn green when we see that color: colors do not exist in the physical world. Presumably chemical reactions correspond to them, since these exhibit the required variety (cf. Köhler 1938).

Isomorphism has proved to be a powerful heuristic, leading Köhler first to the investigation of figural aftereffects, then to the demonstration of steady cortical currents hypothesized to correspond to such effects and to the perception of segregated forms in general. Naturally, the theory of cortical currents has come under attack, notably by Lashley and by Sperry, with their co-workers. Why does everybody quote these criticisms, and why does nobody read Köhler's (1958, 1959, 1965) replies? One of the current texts I have been using, after summarizing the work of Lashley and of Sperry, does, in fact, include the sentence: "There are, however, certain questions that can be raised concerning these experiments" (Rock 1975:445). What these questions are is never indi-

cated. Another recent writer simply dismisses the theory of figural aftereffects as "no longer accepted," presumably because of
Sperry's work (Kaufman 1974:511). It is interesting to note that
the latest reference to Köhler's work in this volume is to a monograph of 1944, although the text was published thirty years later.
Still another well-informed writer refers to the objections to the
satiation theory already mentioned, omits Köhler's replies, and
concludes (a bit more mildly than the others quoted): "While it
cannot yet be discarded in its entirety, it is now evident that it
cannot be retained intact, either as to substance or promise"
(Hochberg 1971:470). Köhler (1965) himself has discussed unsolved problems in the field of figural aftereffects and has refined
his concepts. But these considerations seem to have escaped the
attention of the textbook writers on perception. It may be noted
that the particular authors cited have been chosen, with one exception, not to be representative, but to be better informed than
the average about the work of Gestalt psychology.

In the case of all the problems I have been discussing, why is
one position so systematically ignored, or so consistently misin-
terpreted? We are concerned with developing a science, not with
winning a debate. Can we afford to ignore or to misinterpret the
hypotheses of one group of scientists, particularly ones who have
made such important contributions?

I turn now to some of these contributions.

It seems to be generally agreed that Gestalt psychology transformed the study of perception. In 1912, when Wertheimer's paper
on stroboscopic motion appeared, the center of investigation was
sensation; what we now call perception was accounted for, in one
way or another, by the intervention of higher mental processes. A
survey of some of the theories on the German scene can be found
in Köhler's critical article of 1913. In America, Titchener was at
his height; his context theory is formally similar to theories criticized by Köhler. While such theories are even now not extinct,
the focus today is on the study of the objects and events of our
phenomenal world. Both by their criticisms of the older views and
by their demonstrations and experiments, Gestalt psychologists
were most influential in effecting this change of direction.

Beginning with stroboscopic movement—which Wertheimer refused to call by its then customary name, "apparent movement,"

because that term accorded it less reality than other movement from which it was phenomenally indistinguishable—Wertheimer and Koffka undertook their perceptual investigations. Köhler was meanwhile studying various perceptual functions in chimpanzees and hens, now criticizing by empirical methods the theories which made of size constancy "apparent size," of color constancy "memory color." Once more, it was the phenomenal object, not sensations transformed by experience or by other processes, with which his work was concerned. I think nobody will deny that it was mainly the Gestalt psychologists who turned the psychology of perception in this new direction. Gibson (1971), as one example, assessing Koffka's (1935) *Principles of Gestalt Psychology* thirty-five years after its publication, comments: "His book, more than any other book of its time, set the psychology of perception on the course it is now following" (1971:9).

Likewise in thinking, Gestalt psychology provided a fresh start. The old psychology of images was already beginning to give way to other approaches, but Wertheimer's (1912a) first use of the Gestalt principle in connection with the number concepts of indigenous peoples represented a more radical departure. Köhler's work, published as *The Mentality of Apes* (1925), is an acknowledged turning point in the psychology of thinking. Departing from most paradigms then in use, Köhler gave his chimpanzees the opportunity to behave intelligently, and they did. But their curiously foolish errors were also illuminating. The concept of *insight* was introduced, and its role in thinking was progressively clarified after this early work. Insight has never been very popular among American psychologists, who even now seem to suspect something mysterious about it. But insight, properly understood, may refer to the most commonplace cases as well as to more notable achievements. Duncker's (1945) work on problem solving is still widely known, and his term "functional fixedness" has become part of our psychological vocabulary. Wertheimer's major contribution to the psychology of the thought processes, *Productive Thinking* (1945), has not yet had the influence it deserves; but it may still have an effect on theory if we ever have the courage to turn our attention from how computers solve problems and look to human thinking at its best.

I will return to theoretical and research contributions of the

Gestalt psychologists, but I would like to mention first another kind of contribution. Since Gestalt theory did not fit the intellectual habits of American psychologists, attempts have repeatedly been made to reinterpret findings of this group in more familiar terms. Thus, issues for controversy were provided which, in turn, inspired new research. For example, the finding that animals and human beings often solve problems suddenly, often without previous fruitless efforts to reach the goal, did not fit the generally held theories of learning as an incremental process. There followed the long controversy over continuity in learning, and the result was much new research. Köhler's work on the nature of associations initiated a controversy, with Postman defending the traditional associationistic position and Asch continuing with experiments in the Gestalt tradition. We have thus acquired much new knowledge about the nature of associations. Attempts were made to reinterpret the Restorff effect (or isolation effect) in terms of association theory, and again new research was produced. Asch's work on the formation of impressions of personality, interpreted by him in organizational terms, led to a good deal of research that attempted to return it to the traditional fold. A very large body of research has grown out of attempts to reinterpret figural aftereffects.

Some of this work is difficult to evaluate at the present time. But however the issues are resolved—if they are resolved—controversy gives rise to new research. The supplying of issues for controversy is thus in itself an important contribution of Gestalt psychology. Controversy is good for psychology.

Some of the directions in which the Gestalt psychologists took their work were left strictly alone by American psychology. This is true of problems as diverse as values and cortical currents. Value seemed to many Americans best ignored in the interests of a value-free science, this despite Köhler's (1938) analysis of the concept within the framework of natural science. For very different reasons, cortical currents were mainly ignored, except for the effort to show that they did not really correspond to perceptions anyhow. Technological advance had made it possible to stimulate the single cell, and attention was shifted away from more molar cortical events. In this case, physiologists will surely some day take up the problems if we do not; in the case of value, we seem to be leaving the task of analysis to philosophers. There are further examples of work that has been ignored. I wonder how many psychologists know that Gestalt psychologists have put forth a theory of recall and one of attention.

I think we must say, in short, that outside of the field of perception and perhaps of thinking, the contributions of Gestalt psychology have been insufficiently utilized. I wonder if it is too optimistic to think that there is change in the air. That cognitive psychology has returned to prominence is well known. Even behaviorism can no longer turn its back on cognitive problems. But concern with cognition is one thing; *how* cognitive problems are dealt with is another. Cognitive behaviorism and computer simulation are still a long way from Gestalt psychology. Still, the stage may be set for a return to some of the conceptions of the Gestalt group.

A promising development is Jenkins' contextualism, as put forth in a paper entitled "Remember That Old Theory of Memory? Well, Forget It!" Jenkins describes the associationistic assumptions from which he started, remarking: "This view is so pervasive in American psychology that it is almost coextensive with being an experimentalist" (1974:786). But his own research forced him to what he calls a contextualist position. "This means not only that the analysis of memory must deal with contextual variables, but also . . . that what memory is depends on context" (*ibid.*). There is no reference in this paper to Gestalt psychology, and the experimental paradigms illustrated differ considerably from those typically employed by the Gestalt investigators. But that Jenkins' own findings led him to abandon the atomism and the mechanistic assumptions of his earlier approach is an event of no little importance. Both atomism and mechanism have consistently been the targets of criticism by Gestalt psychologists.

Another small indication of change is what today is called interactionism in personality and social psychology. After a critique of the situationism of behavior theorists, Bowers defines his own position: "Interactionism argues that situations are as much a function of the person as the person's behavior is a function of the situation" (1973:327). Of course, there is nothing new in this statement, and it took the Swedish psychologist Ekehammar (1974) to point out that it has a history. Certainly the most relevant previous formulation is that of Kurt Lewin who, forty or more years earlier, not only stated the relationship just quoted, but worked out concepts for person and environment that seem to be lacking in contemporary interactionism (Lewin 1935). Still, here is a small step toward where we were forty years ago.

Was Gestalt psychology ahead of its time—as some of these examples might suggest—or simply uncongenial to the American intellectual scene? Can we today make better use of the contributions of Gestalt theory than we have done in the past? Before trying to answer these questions, I would like to take another brief look back into history.

Gestalt psychology arose, not only as a protest against the traditional psychologies of the time, but also as a response to a much more general intellectual situation. This was called the crisis of science; the German phrase, die Krise der Wissenschaft, is more exact, since it was not only the sciences, but academic knowledge in general that was involved. The academic disciplines could no longer take for granted the respect they had previously enjoyed. Why the crisis of confidence? Because scholars seemed to be unable to contribute to matters of human concern, and indeed seemed to be uninterested in them. Science, by its very nature, seemed to exclude meanings and values and thus to exempt itself from pressing human problems.

In psychology, one solution to the crisis of science was to develop an understanding psychology that gave up scientific explanation and hoped, through understanding, to find an avenue to real life human concerns.

The solution of Gestalt psychology was different. Rather than abandon the scientific method, it undertook to reexamine it. It discovered that certain assumptions being made about this method were not a necessary part of it, that science did not require the atomistic and mechanistic approach prevailing in psychology. Problems excluded by these assumptions might be dealt with if psychology concerned itself with molar events, employed more natural methods of analysis, and adopted the scientific stance of field theory.

It seems to me that we are again in a crisis of science, at least in psychology. To a large extent, we see the massive problems facing us today as human problems, and as psychologists we are able to do little about them. There is, it is true, one big difference from that earlier crisis of science: we want to help. The cry for relevance comes from within psychology itself. We have developed new fields of psychology in the face of our crisis: environmental psychology, community psychology, psychology of aging, population psychology, and so on. It is my impression that we have not learned how to formulate problems well out of practical necessity and that our new "relevant" psychologies are as much an expression of our own concern as areas of scientific achievement.

One solution to that earlier crisis is with us again. With the apparent failure of scientific psychology to solve human problems, we find advocates of an understanding approach to these problems. Occasionally such an author presents his program with a knowledge of that earlier history (e.g., Giorgi); more often, not. I hear from students today a question that was simply not expressed in the university a decade ago: Must psychology be a science? The understanding approach abandons or supplements the rational methods of natural science. It does not necessarily imply irrationalism, but today irrationalism is often one of its ingredients.

What is missing in our contemporary crisis of science is a radical reexamination of the scientific method. A reexamination of research paradigms—yes: field research vs. experimental research, multivariate vs. conventional analysis. We no longer want to deceive our subjects; indeed, we do not like to call them subjects, but rather research participants. We hear a great deal about paradigms these days. More important, there is discussion of outmoded philosophies of science on which we have relied in the past: positivism, operationalism, and so on. But in a positive direction, what shall we do?

Here is my suggestion. It has been the theme of this chapter that, except for the field of perception and, to a lesser extent, that of thinking, Gestalt psychology has not been given a real hearing. It has been misunderstood, its findings reinterpreted as if nothing new had happened, parts of it have been ignored.

In this present crisis of science, let us see how far the scientific method will take us in psychology. But let us examine the method we use. It would be reasonable to start in the direction of Gestalt psychology's reexamination of science—which, if I am correctly interpreting the contemporary scene, has yet to be followed up. Perhaps terminology will have to be changed; doubtless, specific concepts require modification. Surely they will be refined with further work. But this is still a direction that deserves to be explored by more than a few people. If such a revised psychological science is really tried and fails, I see two other courses open to us: a different kind of reexamination of science; or, failing that, being forced to agree with such thinkers as Sigmund Koch (1971) that a coherent discipline of psychology is not possible.

Chapter 11

Review of
R. L. Gregory,
The Intelligent Eye

Richard L. Gregory, professor of bionics at the University of Edinburgh, delivered the distinguished Royal Institution Christmas Lectures in 1967–68 under the title "The Intelligent Eye." The present book is an essay of the same title rather than a record of the lectures. It is a lively and provocative discussion of the nature of visual perception, with a theory of its relation to the thought processes. The experiments here reported show Gregory to be an unusually talented and ingenious experimenter, and the illustrations and demonstrations with which the book is richly provided enhance it greatly. The stereoscopic drawings, for example, are exceptional (a viewing device for these is provided), and well-chosen engravings, op paintings, and many other kinds of illustration contribute to the interest of the book.

Quoting a paragraph from Helmholtz which contains the famous doctrine of the role of unconscious inferences in perception, the author comments that his book "may almost be regarded as an extension of this passage from Helmholtz" (p. 31). Perception is considered to be a matter of building up and testing hypotheses; it involves inferences from sensory data to the external objects which gave rise to the sensory pattern. Thus perception, for Gregory, involves a kind of problem solving; it is in this sense that the eye is intelligent.

The identification of the correct object presents a problem because a given retinal image could have been produced by any number of things. Hypotheses about the most likely object are provided by past experience: "Retinal images evidently serve to select from a stored repertoire of objects represented symbolically in the 'visual' brain. Perception must, it seems, be a matter of seeing the present with stored objects from the past" (p. 36). In some cases, the ambiguous figures, alternative hypotheses are equally likely, and "the brain never makes up its mind" (p. 38).

As with other accounts that assign to previous experience a major part of the responsibility for perception, two questions must be faced: How were the first perceptions possible—that is, before past experiences existed to account for them? and, How is this experience itself acquired? Gregory does not deal adequately with either question. In connection with the first, he seems to admit "the possibility that some perceptual organizing processes are 'wired in' at birth" (p. 22). This possibility does not figure in his subsequent discussion, however, and, for a reason to be indicated below, will not solve our problem in any case. The author fails to see the problem of how experience is acquired because he does not face the problem of organization. No retinal image can select a memory trace from "a stored repertoire of objects," since the retinal image is not itself organized; it is a mosaic of excitations indifferent to one another, excitations which do not themselves constitute a form. Only an organized process can make contact with the organized memory trace of a previously perceived object; thus organization in the visual cortex is prior to trace selection and must be considered before any use can be made of past experience in accounting for perception. Effects of past experience presuppose, they cannot produce, organization.

Apart from the failure to deal with organization, the author's persistent failure to understand Gestalt psychology is unfortunate in yet other respects. (See also his review of *The Task of Gestalt Psychology* by Wolfgang Köhler, *Science*, May 8, 1970.) While not rejecting the principles of organization formulated by Gestalt psychologists, Gregory attributes them to inductive generalization from instances; he describes the Gestalt view of them as "innate, inherited" (*Eye*, p. 20). But Köhler breaks out of the nativistic-empiristic dichotomy, distinguishing in addition those factors that organisms share with the rest of nature, thus factors independent both of heredity and of individual experience. These are factors concerned with action and include, of course, the cortical events corresponding to perception. It is incorrect to describe Gestalt psychology as nativistic; it takes into account inherited structures, influences of experience, *and* invariant dynamics. Gregory's organizing processes "wired in at birth," on the other hand, presumably refer to innate structures, not to invariant dynamics, and thus could not account for *processes* of perception, any more than wiring arrangements could provide the power that runs the computer.

The eye is intelligent not only in the sense of engaging in problem solving, but also because abstract thinking is seen as emerging from vision. In this connection, the problem of the relation of language to thought is given a novel twist by the author, since abstract thinking seems to be derived from *written* language. The progress is one of increasing abstraction from pictures (such as stylized cave paintings) to increasingly simple and abstract pictographs, and finally to cuneiform characters or hieroglyphic or letter symbols, in which only "distant echoes" of the original pictograms remain. "Granted that, with the development of written language, thinking gradually became abstract, freed from perceptual situations, we can only speculate that the symbols were necessary for the thought; that the symbols freed the brain from the tyranny of sensory perception" (p. 147).

It is usual for students of language to regard spoken language as primary, written language as a later and secondary development. Thus it seems more likely that writing became a vehicle for the abstractions first expressed in spoken language than that it led to the development of these very abstractions. In any case, it is hazardous to infer from the contents of early writings—lists of possessions, commercial accounts, and the like—that earlier civilized man was incapable of, or uninterested in, abstractions.

Gregory sees the separation of thought from perceptual experience as culminating in modern science. Science's use of "'observational data' which can only be 'observed' with instruments" presents a paradox, he says, since "the senses can no longer be said to be the sole source of direct knowledge" (p. 15). But observation with instruments depends ultimately on reading these instruments, thus on sense data. The development of science is further characterized by increasingly abstract theories; perceptual models of reality become inadequate. Thus "perhaps thought in terms of the brain's perceptual hypotheses becomes inadequate as theories become more general and abstract" (p. 152). Or, in other words, "the physicist in a sense cannot trust his own thought" (p. 150).

In these ways Gregory sees science as increasingly distant from man's perception and his thought processes. Since these are the basic tools of the scientist, the whole of science would be undermined if this theory were correct. Indeed, the author himself comments: "We are left with a question: how far are human brains capable of functioning with concepts detached from sensory experience?" (p. 154). It is true, of course, that the scientist has no direct access to the physical world. But his inferences about it *are* based on observation, as mentioned above: pointer readings and the like are his link to hidden physical facts. These perceptual data are assumed—must be assumed—to share characteristics with the physical facts in question; it is only on this basis that theory building can proceed. And theoretical constructions, in turn, are tested experimentally—that is, against new perceptual facts. A theory of perception and thought that denies the basis on which science proceeds, the only one on which it can proceed, would seem to require revision.

It is only deductive inferences that, according to Gregory, thus become detached from perception. These are the inferences involved in abstract thinking, in communication, and in the hypotheses of formalized science. Deduction, which requires a formal symbolic language, would thus be a uniquely human possession (or one shared by human beings and computers). Perceptual hypotheses, on the other hand, are essentially inductive. "We may say that deduction is non-biological—for there cannot have been deduction before there was formal language" (p. 161). Again, "It is the incredible invention of deductive thinking . . . which has given unique power to the human brain: allowing us to transcend our biological origin" (p. 162).

A number of issues arise in connection with this view. The author undoubtedly does not mean to say that formalized science is exclusively deductive, so comment here is unnecessary. But it needs to be shown, not merely asserted, what kinds of abstract thinking and communication involve deductions in what ways and to what extent. Nor is it clear why perceptual hypotheses are inductive if the problem to be solved is, "What is the object giving this projection?" (p. 36). Indeed, the author illustrates Helmholtz's doctrine of unconscous inference, of which his own theory of perception is said to be an extension, by way of a deduction (p. 30). Once more, it is difficult to see why a process that depends on language is "non-biological." Has not language a biological basis?

Many particular discussions in this book deserve mention. A single example of special interest is Gregory's treatment of the contrast between pictures and perceptual objects. Although, as he points out, most perceptual experiments have used pictures rather than objects, he shows important functional differences between the two. This discussion needs, of course, to be continued with a focus on similarities as well as differences between pictures and things. Metzger's work on three-dimensional illusions is relevant here, as well as the author's own ingenious "impossible object" constructed after the model of the "impossible triangle" of the Penroses.

The mixture of physiological and psychological terminologies in this book I find particularly disturbing. Such expressions as "pictures in the eye" (p. 15), "The brain never makes up its mind" (p. 38), "Colour is transmitted to the brain" (p. 75), can only be confusing. The difficulty is not merely stylistic. To speak of "pictures in the eye" makes it easy to overlook the fact that the retinal image is a mosaic, and thus to bypass the problem of organization, as the author in fact does.

Gregory is obviously in command of the facts of perception, and his experimental contributions are excellent. His major thesis, that perception is intelligent, is an important and interesting one. It deserves better treatment.

R. L. Gregory, *The Intelligent Eye*. New York: McGraw-Hill, 1970.

Part IV

On History as Problem Solving

Chapter 12

E. B. Titchener and the
Case of the Missing Element

"In the last twenty years," Boring wrote in 1933, "the pendulum has been swinging away from the multiplication of mental elements."

> The images never quite gained an independent status. . . . The feelings, too, began to give way before the sensations. James . . . had held that emotions are characterized by their sensory content. Other psychologists (e.g., Stumpf in 1907) had argued that the simple feelings are sensations. Finally Nafe (1924), in Titchener's introspective laboratory at Cornell, came experimentally to the conclusion that the simple feelings, pleasantness and unpleasantness, are simply bright and dull qualities of sensory pressure. No wonder Titchener could conclude (posthumously, 1929) that introspective psychology deals solely with sensory materials. Sensation had won the day. Conscious content is *ipso facto* sensory. (1933:18–19)

Now this would have been quite a trick even for Titchener. I have seen him described as a "Jehovah in black broadcloth" (Gibson 1967:130), but I have nowhere else seen posthumous conclusions ascribed to him even by his most ardent admirers.[1]

My warm thanks go to Professor Rand B. Evans, who referred me to the letters from Titchener to Young quoted here, and who sent me copies of them (letters in the Cornell University Archives). I am grateful to him also for information about the status of the element of affection in Titchener's Elementary Lectures, and for his helpful interest in this project.

A closer look into the chronology will make unnecessary this excursion into spiritualism. Nafe's experiments, published in 1924, were begun in October 1922. The passage in the *Systematic Psychology* to which Boring refers is to be found in the third chapter. This chapter engrossed Titchener, Weld, his editor, assures us, from May 1918, when chapter 2 was completed, until December 1919, when Titchener put it aside as complete (Titchener 1929:v). Thus Boring cannot be correct when he tells us:

The convincing identification of feeling with sensation came about, not from the arguments of Bourdon, von Frey and Stumpf . . . but from the introspective experiments of J. P. Nafe. (1933:32)

It would seem, on the contrary, that these experiments were undertaken to support a conclusion Titchener had already reached; they were not the grounds for that conclusion. Yet Boring is undoubtedly right that it was not the arguments of his opponents that convinced Titchener that elementary affections must go: of the arguments of Stumpf, for example, he leaves not much standing (Titchener 1908). Thus we are faced with a mystery: what led to the disappearance of the affective elements of pleasantness and unpleasantness from Titchener's system?

I will try to support the hypothesis that in the *Lectures on the Elementary Psychology of Feeling and Attention* of 1908, in which Titchener weighs the arguments for the independent status of affections as elements, he simultaneously adumbrates the considerations that were to undermine that elementary status.

It is not unknown for Titchener buffs to take as autobiographical some passage that Titchener had written about Wundt. Without recommending it as a general historical procedure, I would like to make use of it in the present connection. Speaking of a change in Wundt's theory—incidentally, his theory of feeling—Titchener remarks:

In cases like this, I always want to trace the motive. Like the lawyer in *David Copperfield*, I assume that in all such cases, there *is* a motive. What was it, then, that led Wundt to his change of opinion?
If my reading of Wundt is correct, the changes that he has made, from time to time, in his various systematic works have never been due, in any

real way, to external causes, but have always represented the climax or culmination of a stage of internal development. The germs of the changes are invariably, I think, to be found in the prior Wundt. (1908:129)

Let us follow the method of Detective Titchener and seek a motive in the Case of the Missing Element. And let us take a cue from him and focus our attention on the prior Titchener. But first, in cases of mysterious disappearances, it is customary to begin the investigation by asking: When was the missing person last seen?

Simple feelings were clearly in evidence in 1914. On April 3 of that year, Titchener discussed Watson's article "Psychology as the Behaviorist Views It" before the American Philosophical Society. At that time he could still say: "Elementary, my dear Watson." The *Beginner's Psychology* of 1915 still includes simple feelings, along with sensations and simple images as the "elementary processes of mind" (1915: e.g., 90). Again, feeling appears as an element in January 1917, when Britz, a critic, is told that "clearness is not an attribute of the simple feeling" (1917a:57). And finally, insofar as I have been able to trace its movements, the affective element makes its last appearance in print in the *American Journal of Psychology* of April 1917. In Titchener's remarks on "Professor Stumpf's Affective Psychology," he refers to his own "present view" that the affective processes are to be classed apart from sensations (1917b:269).

Professor Rand Evans informs me that Titchener's lectures in the fall of 1917 included the element of affection; and that the element remained in his lectures through the fall of 1919. The term is missing, he adds, in the fall of 1920. Dr. Evans remarks that Titchener's thinking was probably a couple of years ahead of his lectures.

Whether we date the disappearance after April 1917 or after the fall of 1919, the elementary feeling slipped out of sight as silently and mysteriously as Judge Crater. We must ask: What happened between April 1917 and December 1919, by which date Titchener had described the subject matter of psychology as sensory? The significant event, it seems to me, was that, as Weld tells us, "in the early summer of 1917, Professor Titchener began writing his Systematic Psychology" (Titchener 1929:v). And, as Titchener remarked: "We are talking of system, and . . . a system must be systematic throughout" (1929:247).

Another fact must be noted before we begin our search into motives: Titchener's affective psychology was, from the beginning, ripe for change. In his *Lectures* of 1908, for example, he laments: "The unsettled state of the psychology of feeling is notorious" (1908:4–5). The same volume contains this remark: "Theories, believe me! sit more lightly on their owners than is commonly supposed; I would cheerfully exchange all my 'views' of feeling for a handful of solid facts" (1908:48–49).

Not only is Titchener willing to make changes in his psychology of feeling, it is also clear that his disposal of the affective element is not unpremeditated. In his reply to Watson, he admits:

My view that affection lacks the attribute of clearness is, he [Watson] says, an assumption "arrived at largely in the interest of obtaining a structural differentiation between sensation and affection." . . . As if a structural system would not be greatly simplified and, as system, improved by the reduction of affection to organic sensation! I only wish that I could see my way clear to it. (1914:12–13 n. 32)

Again, in the paper containing the final printed appearance of the affective element, Titchener suggests that if his view is wrong, that affective processes are to be distinguished from sensations, then it is his belief "that they must reduce, one and all, to complexes of organic sensations" (1917b:269). Thus he is ready with an alternative before the element has been decently buried.

After 1917, except in his lectures, Titchener maintained silence about the nature of affective experience. Thus we can only examine the experimental output of the Cornell laboratory. This work seems to tell the same story of a change in Titchener's thinking about affections long before Nafe's work. The number of publications is small, but there is a clear difference between studies of the affective processes undertaken before, and those done after, 1918—that is, before and after the disappearance of the feeling element. The *Lectures on Feeling and Attention* seem to set the problems for investigation in this area for the decade following their publication: such problems as methods of investigating affective processes (Nakashima 1909a); the nature of the affective judgment (*ibid.*); the controversy over the existence of mixed feelings (*ibid.*; Young 1918a); time relations of the affective processes (Nakashima 1909b); affective localization (Nakashima 1909a; Young 1918b); the tridimensional theory of feeling (Roese and Foster 1916).

The next study to be mentioned is not under Titchener's editorship, but it surely belongs in the series. P. T. Young received the Ph.D. from Cornell in 1918. Shortly afterward he went to Minnesota and, in 1919–1920, there obtained observations intended to answer the question: "Is there any characteristic difference between the organic-kinaesthetic factors of P and U feeling?" (Young 1921:38). It is difficult to dismiss as coincidence the fact that, just about the time that Titchener had decided that the subject matter of psychology is sensory, one of his most recent Ph.D.s (the only recent Ph.D. primarily interested in affective experience) began to search for a sensory basis of pleasantness and unpleasantness.

The findings must have been disappointing to Titchener. Young found "no sensory *sine qua non* of P and U" (Young 1921:40). He did obtain a tendency for unpleasantness to be correlated with muscular strain, pleasantness with relaxation. But relaxation, he concluded, "is negative and passive, a letting-up of strain" (1921: 52). Young adds:

P . . . so far as our data go, is organically-kinaesthetically negative. P is felt when one relaxes, or simply "does nothing"; there are no reflex responses to the stimulus-object and no bodily "reverberations." (1921:53)

Thus Young had found a possible (though not invariable) sensory correlate for unpleasantness, but not for pleasantness. Titchener went into action. As he put it later:

It seemed to us that it would be fairly easy to set up conditions that should show P as "organically-kinaesthetically" positive: and Corwin published our results later in the same year. (Titchener 1923:149)

Corwin altered the conditions of Young's study and did obtain positive results for pleasantness (Corwin 1921).

Once more this line of research ended in disappointment. In 1922, Young published a paper that cast serious doubt on the interpretation of Corwin's results as expressions of pleasant feeling; they might rather be accounted for, Young showed, in terms of sensory attention (Young 1922). Titchener subsequently commented on Young's paper, but it is interesting that his note does not so much as mention that author's findings (Titchener 1923). He limits his critique to the manner in which Young quotes a sentence of Corwin, a quotation that makes the latter's interpretation appear to be teleological. Titchener's statement is characteristic: "When I read this quotation, I wondered that any student of mine should have made the statement, and not less that I should have allowed it to appear in print" (Titchener 1923:149). Titchener does not challenge Young's reinterpretation of Corwin's data. The existential, nonteleological character of structural psychology is here reaffirmed—but meantime pleasantness appears to lack a sensory basis.

It was during this period that Nafe's study was being conducted. Titchener was still thinking, at least in part, in terms of organic sensations, as a letter to P. T. Young indicates. The affective qualities, he writes, may "turn out to be psychological integrations, as Watt supposes, of a new and distinct kind; or they may be familiar organic integrations to which the meaning of 'feeling' has attached itself" (February 13, 1923; letter in Cornell University Archives).

But another process may have been going on at the same time. As Titchener wrote to Boring in another connection:

You know yourself how it is, that an accumulating number of tiny indications gradually get possession of one, until a cranky idea formulates itself, and then the idea sticks and takes on more and more the colour of possibility, until presently one almost finds oneself regarding it as probable. (Boring 1937:478)

Nafe, it will be recalled, reduced pleasantness to bright pressure, unpleasantness to dull pressure (Nafe 1924). But there was earlier "an accumulating number of tiny indications" of the role of pressures in affective experience. "Pressures referred to the chest, heart and trunk" were reported by Young's observers (Young 1921:39). The introspections of Corwin's observers contain even more specific anticipations of Nafe's results. Here are a few reports on pleasantness:

Rather a bright-like pressure. (Corwin 1921:566)

There was a general liveliness of pressure-quality. (1921:567)

I experienced a diffuse quality that was bright and lively. (1921:569)

There was a diffuse bright pressure. (*Ibid.*)

Nafe himself reports: "Dr. Titchener remarked that he had a vague recollection that mention had occasionally been made of pressure in old Laboratory Reports of affective experiments" (1924:510n). For this reason, Nafe used an untrained observer, whose introspections could not possibly be affected by any such recollection, and whose results could then be compared with those of the trained observers.

Of his results, Nafe remarks that they "were as unexpected by us as they will probably be strange to the reader" (1924:542). One might guess that one reader who did not find them strange was Titchener himself. In any case, this survey of the empirical literature suggests that, for Titchener, Nafe's work was the reward of some five years of searching for a sensory basis of affective experience.

Why did Titchener want to dispose of the affective elements? It is time to search for motive. We may eliminate, at the outset, those motives that figure most in detective fiction. For example, "The reduction of pleasantness-unpleasantness at large to sheer sex-feeling is to me nothing else than nonsensical," says Titchener in his discussion of Watson's papers (1914:12 n. 32).

A more serious possibility is the motive of parsimony and systematic elegance. We have seen that improvement of the system in this manner was tempting to Titchener. But he sternly rejects this way out of the difficulties of affective psychology and criticizes Stumpf for taking it: "The appeal to a 'principle of economy' is worth very little, because the appeal in science lies always to the facts of observation" (1908:87). The criticism is repeated in 1917: "If the facts are complex, no twist of logic can make them simple" (1917b:273). Again, Titchener comments austerely: "To aim at simplicity for simplicity's sake would be to follow an aesthetic, not a scientific ideal" (1929:64).

Nor can it be the appeal to observed fact that led Titchener to discard the feeling element, as we have seen. Nothing seems to remain but to look to the prior Titchener, the Titchener of 1908.

It is interesting that the *Lectures* given in that year are on feeling *and* attention. Why not sensation and attention? Attention, we remember, is sensory clearness for Titchener, the attribute of clearness or attensity (Titchener 1924); and feeling is the one kind of element that does not possess this attribute. "Attention to an affection is impossible," wrote Titchener in 1908 (1908: 69). In the same volume, he quotes a passage by Meumann to the effect that "anybody at any time may convince himself that he can attend to his feelings," and he remarks: "I must confess that this passage staggers me" (1908:74). Titchener must have had little doubt about the matter: I cannot imagine that he was easily staggered. Again, he speaks of the incompatibility of affection and attention (1908:180); and many other statements to the same effect could be cited.

Pairing feeling and attention is thus like talking about elephants and forgetting, because elephants never forget; or about watches and butter, because even the best butter will not make a watch run.

The lectures on feeling differ in character from those on attention. Titchener himself describes the former as "almost wholly critical" (1908:285). He examines critically the various criteria that had been proposed to distinguish affection from sensation. Then he turns his critical eye to the theories of Stumpf and of Wundt. The approach to attention, on the other hand, is to a greater extent oriented to empirical research. A final lecture is devoted to tying together what amount to two sets of lectures concerned with incompatible subjects treated in different manners.

The two are related since "no one will deny that pleasantness and unpleasantness appear often and often again . . . as the accompaniments of attention" (1908:298)—although there may be attention without feeling. More important is an intrinsic relation between attention and affection: Titchener finds that "whenever we are moved and stirred to feeling, the sensible factors in the total process are relatively clear" (1908:303). In this sense there is no feeling without attending.

The nature of this solution is of less interest than the tension between affection and attention, their incompatibility, so apparent both in the form and the content of the *Lectures*. It is in this tension that I think we will find the motive we are seeking.

For observation, "the universal and peculiar method of scientific work" (Titchener 1929:38), depends on attention. In the *Text-book* Titchener writes:

Observation implies two things: attention to the phenomena, and record of the phenomena; that is, clear and vivid experience, and an account of the experience in words or formulas. (1910:19–20)

The definition is elaborated, but otherwise unchanged, in the *Beginner's Psychology* (1915), and in the period of our special concern (1917–1923), when the first chapter of the *Systematic Psychology* was being written and revised, observation is described as "a clear and sympathetic awareness" (Titchener 1929:39). Thus observation depends on attention, and attention and affection are incompatible.[2]

Titchener is, from the outset, aware of the difficulties this incompatibility makes for the investigation of affective experience. In the *Outline* of 1896 he says:

We cannot attend to a pleasantness or unpleasantness; and we can describe our affective experience only in a roundabout way. Hence if we were confined exclusively to the employment of psychological method,— the method of experimental introspection,—we should find it very hard to give an adequate account of affective experience. Fortunately, we can supplement this direct method by an indirect, physiological method, which allows us to infer the presence and intensity of affective processes from their bodily consequences. (1898:101)

By 1901, this method of expression seemed less valuable to Titchener. The curves of physiological changes so obtained "doubtless tally with the variations and trends of affective consciousness. But until we know the affective consciousness itself, how are we to be sure of interpreting our curves?" (1901, part II:149). Nor does the method of impression hold out "promise of ever settling the question of the number of affective qualities" (*ibid.*).

In the *Text-book*, a more sanguine view is taken of the method of impression: "It is, indeed, to this method that we must mainly look for a settlement of the vexed questions of affective psychology" (1910:243). Here, too, Titchener asserts that attention to an affection is not necessary for affective introspection (1910:472); and in the *Beginner's Psychology* he remarks that the study of feeling is not difficult in practice.

But this last statement is difficult to reconcile with the discrepancy between Titchener's expressed concern with affective psychology and the small amount of empirical work on it that came out of the Cornell laboratory. In the *Text-book* he wrote:

The reason, then, that our descriptive psychology of emotion is schematic rather than analytical is, simply, that experimental psychology has so far found neither the time nor the courage to take emotion into the laboratory. (1910:473)

Titchener was well supplied with courage, and his large number of graduate students might have been expected to provide the requisite time. But I have been able to find only five empirical studies between this call to action in 1910 and Nafe's settling of the problem in 1924.[3] Titchener *must* have been concerned with the scientific status of the psychological investigation of feeling.

The method employed is perhaps best described in the *Beginner's Psychology*:

In the case of feeling, the observer is set to attend to sensation, but to report upon the feeling which accompanies the sensation; the sensation comes and is attended to; and the report then describes, under the influence of the preliminary set, the feeling which accompanied the sensation. That sounds a little paradoxical; but the method is not difficult in practice; and it has the advantage that we can use all manner of sensory stimuli . . . in our study of feeling. (1915:80)

It not only sounds paradoxical—it *is* paradoxical. Psychological observation requires a psychological attitude, "a vivid experience of the particular phenomenon which is the object of observation" (1915:19), and a report on this experience. It is *not*, according to the definition, a matter of a vivid experience of one phenomenon and a report on another. Either the definition must be changed or the method here described is not psychological observation of affective experience.

But the definition, we have seen, was not changed. Indeed, in the *Systematic Psychology*, the discussion of observation is clarified and strengthened:

Observation is the elementary way of gaining scientific knowledge, and its result is a direct "acquaintance with" the object observed.

Science is not concerned to go behind this statement; it is concerned only that nothing shall pass muster as fact which has not, in the strict sense, been observed. . . . Observation is a clear and sympathetic awareness . . . of some item of the existential universe. (1929:38–39)

The data obtained by the method of impression do not pass muster as scientific facts. The whole psychology of affective experience, therefore, *had* to come under review.

Titchener must have been aware of the specific difficulty being discussed, and he was ready for that review. I have referred to his uncertainty about feeling as expressed in the *Lectures on Feeling and Attention*. Both before and after 1908, he would cheerfully have exchanged all his "'views' of feeling for a handful of solid facts." I will only add a couple of statements from the period of our present concern, the period during which the *Systematic Psychology* was being written and the affective element disappeared.

Titchener's letter to Young of February 13, 1923, begins: "It is very difficult to give any advice as regards the investigation of feelings. I am myself, if anything, more fluid in my attitude to them than I was in your day."

Young's "day" was 1916–1918, thus at the close of the period when feeling enjoyed elementary status. His dissertation, which was completed and published in 1918, was the last in the old tradition of the *Lectures on Feeling and Attention*. What was Titchener's attitude to feelings in Young's day? In his reply to Britz in 1917, he conceded: "I realize that the whole psychology of feeling is debatable ground" (Titchener 1917a:57). In 1923, his attitude must have been very fluid indeed!

Affective experience could not be excluded from psychology. Motivation, for example, was a different story: "The detailed study of instinct belongs to physiology and general biology. The psychologist is concerned with it only in so far as the innate tendencies guide and form the stream of thought" (Titchener

1915:207). Likewise, determining tendencies are affairs "not of mind but of body" (1915:213). But feelings and emotions are conscious contents, and structural psychology had to face up to them.

Such contents could enter into Titchenerian psychology only if they were observable. Thus the affections *had* to be reduced to sensory data. Nafe tells the story in 1924:

We undertook this Study on the assumption that the affective qualities, whatever they may be, must be palpable. . . . The presence of impalpables in a scientific subject-matter is, indeed . . . anomalous, if not contradictory. We decided, therefore, to show the courage of our scientific convictions, and to assume that the affective qualities are palpable. (1924:507)

One can imagine Titchener's editorial pen behind these words. Indeed, not much imagination is required. In Titchener's letters to Young a year earlier (February 13 and 20, 1923), the issue is stated in the same terms:

We are ourselves taking up the general problem of feeling over again, with the very simple object of determining, first of all, whether the affective qualities are palpable. If they are not, then they cannot be (in my opinion) elementary psychological qualities.

I am sorry not to be more illuminating; I am, in fact, convinced only of the one point,—that, if we have affective qualities, they must be observationally palpable. (February 13, 1923)

Young apparently wrote to ask what was meant by palpable; remember that, with respect to affective psychology, he belonged to an earlier tradition. Titchener replied on February 20, 1923:

By "palpable" I mean anschaulich, in the sense in which Messer and the rest of them use that term. I have no objection to the periphrasis "attentively observable" except that your observers are not likely to take the adjective in the strict scientific sense.

Nafe complained, a few years after its publication, that his work had not been understood:

The assumption that the terms [bright pressure and dull pressure] were generally understood proved to be a grave mistake. They originated with Titchener evidently about 1919 and are familiar only to Cornell students since that time and to a few others who have inquired about them. (Nafe 1927:370)

But generally understood or not, Nafe's experiments had served their purpose: the affective qualities had been shown to be palpable, even if they were no longer elementary or even specifically affective.

How well they served their purpose may be seen in the change in Titchener's attitude to feelings between 1919, when the subject matter of psychology had been described as sensory, and after 1924. In the *Systematic Psychology* he does not prepare the reader for this characterization of psychological phenomena. He rejects the terms *"Erlebnis"* and *"experience"* as too vague; and he continues:

All things considered, it would perhaps be the part of wisdom to put off the material characterisation of psychological subject-matter until such time as the accumulated facts point to their natural adjective. Since, however, the very nature of these facts is in dispute, and the postponement must therefore be altogether indefinite, we venture a leap into the half-dark, and choose the term "sensory." (1929:265)

Nor does Titchener justify this characterization. He merely remarks that the technologists will not like it, but that in the long run even technology will benefit from the aloofness of science (1929:268). Meantime, we had better get on with the work of science.

The passage that I have just quoted, in limiting psychological phenomena to sensory ones, in effect eliminates the elementary affections. But it is still a "leap into the half-dark"; and we have seen how fluid was Titchener's attitude to feelings at least into 1923. But after Nafe's work, his attitude changed. In a letter to Boring on May 4, 1927, he gives specific directions for finding the pressures that constitute pleasantness and unpleasantness. If the experiment is successful, the observer will find, in addition to the quality of the stimulus,

and mixed all up with it either something buoyant, light, flimsy, filmy, diffuse, or else something heavy, dull, thick, oppressive. . . .
When you have once put your finger on this addition to the . . . [stim-

ulus] quality, it is only a matter of time and repeated observation to realise that its own quality is that of pressure. A good many trials may be needed; but the outcome is quite sure. (Boring 1937:476)

The outcome is quite sure—this is far from a leap into the half-dark. The transformation of pleasantness and unpleasantness into sensory content had been completed; the elementary feelings had disappeared.

We may summarize: we have found the approximate time of the disappearance of the affective element; we have reconstructed a motive; and we know the means employed: indeed we have detailed instructions for disposing of what once was a troublesome element. Although I have not previously mentioned opportunity, it is clear that the patient introspections of the Cornell observers provided ample opportunity to eliminate the problematic simple feelings. Much of our evidence is circumstantial; but this limitation is unavoidable when one reopens a case after some fifty years. And circumstantial evidence—if my reading of detective fiction has not failed me at this point—must be taken seriously. Given motive, means, and opportunity, I suggest that we may at last remove the folder from the Pending File and write "Closed" to the Case of the Missing Element.

Part V

Historical/Systematic Approaches to an Empirical Problem: Thinking

Chapter 13

Fishing for Ideas

When Gulliver visited the Grand Academy at Lagado, he met a Professor whose exalted project it was to improve "speculative Knowledge by practical and mechanical Operations." Bypassing the usual laborious means of mastering the arts and sciences, "by his Contrivance, the most ignorant Person at a reasonable Charge, and with a little bodily Labour, may write Books in Philosophy, Poetry, Politicks, Law, Mathematicks and Theology, without the least Assistance from Genius or Study."

He showed Gulliver his apparatus, which was a large frame, twenty feet square, covered with bits of wood linked together by wires. Each surface of each piece of wood was covered with paper, and on these papers were written all the words of the Lagado language, in their several moods, tenses, and declensions, but without any order. Each part of speech was represented in its proper proportion in the language. At the Professor's command, each of forty pupils took hold of an iron handle fixed around the edges of the frame and gave it a sudden turn, thus scrambling the words on the frame. Now the students read the various lines, and whenever they found three or four words together that might

Because this article examines a general line of thinking about creative thinking, the specific authors cited in the text, while representative, are not themselves the focus of attention. Therefore, a reference list is not included, and quotations are not identified.

make part of a sentence, they dictated them to scribes who duly recorded them. The Professor had already collected several volumes of these fragmentary sentences "which he intended to piece together; and out of those rich Materials to give the World a compleat Body of all Arts and Sciences."

The problem of creativity has not always enjoyed its present popularity. But since this Contrivance was intended to give a compleat Body of all Arts and Sciences, I think we may fairly interpret the underlying implicit theory as a theory of creativity. As such, it bears comparison with contemporary theories of the same phenomena. One popular theory defines the creative thinking process as "the forming of associative elements into new combinations which either meet specified requirements or are in some way useful."

There are three aspects of this definition, all of which would be acceptable to the Professor at the Grand Academy. First, creativity is viewed in terms of elements—these are the individual words of the Lagado language. Next, the elements are to be formed into new combinations—these are achieved by turning the iron handles. Finally, the new combinations must meet specified requirements or be useful in some way. In the case we are examining, these combinations must form parts of sentences; and the Professor is fully sensible of the usefulness of achieving a complete body of knowledge without the necessity of either genius or study.

How are creative solutions achieved? In the contemporary theory that I am using for illustration, they are brought about by anything that will bring "the requisite associative elements together." Although several ways of achieving such combinations are discussed, only one is shown to have any important bearing on the creative process—serendipity or chance:

This is the manner of discovery to which is popularly attributed such inventions as the X ray and such discoveries as penicillin. One physicist has described how he has reduced serendipity to a method by placing in a fishbowl large numbers of slips of paper, each inscribed with a physical fact. He regularly devotes some time to randomly drawing pairs of these facts from the fishbowl, looking for new and useful combinations. His procedure represents the operational embodiment of this method of achieving creative solutions.

It is noteworthy that chance is likewise relied upon by the scholars at Lagado. The words are initially arranged without any order, and new random combinations are subsequently achieved by the successive turning of forty unrelated handles. And it might be added that while the physicist can only hope, by his method, to make discoveries in physics, the Grand Academicians are inspired by the nobler goal of a complete body of knowledge. Indeed, it is the Professor, not the physicist, who deserves credit, as Gulliver points out, "as the sole Inventor of this wonderful Machine."

The Professor, it must be admitted, is relying on more than mere chance, since his pupils are required to distinguish sensible combinations from useless ones. This failure to rely on chance alone is a departure from strict association theory and is found also in some of his contemporary successors. I will return to this issue.

Before we proceed, it may be remarked that if we were to translate the theory into stimulus-response terms, our Lagado Professor could have no objection. Indeed, John B. Watson might consider the Professor a behaviorist. He raised the question, "How do we ever get new verbal creations such as a poem or a brilliant essay? *The answer is that we get them by manipulating words, shifting them about until a new pattern is hit upon.*" Here we find the same kind of thinking in terms of specified elements (words), forming them into new combinations and, as the subsequent discussion shows, continuing to do so until specified requirements are met. All that is missing in Watson's account is a Machine that would eliminate learned differences in ability to manipulate words; such differences, he considers, are what distinguish the literary man from the man in the street.

It is now, of course, more fashionable to speak of response hierarchies; and reinforcement often occupies a prominent place in theories of creativity; for example, "The amount of reinforcement is inversely related to the initial probability of a verbal stimulus evoking a verbal response. Originality is more reinforcing than commonplace responding." In this instance, too, specific analysis would show the same features that characterize the implicit theory underlying the Professor's procedure.

We have become so used to thinking about creative processes in associationistic or stimulus-response terms that we sometimes forget to examine their implications. Now, because I agree with Gulliver that the Professor at Lagado "should have the Honour entire without a Rival" to claim his invention, I should like to address my initial remarks to him. I will try at first to remain specifically within the framework of his assumptions; I will, for example, omit for the moment twentieth-century criticisms of elementarism.

The Professor ingeniously assured that all the requisite elements would be present by employing all the words of the Lagado language. And it is generally assumed in theories like his that the individual has in his response repertoire all the elements needed for a creative solution. Then the novelty of the creative process is only a matter of combining old responses in new ways. But can this always be assumed? Why, for example, did it take Einstein so long to arrive at the theory of relativity? Would he have done better to draw cards from a fishbowl, like the physicist described earlier? Or was his task, perhaps, *not* a matter of combining elements, but of finding a new view—within which the known facts would then take their place? There are no new views in the physicist's fishbowl. Again, how did the Professor's own noble and exalted Thought spring into his head, that is, before he had the machine with which to combine the component elements? I would remind him that it is unwise, at the outset, to eliminate the possibility of novelty on what I suppose he would call the response side.

The Professor himself recognized that his procedure would take excessively long; he told Gulliver that his work would be expedited "if the Publick would raise a Fund for making and employing five Hundred such Frames." Even 500 might not be enough. Although there are only six of them, and although they are combining letters, not words, the monkeys at their typewriters require an infinite period of time to produce all the books in the British Museum. There are simply too many combinations of large numbers of elements, and most of them, as the Professor must know well, are not interesting. Indeed, his project might have profited in this respect from another one going on in his own Academy. This was a project to shorten discourse by cutting polysyllables and by eliminating all verbs and participles, for the obvious reason that "in Reality all things imaginable are but Nouns." On the other hand, a concurrent scheme to abolish all words whatsoever would have left his pupils little to do.

Why are some individuals more creative than others? The Professor at the Grand Academy has neatly eliminated the problem: I cannot think of any individual differences that could matter for him beyond the physical stamina required to turn the iron handles, persistence in this noble task, and perhaps ability to pay any small fee charged for the use of the Machine. But contemporary theorists, whose machines require programming, must face this problem. Fortunately, individuals differ in the nature of their associative hierarchies, in the number of their associations, and in other respects less well defined. Let us consider the first two.

1. The nature of the response hierarchy varies. Some persons may be said to have an associative hierarchy with a relatively steep slope around a given idea. After the first couple of conventional responses to it, the strength of associations drops rapidly. Thus, these individuals will have a few associations of considerable strength to that idea and will be restricted to stereotyped responses to it. If the idea be *table*, for example, the Steep Slope may not get beyond the associations *chair* and *spoon*. But there are other individuals whose response hierarchy may be represented by a flatter slope. Such persons are more likely to get past the conventional associations to more remote ones. A Flat Slope might get from *table* to *random numbers* without difficulty. Such persons are more likely to find a creative association than are possessors of steep slopes.

If different kinds of associative hierarchy are factors in creativity, we need to know how such differences arise. How does one individual come to possess a flat slope, another a steep one? Either we are arguing in a circle from creativity (the creative individual is the one who has a flat slope, which makes him creative), or else we are pushing the whole problem of creativity back into an unknown past when associative hierarchies were formed.

But let us not be stopped by the mere circularity of an argument. It is instructive to look at its more concrete implications.

Among our examples of creative solutions popularly ascribed to chance was the discovery of the X ray. It is well known that Roentgen was not the only scientist to find his photographic plates fogged. Let us imagine how this disturbing fact might be dealt with by individuals whose associative hierarchies have different slopes.

Suppose that we are in Schultz's laboratory, not yet in Roentgen's, and that he finds his photographic plate fogged. And suppose further that he is a Steep Slope type. He starts associating: "Fogged plate. Gott in Himmel, what a nuisance. I can't work with a fogged plate. I'll have to start all over again." Note that Schultz's associations have led him to no discovery except a very pedestrian practical one. So far the theory seems to be working.

Now we visit Schmidt's laboratory. Perhaps his associations assume a flatter slope than Schultz's, but he is inclined to be paranoid. We would say that he is a Deviant Slope. Again, he finds his plate fogged:

Fogged plate. Gott in Himmel, who did it to me? I'll bet it was that lazy no-good assistant Johannes. I'll fire him and get a new assistant. I hear that Schultz has a good assistant—too good for him. Won't Schultz be angry if I take his assistant! I'll get even with him for writing that unfair review of my Lehrbuch! usw.

Again Schmidt, with his flat but deviant slope, has added nothing to his or our knowledge except a very questionable hypothesis of no scientific interest whatever.

Next we visit Roentgen's laboratory and listen as he associates to his fogged plate: "Fogged plate—how can that have happened?" Our fictional Roentgen has never encountered this situation before and, despite his flat slope, *he has no associations to it*. Lacking associations, he is free to enter on a productive search.

Perhaps you will say that as long as we are reconstructing Roentgen's associations, we might just as well do it differently: "Fogged plate—unusual situation. How could it have happened?" But even Roentgen probably did not associate "How could it have happened?" to every unusual situation. (If he did, he would be a Steep but Deviant Slope, and unlikely to be creative except as a one-shot affair.) Suppose that he commutes to his laboratory and that the train is, for once, on time. It is unlikely that his associations would be: "Eight-oh-two on time—unusual situation. How could it have happened?" But more likely: "Eight-oh-two on time. Gott sei dank!"

Returning to the fogged plate, suppose we have approximately reconstructed Roentgen's associations. This process takes us only to the problem, by no means yet to the solution. An associative theory of creativity assumes that all the elements in the creative solution are in the individual's response repertory, needing only to be combined. But X rays were unknown until Roentgen discovered them. There were *no* relevant associations, to be combined or not.

2. Another factor making for individual differences in creativity is said to be the number of associations a person has: "The greater the number of associations that an individual has to the requisite elements of a problem, the greater the probability of his reaching a creative solution." In other words, the more items in your fishbowl, the more likely you are to find the one needed for a creative combination.

This factor raises a now-familiar problem. How do we know that one individual has more associations than another? Presumably we know by his ability to produce a creative solution, so we have not explained the creative solution. More important than the circularity of the argument is another consideration: without a principle of selection, mere number of associations gives us nothing more than flight of ideas. If we may venture into another imaginary laboratory, we might find ourselves in the presence of Braun, who, whatever the shape of his slope, is well equipped with associations. He, too, finds his photographic plate fogged: "Fogged plate. Might be some kind of radiation. Radiation is harmful to health. That reminds me, I haven't seen my doctor for a year; I must get a checkup. That one is certainly a robber. And speaking of robberies . . ." usw. Here our friend has hit upon the relevant point without even noticing it and has lost it in his wealth of associations.

3. Another respected associationist believes that individuals can be trained to be what he calls original. Because this is a matter of no small social significance, I will outline his basic procedure briefly. He asked twenty-five subjects to respond to

each word of a list of twenty-five with the first word that came to mind. Control subjects were given the training list and then a test list. The experimental group was given the training list; then this list was repeated five times with instructions to give a different response each time to any given stimulus word. Finally, the experimental subjects were given the test list.

Responses were scored in terms of their frequency in the subject population. The two groups did not differ in their scores on the training list, but the experimental subjects were more "original" on the test list. In the course of five brief trials, we witness Steep Slopes being transformed into Flat Slopes. And lest you think this was a transitory phenomenon, I will add that the effects of the training were shown to persist to a significant degree for at least two days under the given experimental conditions. Unfortunately, this otherwise sturdy effect could not be replicated in the one attempt at replication of which I know.

There is no point in examining additional examples of associationistic approaches to creativity. Whether they are formulated in associationistic or in behavioristic terms, they have a number of features in common:

1. They eliminate the role of novelty, the hallmark of productive thinking. It is assumed that the needed element is already present in one's response repertoire, waiting to be combined with something else. You can only fish out of your fishbowl what is already in it. But it is often just this x that is missing and has to be discovered. To assume that it is there all the time does violence to the facts and begs the question of creative thinking.

2. To assume that what is needed for solution is an *element* is to stretch the term *element* beyond any reasonable meaning. We need only extend our gaze beyond the restricted experimental paradigms usually employed by advocates of an associationistic view; if we consider such solutions as a new scientific theory, an idea for experimental investigation, the conception of a work of art—these are hardly elements in any useful sense of the term. The use of the same term for a word association and a new approach to physics can only obscure important differences. Although I promised not to bother the Professor at the Grand Academy with twentieth-century criticisms of elementarism, I

do think that contemporary associationists need to be reminded that some parts of psychology have been transformed by these criticisms.

3. These associationistic approaches eliminate the role of the problem or the question, which is usually the starting point for productive thinking. Indeed, as some of our hypothetical examples showed, associating to the given data may actually take one away from the problem. But, as James Stephens has remarked, a well-packed question carries its answer on its back as a snail carries its shell. Many scientists have pointed to the role of the problem in scientific work, and something analogous cannot be ignored in the arts.

This is a whole new story, which I cannot go into here. As an example of the simplest kind of problem, I will merely refer to William James' description of the attempt to recall a forgotten name. There is a gap in experience, but it is "no mere gap. It is a gap that is intensely active . . . beckoning us in a given direction." The problem does more than beckon in a certain direction; it demands its solution. "Some problems are very stubborn," said Max Planck; "they just refuse to let us in peace." I need not multiply quotations; the experience is a common one. Vectors arise from the perceived problem in the direction of solution. The problem demands its solution, and the individual lends himself to these demands and to the directions implicit in them. This is where we need to begin a study of creativity, not with what can be caught in the fishbowl, but with what can never be found there. Why have psychologists paid so little attention to the nature of the problem or of the question? or to what precedes the problem: doubt, uneasiness, wonder?

4. The role of chance is magnified in associationistic theories of creativity. It cannot be denied that chance often plays a large role in discovery. Mach cites a German expression intended to cast doubt on the abilities of a person: "He was not the inventor of gunpowder" (Er hat das Pulver nicht erfunden). This is perhaps not the most apt expression, Mach remarks, because "there is probably no invention in which deliberate thought had a smaller, and pure luck a larger, share than in this." But he continues: "Are we justified in placing a low estimate on the achievement of an

inventor because accident has assisted him in his work?" No, says Mach, because so much is required of the discoverer or the inventor if he is to be able to use what chance has presented to him. There has now been sufficient discussion of fogged photographic plates. What is clear is that not everybody recognized their significance. A chance solution to a problem must still be recognized as a solution to that problem; the relevance or significance of an unusual event has still to be grasped. These things cannot be taken for granted. Mach was so impressed with the active role of the scientist in utilizing chance occurrences that he concluded: "It is permissible ... to ask whether accident leads the discoverer, or the discoverer [leads] accident, to a successful outcome in scientific quests."

Associationists, too, have realized that the selection of just the creative combination of elements, among the many which may occur to the individual, presents a problem. How do they deal with it? Here is one solution: "When the set of consequents of a new combination achieves a close fit with the set of problem requirements, this combination is selected. When there is complete overlap of sets, 'search behavior' is terminated." About this solution I have two remarks to make. 1) It departs from associationism. I am happy to see such a departure, but a theory using the implied recognition of closeness of fit or appropriateness or relevance cannot properly call itself consistently associationistic. 2) It implies a theory of similarity (or closeness of fit). We really do not know much about similarity, but we do know that it cannot be defined in terms of the elements that an associationistic theory would require.

I conclude that the undoubted role of chance in productive or creative thinking does not constitute a theory nor relieve us of the necessity of developing one.

If associationistic theories are as faulty as I am suggesting, why bother to criticize them? Because—unless you want to talk about sublimated sex and aggression or about man's existential despair—this is, by and large, how creative thinking is being viewed by psychologists today. These associationistic theories at least have the advantage of being concerned with the *processes* that are said to constitute productive thinking. Now we have only to broaden that view. Let us not, in advance, rob creativity of its novelty. Let us not, in advance, limit the nature of the creative solution to the word association or other specified element. Let us recognize the operation of principles other than chance. And let us recognize the role of the problem in the productive process. Then perhaps we can begin to think about creative thinking.

We have been told nothing of the success of the physicist who grimly fished for ideas. Nor have we heard of the composer who used to drop pennies at random on a staff of five lines; have any of his compositions been performed? I fear for the safety of the chemist who mixes liquids out of curiosity. And the Professor's pupils have been turning their iron handles for nearly 250 years. I wonder if they have produced a single coherent paragraph.

Appendix

Harvard University
Department of Psychology and Social Relations

William James Hall
33 Kirkland Street
Cambridge, Massachusetts   02138

August 19, 1975

Dr. Mary Henle
Box 404
Ridgefield, Connecticut   06877

Dear Dr. Henle:

I wonder if you have thought how your argument about creativity would have applied to Darwin? Would you not have insisted that it was necessary to return to a creative Mind?

I am no more impressed with what psychologists have done with creativity than you are, but I would want to amend your statement that, "This is, by and large, how creative thinking is being used by psychologists today." I am not an associationist or stimulus-response psychologist (though many people do not realize that) and I believe I have answered your objections to a psychological theory in my book *About Behaviorism*. See particularly pages 100–101, 113–115, 158, and Section 6 on page 224. Two articles of mine in the third edition of my *Cumulative Record* on pages 333–355 are also relevant. One is called "On Creating the Creative Artist" and the other on "Having a Poem."

Yours sincerely,

B. F. Skinner

New School for Social Research
66 West 12th Street
New York, N. Y. 10011

The Graduate Faculty
Department of Psychology   September 7, 1975

Professor B. F. Skinner
Department of Psychology
Harvard University
Cambridge, Mass. 02138

Dear Professor Skinner:

I want to tell you again how much I appreciate your taking the time to comment on my paper "Fishing for Ideas."

The question you raise is indeed an interesting one: what would be the consequences of the argument in that paper for Darwinian theory? I do not believe that the alternatives are exhausted by chance variations vs. a creative Mind. Like you, I reject vitalism, but I do not therefore feel forced into mechanism. (The question of mechanism must enter since the chance variations of evolutionary theory produce anatomical constraints of various kinds.) Free dynamics produce remarkable effects: electrodynamic interactions, the soap bubble, the order of the heavenly bodies without the assistance of Aristotelian crystal spheres. In the organism (and in the nervous system) there are obviously many constraints; but within the limits set by these constraints, invariant physical processes produce order without the help of mechanical arrangements or of a creative Mind. We accept such dynamic equilibria in physics, why not also in the nervous system, which is itself a physical system? It may be that evolution will one day be seen, not in terms of environmental selection *after* an organ has appeared (or has been modified) by chance. Rather, the structural change may be the consequence of the selective processes of the organic system itself and may be of such a nature as to assist these processes to reach a better balance in relation to normal environmental conditions. Köhler has suggested this possibility in his 1924 paper, "Gestaltprobleme und Anfänge einer Gestalttheorie."

I do not have *Cumulative Record* at hand and will have to do the rest of my homework when I return to the city. But I have reread the relevant passages in *About Behaviorism*, and in light of the above, you will not be surprised that I am still not satisfied. Naturally, I agree with your criticism of stimulus-response psychology on page 114. But you rely exclusively, so far as I can see, on chance to produce novel behavior. (I certainly do not deny a role to chance, but cannot see it as the exclusive determinant of novelty.) Nor will reinforcement alone account for selection. The result must be recognized as beautiful or successful before it can be reinforcing. This recognition—a seeing of relations or of fit between problem and solution—is a selective process that must come before reinforcement. In the case of novel problems, which is mainly the issue, such a selective process is unlikely to be explainable in terms of the individual's history of reinforcements (which we usually do not know anyway). And why were the leaders of the Enlightenment in France influenced by those particular English ideas? Why not, say, by contemporary German ideas? Again there is a selective process that precedes any reinforcement.

Of course I agree with you that appeal to a creative mind or to a trait of creativity or the like explains nothing. It does not help to cover over with words what we do not understand. And one of the remarkable things about creative ideas is that they so often come "out of the blue," as in your example of Bruckner's theme which "came to him." It can only come from some realm beyond the phenomenal realm; dynamic processes in his nervous system must have taken a new form, perhaps under the pressure of whatever vectors in the brain correspond to sadness. (Since we know so little of this kind of brain function, I am certainly not proposing a solution here, merely indicating an area of investigation.)

May I summarize. If Darwinian theory should require some modification in the processes it envisages, it will not differ in this respect from most major scientific theories. And creativity still seems interesting to me because we have so much to learn about it.

Sincerely,

Mary Henle

Chapter 14

The Snail Beneath
the Shell

Apart from the huge amount of work undertaken to develop tests of creativity and to identify and characterize creative persons, studies of creativity have been concerned largely with the nature, criteria, and conditions of the creative work and the processes by which it is produced. What distinguishes a creative from a routine solution to a problem? And how is the creative solution achieved? Neglected has been the prior matter of how problems arise.

And yet posing the right question may be the most creative part of the whole process. As James Stephens once remarked: "A well-packed question carries its answer on its back as a snail carries its shell" (1920:68). In connection with scientific work, Szent-Györgyi observes: "Posing a good problem, asking a good question, is already half the work" (1962:178); for the problem points out the direction in which its solution is to be found.

Before the answer is achieved, the solution found, a space remains to be traversed; a gap exists in experience. William James has described gaps in experience in connection with the attempt to recall a forgotten name. But this is "no mere gap. It is a gap that is intensely active. A sort of wraith of the name is in it, beckoning us in a given direction" (1890, 1:251). That the gap has a shape is shown by the rejection of wrong names even before the right one has occurred:

If wrong names are proposed to us, this singularly definite gap acts immediately so as to negate them. They do not fit into its mould. And the gap of
one word does not feel like the gap of another, all empty of content as
both might seem necessarily to be when described as gaps. . . . There are
innumerable consciousnesses of emptiness, no one of which taken in itself
has a name, but all different from each other. (James 1890, 1:251–252)[1]

The attempt to recall a name may be regarded as a question we
put to our memory. And questions may be treated in the same way
as James treats such efforts to recall: they are gaps in our knowledge or understanding, gaps that likewise possess more or less
definite shapes and thus "beckon us in a given direction."

This paper will deal with the characteristics of questions. It
will be concerned with how questions arise, how we find or introduce these dynamic gaps, these beckoning gaps in our experience.
Under what conditions do we see problems? And what conditions
prevent us from seeing them?

Our area of interest may not be designated simply by the presence of the question mark. Many queries are only formally interrogative. (How do you do? How dare you?) On the other hand, the
developing question is often not definite enough to be put into
interrogative form. (There is something not quite right about this
argument.) Furthermore, since creative questions are the most
interesting ones, we will deal only with questions whose answers
are not known when they are asked.

The issue then becomes: How do gaps, whose shape we do not
yet know, arise in our experience? And how do they acquire their
shapes?

THE PROPERTIES OF GAPS

The shape of the gap has been mentioned as that most characteristic property by which the question itself is defined. It can be
recognized by the fit or lack of fit of proposed answers. In addition, gaps possess the properties of size or width, location, and
dynamic properties.

Width of the gap here refers to the difference between a problem
area and a specific problem, between a problem that spans disciplines and one that fits snugly into a corner of science, between a

problem that has implications for many phenomena and one that keeps discretely to itself.[2] This is the aspect of problems that Szent-Györgyi is discussing when he remarks:

> As to myself, I like only basic problems, and could characterize my own research by telling you that when I settled in Woods Hole and took up fishing, I always used an enormous hook. I was convinced that I would catch nothing anyway, and I thought it much more exciting not to catch a big fish than not to catch a small one. I have reduced, since, the size of my hook, and am catching fish. (1962:178)

As this author indicates, problems must be sufficiently limited if they are to yield solutions (though it will be pointed out below that they must be broad enough for their shape to be seen): "The bigger, the more fundamental the problem, the better, but this has its strong limits, and too big a problem is no good either" (*ibid.*). Once a problem has been seen, the first step toward solution is often cutting it down to appropriate size.

In addition, a gap has a certain location. This property of questions has hardly been discussed explicitly, though it is clearly recognized that one point of attack on a question is more promising than another. When he discovered an essential link of a solution missing, Max Planck wrote: "I had no other alternative than to tackle the problem once again—this time from the opposite side" (1949:37). Locating the gap in a different place, he was able to find a solution that was an important step on the way to the quantum theory.

Some investigators are said to have a "nose" for problems, and this seems to have to do, at least in part, with the ability to find the right point of attack, to find a gap in the right place. Speaking of both the explorer and the theorist in science, Lord Adrian writes:

> They need the insight and the sense of values or whatever quality it is which makes them pursue the problems which are ripe for solution. Rutherford had that quality very well developed. He saw where the great advances could be made and simply could not understand how an intelligent physicist could waste his time on anything but the nucleus. (1962:274)

The dynamic property of gaps remains to be discussed. As James

describes the gap, it is "no mere gap. It is a gap that is intensely active . . . beckoning us in a given direction." The problem
not only beckons in a given direction, it demands its solution.
Einstein, we read, was intensely concerned for seven years with
the problem that was to yield the theory of relativity as its solution (see Wertheimer 1959:214). Again, "The problem [raised by
Michelson's experiment] was an obsession with Einstein although
he saw no way to a positive solution" (Wertheimer 1959:218). For
four years Gauss worked to prove a theorem (see Humphrey 1948:
129). "Some problems are very stubborn," said Max Planck; "they
just refuse to let us in peace" (1949:52). The same author remarked: "I had no other alternative than to tackle the problem
once again" (1949:37); and Szent-Györgyi testifies to the same
aspect of scientific research: "In a way, it is a passive thing, like
catching a cold. Somehow, problems get into my blood and they
don't give me peace, they torture me. I have to get them out of my
system, and there is but one way to get them out—by solving
them" (1962:176).

Vectors in the direction of solution thus arise from the perceived problem itself. Of course, the problem must engage the
energies and the abilities of the individual who finds himself
caught up in it. The problem demands its solution and the individual lends himself to these demands. Secondary motives, Szent-
Györgyi points out, probably play no great role in real discoveries
and, in any case, they could not account for the solution of any
particular problem.

HOW DO QUESTIONS ARISE?

The ancients were well aware of the central role of questions in
creative thinking. "This sense of wonder is the mark of the philosopher," says Socrates in the *Theaetetus* (155d). "Philosophy indeed has no other origin." And Aristotle: "For it is owing to their
wonder that men both now begin and at first began to philosoph-
ize. . . . For all men begin, as we said, by wondering that things
are as they are" (*Metaphysics*, I:982b–983a). We ask questions to
"escape from ignorance."

Ignorance plays a special role for problems. So, too, does knowledge. The relation of knowledge to questioning is seen, on the one hand, in the fact that the question is itself a productive achievement; "to see a problem is a definite addition to knowledge" (Polanyi 1958:120). Or Socrates: "If we go on like this, either we shall find what we are after, or we shall be less inclined to imagine we know something of which we know nothing whatsoever; and that surely is a reward not to be despised" (*Theaetetus*:187b–187c).

A more relevant point in the present connection is that knowledge is needed if we are to pose meaningful problems. It is generally recognized that immersion in a field and preoccupation with a problem area are conditions of creative work. The requirement of a sufficient background holds not only for the individual thinker, but also for a science, which must be ripe for certain kinds of questions. Adrian makes this clear in the case of Newton:

> That genius alone is not enough is shown, I think, by Isaac Newton's achievements in science. In physics his achievement was supreme, for the background was enough for his purpose, and he could say, "If I have seen further it is by standing on the shoulders of giants." It was the tragedy of his career that he turned from physics to chemistry, for there the background of alchemy was all that he had to stand on. . . . He worked . . . day and night and in the end his health failed and his achievement in it had been negligible. (1962:273)

Ignorance, then, is not a sufficient condition of the productive question. A question is, rather, ignorance with a particular shape; and a sufficient background—of knowledge and of experience of the difficulties in the field—is necessary to provide that shape. That knowledge is a necessary condition of questions has been pointed out by Köhler: "Problems commonly arise in places in which the implications of established information tend to penetrate into a less known environment. In other words, problems issue from knowledge" (1943:77).

Ignorance and knowledge—these are the conditions of asking questions. Can we characterize more specifically the situations in which problems are seen?

1. Contradictions of all kinds provide one of the most fruitful sources of questions. Contradicted may be the expectations, assumptions, previous experience, or current knowledge of the questioner. In research, contradictory findings, unpredicted ones,

negative cases, and contradictory theories are all occasions for posing new problems. A few examples from this rich source may suffice.

Nathan Isaacs sees such situations as the basis of the "epistemic why" questions of young children. There is

a sudden clash, gap or disparity between our past experience and any present event. Some fact is met which is contrary to expectation. . . . Something has gone wrong with our habitual knowledge or assumptions. We need to find out what it is and to put it right. . . . There is a contradiction to be resolved, an obstruction to be overcome. Some x has to be found which will actually achieve this. (1930:295)

When, for example, a four-year-old asks, "Why does it get lighter outside when you put the light out?" the perplexity arises out of just such a contradiction. When the light is turned off, it makes the room darker—why not also the outside? Why does this action, which makes one thing darker, make something else lighter (Isaacs 1930:308)?

In exactly similar situations, adults, too, ask "why?" Since the adult's everyday assumptions and expectations about the world tend to be tested in a long history of such situations, and since he has in addition acquired considerable skill in evading contradictions (see below), it is easiest to see in scientific work the power of the contradiction in the creation of questions.

Parallel to the contradictions of prior expectations by the phenomena of everyday life are the difficulties encountered by scientific theories in the face of unpredicted findings. Here, too, the contradiction may lead to a question and, subsequently, to discovery. Adrian writes: "Sooner or later we can hope for the results which are unexpected and puzzling because they do not seem to fit into any of the pictures we have made. These are the discoveries which will create the new outlook and make the decisive advances in science" (1962:270). They lead to these advances, it may be added, by way of the productive question to which the contradiction gives rise. In a similar connection, Claude Bernard (1927) remarks that there are no unsuccessful experiments.

A well-known example is the part Michelson's findings played in the development of Einstein's thinking. Michelson's result "in no way fitted the fundamental ideas of the physicists. In fact the result contradicted all their reasonable expectations" (Wertheimer 1959:217).

Contradictory findings in the scientific literature are a recognized source of problems. The failures to replicate, so familiar to psychologists, provide numerous examples. As a single one, in the last twenty-five years most attempts to replicate the Zeigarnik effect, so impressive in the late 1920s, have been unsuccessful. At the very least, this must indicate that the conditions of this effect are unknown.

Another source of contradiction in science is the opposition of theories. The large quantity of polemical literature attests to the effectiveness of controversy in giving rise to research. For reasons that will later be apparent, such research, at least in the short run, does not necessarily resolve the issues in question.

In all these instances, the contradiction indicates the presence of a gap in knowledge or understanding. It may also indicate the location of the gap. (For example, what are the specific conditions of the effect that resists replication?) Thus the contradiction provides the occasion for a problem. If a specific question is to develop, however, this gap must acquire a definite shape.

2. Just as contradictions lead to problems, so, too, do unexpected similarities. Köhler (1920) made significant progress in the development of his psychological thinking when he began to notice the similarities between the behavior of perceptual structures and that of simple physical systems. This line of thinking, for example, gave increasingly specific content to the idea of isomorphism and led eventually to the physiological work to be discussed below.

Sometimes startling results arise in science when the explanation of one set of phenomena is shown to hold in another, very different area. Here it is not the apparent similarity of phenomena that poses a problem; what is decisive is the similarity of answers to what at first looked like quite different questions. "Sometimes we have the application of the same set of *ideas* to problems which may appear entirely unrelated at first sight," writes Chandrasekhar. "For example, it is surprising to realize that the same basic ideas which account for the motions of microscopic colloidal particles in solution, also account for the motions of stars in clusters" (Heywood 1947:168). The same author, discussing Herschel's extension of the laws of gravitation from the solar system to the distant stars, comments, "It is difficult for us to imagine how tremendous the impression was which this discovery of Herschel made on his contemporaries" (1947:165).

In the case of such solutions, it would be interesting to read accounts of their development; I have found none. In the absence of such accounts, one might guess that such cases are similar to the ones mentioned earlier: an investigator sees similarities, not previously noticed, between phenomena and seeks to determine whether or not the unknown events can be explained in the same manner as phenomena already understood.

3. Questions arise when we encounter strange, unusual, striking, or new phenomena. Phenomena that are commonplace do not ordinarily excite our wonder.[3] "For as the eyes of bats are to the blaze of day, so is the reason in our soul to the things which are by nature most evident of all" (Aristotle, *Metaphysics*, II: 993b). Unusual events, on the other hand, force our attention and we wonder how so strange a phenomenon can come about. For example, the rainbow was a conspicuous phenomenon that demanded attention of thinkers, and there were a number of theories of it between Aristotle's and Newton's. Likewise, epilepsy doubtless received more and earlier scientific attention than did the common cold.

Chandrasekhar, discussing the discovery from which Rutherford was led to the nuclear model of the atom, quotes him as saying: "This was quite the most incredible event that has ever happened to me in my life." This astonishing observation led to consideration of the kind of event that could produce it—what kind of event will fill a gap of this particular shape? Calculations then showed that the results demanded the assumption of an atom most of whose mass is concentrated in the nucleus (Heywood 1947:161).

The unusual phenomenon that leads to inquiry need not, of course, be of the intensity of the instances cited so far. Bartlett (1958:140) reports, for example, that it was the oddity of the results of certain perceptual demonstrations that led him to the first steps of his research on remembering. Most researchers can give instances of "something odd" that set them off in a particular direction of exploration. Claude Bernard (1927:152) relates how, from chance observation of the unusual characteristics of the urine of rabbits brought to his laboratory, he was led to a series of experiments and thus to an important conclusion. Once more, the eland and the oryx "can survive indefinitely without drinking. How do they do it?" (Taylor 1969).

Again, new techniques have played a continuing role, not only in solving problems, but also in raising questions, precisely because they have made new phenomena available for observation. The microscope extended the range of known biological phenomena, for example, as the telescope opened up new heavenly phenomena for study. This is not the place to retell the story of how these and other technologies played their role in the posing of problems.

Strange or new phenomena, in short, arouse our wonder and raise questions. On the other hand, this seems not to be true of things that are too strange. "We feel neither curiosity nor wonder," writes William James, "concerning things so far beyond us that we have no concepts to refer them to or standards by which to measure them" (1890, 2:110). As an example, we may cite the report of an early traveler who sees a volcano for the first time, Hanno the Carthaginian (probably c. 500 B.C.): "Sailing . . . onward, we passed along a burning region, filled with sweet scents, from which fiery streams poured . . . into the sea. The land was not to be trodden for very heat. And from it we hastened on our way, seized with a great terror" (quoted by Leithäuser 1955). Clearly, this experience was too strange and too terrible to arouse scientific curiosity.[4]

Still, care is needed at this point. It may be that we do wonder, but have not yet asked a question; in the case of the too-strange, it is possible that the gap is there but has not yet acquired a shape. In those instances in which striking phenomena lead to investigation, they do more than indicate the presence of a gap. The gap already possesses a particular shape that any explanation of the event must fit.

4. In science, except perhaps in its earliest stages, the most

common form of question is the hypothesis. A theory has certain implications for reality, and the hypothesis is the statement of these implications. It is the expectation that, under particular conditions, a certain kind of event will occur. To test the hypothesis, the conditions in question are set up, and the presence or absence of the predicted events is noted. The hypothesis, in short, is a gap of a very particular shape, one that can be filled only by the predicted result. If the result is not obtained, if the hypothesis is not confirmed, we have been trying to fill a gap of the wrong shape; and further work is needed to determine whether the larger theory itself is wrong. A well-known example of a theory with holes of very specific shapes is the periodic table, a table that not only ordered the elements known at the time of its construction, but also contained empty spaces for elements not yet discovered. Similarly, Fraser Harris remarked, "Harvey made the existence of capillaries a logical necessity, Malpighi made it a histological certainty" (quoted by Schwartz and Bishop 1958, 2:595). But since the making and testing of hypotheses constitute the everyday business of the scientist, further illustrations are perhaps superfluous. It need only be added that a situation particularly favorable for research is presented by a conflict of theories. Then two opposed hypotheses, two gaps of different shapes, are tested for fit of the data.

5. Difficulties arising out of the formal characteristics of prevailing theories may initiate the sequence: new question—discovery or new theory. A classic example is the work of Copernicus, who was looking for a theory less cumbersome than the Ptolemaic doctrine, one mathematically more harmonious. Max Planck, describing the work that was to lead to the quantum theory, reports:

But even if the absolutely precise validity of the radiation formula is taken for granted, so long as it had merely the standing of a law disclosed by a lucky intuition, it could not be expected to possess more than a formal significance. For this reason, on the very day when I formulated this law, I began to devote myself to the task of investing it with a true physical meaning. (1949:41)

Wertheimer describes a similar situation when Einstein considered Lorentz's solution to the paradox of Michelson's result. "But for Einstein the situation was no less troublesome than before; he felt the auxiliary hypothesis to be a hypothesis *ad hoc*, which did not go to the heart of the matter" (Wertheimer 1959:218).

6. Up to now, a variety of conditions have been discussed that lead to new questions. These have been structural indications of gaps in our knowledge and understanding. One more condition will be mentioned, without which many questions are lost; this is an attitudinal, not structural, condition of problems. Questions occur to the welcoming mind. Commenting on chance discoveries, Bronowski writes:

Why does chance enter in this way? The answer is simply that the mind is roving in a highly charged, active way and is looking for connections, for unseen likenesses in these circumstances. It is the highly inquiring mind which at that moment seizes the chance and turns what was an accident into something providential. The world is full of people who are always claiming that they really made the discovery, only they missed it. There were many people whose photographic plates had been fogged before Roentgen in fact asked himself, "Why is the plate fogged?" . . . It was chance; but it was the chance that was offered to the highly active and inquiring mind in this creative state when it was looking for hidden likenesses. (Summerfield and Thatcher 1964:102)

Claude Bernard remarks that nothing is more common than experimental ideas born by chance. "We take a walk, so to speak, in the realm of science, and we pursue what happens to present itself to our eyes" (1927:151–152). This we can only do, of course, if we keep our eyes open during this walk.

"The world is teeming with problems," writes Planck. "Wherever man looks, some new problem crops up to meet his eye. . . . And some problems are very stubborn; they just refuse to let us in peace" (1949:52). Why, then, do we consider it a creative achievement to raise new questions? Why, in a world teeming with problems, are good questions not an everyday affair? Some of the conditions will be discussed that work to keep us from seeing problems.

1. A number of authors have discussed the manner in which information is shaped by attitudes, hypotheses, or convictions. These interactions between beliefs and facts can be seen to obscure contradictions, one of the most powerful sources of new questions. It is easy, for example, to ignore facts that contradict

one's view if one can question their source, the conditions under which they were obtained, and the like. In psychology, the demonstration of experimenter effects and other sources of difficulty in replication make it a matter of course to raise such doubts when contradictory data appear. Polanyi cites an example from physics and comments, "Little attention was paid to the experiments, the evidence being set aside in the hope that it would one day turn out to be wrong" (1958:13).

Or contradictory facts may be recognized, but their relevance to the issue questioned. An example from the history of psychology is the Baldwin-Titchener controversy on reaction time. Titchener argued that Baldwin's data, obtained with untrained subjects, were not of scientific value, while Baldwin held that it was precisely the training in observation that obscured the individual differences in which he was primarily interested (cf. Boring 1929). In other words, each contestant recognized the data of the other, but denied their relevance.

Still another means of disposing of contradictory evidence is interpreting it in line with one's own hypothesis. In the long controversy over continuity in learning, for example, there was no dispute about the facts, only about their significance. The data could be interpreted in terms of competing views; as the problem was formulated, it did not permit a crucial experiment. This is by no means a special effect: it is commonplace in discussions between persons holding different attitudes. For example, one meaning rather than another may be selected when an item allows several interpretations, or an item may look different in the contexts of opposed views (cf. Henle 1955).

One particular way of reinterpreting contradictory evidence is by means of the ad hoc hypothesis. Again an example may be taken from the history of psychology. When it was recognized that many perceptual phenomena did not behave as they ought to have behaved in terms of the atomism prevailing in earlier psychological theory, nothing was easier (or more misleading) than to bolster up the conventional explanations with added assumptions about the effects of previous experience. It is easier to explain puzzling phenomena by recourse to ad hoc hypotheses than to recast one's entire line of thinking.

Another type of interaction between fact and theory deserves mention: the one is simply identified with the other. Polanyi reports: "During the eighteenth century the French Academy of Science stubbornly denied the evidence for the fall of meteorites which seemed massively obvious to everybody else. Their opposition to the superstitious beliefs which a popular tradition attached to such heavenly intervention blinded them to the facts in question" (1958:138).

It is to be noted that the processes described here, and doubtless others, are *cognitive* means of avoiding contradictions. While it is not to be denied that personal involvement with an attitude or point of view may make it harder to revise it in the face of contradiction, such involvement is not necessary. Simply because of the interaction between items and their context—interaction that is necessary for any theoretical thinking or indeed any consistent view of the world—contradictions are often difficult to see. Furthermore, when personal involvement enters, it is very likely by way of processes such as the ones here discussed (cf. Henle 1955).

2. While contradictions are an important source of problems, only assumptions or propositions clear enough to be contradicted can yield questions. Many of our assumptions are unformulated or implicit; these include what we take for granted. Although Isaacs (1930:299) sees local contradictions of such assumptions as a source of epistemic questions, it must be added that such unverbalized positions may be too loose, too vague, to permit contradiction. Even scientific writers sometimes obscure issues, and thus eliminate the possibility of problems, in the effort to reconcile opposing points of view (see Henle 1957).

On the other hand, clarification of terms may show that what appeared at first to be a contradiction is not one at all. What Planck calls phantom problems (*Scheinprobleme*) provide examples. These include questions "so vaguely worded that they must remain phantom ones because they are inadequately formulated" (1949:57).[5] The following is an instance of a phantom problem:

The room in which we now sit, has two side walls, a right-hand one and a left-hand one. To you, *this* is the right side, to me, sitting facing you, *that* is the right side. The problem is: Which side is in reality the right-hand one? I know that this question sounds ridiculous, yet I dare call it typical of an entire host of problems which have been, and in part still are, the subject of earnest and learned debates, except that the situation is not always quite so clear. (Planck 1949:57–58)

Here the contradiction is an apparent one only. Once the terms are properly defined, it disappears—and the problem along with it.

3. In order to be able to see the shape of the gap in our understanding, we must look at the data in a sufficiently wide context. Too limited a view will work against seeing the problems. Relevant contexts are not always confined within the limits of a single discipline. Köhler writes: "It would be interesting to inquire how many times essential advances in science have first been made possible by the fact that the boundaries of special disciplines were *not* respected. . . . Trespassing is one of the most successful techniques in science" (1940:115–116).

An impressive example is Köhler's own work on figural aftereffects and cortical currents. Observing the strange behavior of reversible figures, he asked what kind of brain process could correspond to it. The nature of the required process—the shape of the gap—is specified not only by the nature of the phenomenon to be explained, but also by the limitations imposed by the medium of the brain. Köhler found one process, and only one, that would fit: the electric current in an electrolyte. If electrical currents correspond to organized perceptions, this fact has certain consequences for perception, and the prediction and investigation of figural aftereffects followed. Finally, direct physiological investigation of cortical currents was undertaken (see, for example, Köhler 1959). In this work, neither a psychological nor a physiological context alone would have been sufficient. The gap in understanding indicated by the psychological observation could be filled only by postulating an isomorphic brain process and, in turn, the consequences of this could at first be tested only by psychological observation.

Within a discipline, too, it must follow that the shape of the gap cannot be seen correctly if the theoretical context is too narrow. Miniature systems of all kinds are for this reason unlikely to provide adequate contexts out of which significant problems can arise.

4. Just as there are attitudinal conditions of seeing problems, so there are other attitudes that prevent us from asking questions. Haste, not caring, and ego orientation are examples. Thus lack of concern may cause us to fail to examine the shape of a gap closely enough, to consider a problem closed whose solution only approximately fits, to overlook a minor anomaly or a minor contradiction, and so on.

FROM WONDER TO QUESTION

It is not my intention to review the literature on productive thinking, but rather—insofar as possible—to apply our knowledge of the thinking process to the formulation of the question. It should be noted, however, that the distinction between solving problems and asking questions is by no means a clear one. Duncker (1945), in particular, has shown this by treating problem solving as a matter of successive reformulations of the problem until the one that carries its solution is achieved.

Questions must acquire a sufficiently precise shape and be of manageable size if they are to yield answers. These requirements, it has been noted, may sometimes be in conflict: if a gap is narrowed to the point at which it is easily bridged, it may at the same time be so narrowed that the investigator can no longer grasp its shape. How are precise shape and optimal size achieved?

The deduction of specific hypotheses from more general theories is one means of producing questions with these properties. Here the precise shape of the gap is shown by the fact that only one type of answer will fit, and appropriate size is insured by the fact that the hypothesis is formulated with a view to specific test.

On the other hand, before hypotheses are possible, the process of formulating questions is often a matter of differentiation. "The process started in a way that was not very clear," says Wertheimer in his account of the development of Einstein's thinking about relativity, " . . . in a certain state of being puzzled" (1959:214). And at a somewhat later stage: "Back of all this there had to be something that was not yet grasped, not yet understood. Uneasiness about this characterized young Einstein's state of mind at this time" (1959:215). Still later:

This simply would not become clear. He felt a gap somewhere without being able to clarify it, or even to formulate it. . . . He felt that a certain region in the structure of the whole situation was in reality not as clear to him as it should be, although it had hitherto been accepted without question by everyone, including himself. (1959:218–219)

From here Wertheimer traces Einstein's thinking as specific questions and solutions gradually replace the initial unclarity.

SCIENCE AND THE ARTS

In the discussion of creative questions, we have thus far taken our examples from the sciences. Has this kind of analysis any relevance to the arts? That it has is suggested first by the fact that many artists view their work as a process of discovery.[6] For example:

Writing . . . is a voyage of discovery. (Henry Miller, in Ghiselin 1955:178)

You will write . . . if you will write without thinking of the result in terms of a result, but think of the writing in terms of discovery. (Gertrude Stein, in Ghiselin 1955:159)

If the poem is a real creation, it is a kind of knowledge that we did not possess before. (Allen Tate, in Ghiselin 1955:136)

The area of discovery, the area of exploration that exists in painting for me, is to me the most intriguing and the most rewarding one actually today. (Ben Shahn, in Summerfield and Thatcher 1964:43)

Stephen Spender even speaks of question and answer in connection with the writing of poetry: "All this sequence of thought flashed into my mind with the answer which came before the question" (in Ghiselin 1955:119).

The idea of a gap that remains to be filled is mentioned explicitly by Amy Lowell in her description of the making of a poem: "Here is where the conscious training of the poet comes in, for he must fill in what the subconscious has left. . . . Every long poem is sprinkled with these lacunae" (Ghiselin 1955:111). That the gap possesses a certain shape is clear from this remark: "He must . . . fill it in as much in the key of the rest as possible" (Ghiselin 1955:111).

Aristotle's treatment of tragedy likewise suggests a paradigm not far from the question-answer configuration:

We have laid it down that a tragedy is an imitation of an action that is complete in itself, as a whole of some magnitude. . . . Now a whole is that which has beginning, middle, and end. A beginning is that . . . which has naturally something else after it; an end is that which is naturally after something itself, *either as its necessary or usual consequent,* and with nothing else after it; and a middle, that which is by nature after one thing and has also another after it. A well-constructed Plot, therefore, *cannot either begin or end at any point one likes;* beginning and end in it must be of the forms just described. (*Poetics:*1450b; italics added.)

An end demanded by a beginning is similar in structure to a question that carries its answer.

Furthermore, size is here a relevant variable, as it was in the analysis of questions (cf. discussion of width of gaps):

To be beautiful, a living creature, and every whole made up of parts, must not only present a certain order in its arrangement of parts, but also be of a certain definite magnitude. Beauty is a matter of size and order. . . . The longer the story, consistently with its being comprehensible as a whole, the finer it is by reason of its magnitude. (*Poetics:*1450b–1451a)

Finally, most pronounced in art is the property that has been described above as the dynamic quality of the gap. Vectors beckoning in a certain direction are experienced as arising from the work of art in progress. The following examples show this quality to be just as conspicuous as in the case of scientific questions:

The key word or line . . . occurs in what seems to be an active, male, germinal form as though it were the centre of a statement requiring a beginning and an end, and as though it had an impulse in a certain direction. (Stephen Spender, in Ghiselin 1955:118)

Each particular carving I make takes on in my mind a human, or occasionally animal, character and personality, and this personality controls its design and formal qualities, and makes me satisfied or dissatisfied with the work as it develops. (Henry Moore, in Ghiselin 1955:77)

There arrives a period during the painting when the painting itself makes certain demands . . . and if you're not hypersensitive to it . . . you're going to lose a good quality of painting. It definitely becomes a living thing. (Ben Shahn, in Summerfield and Thatcher 1964:43)

These artists are clearly not referring to the influence of unconscious processes so often reported by creative persons, but are here concerned with the dynamic properties of the developing work itself and the directions they contain for its completion.

In a number of respects, then, the present discussion of questions and their properties seems to have relevance to artistic as well as to scientific work. This is by no means to identify these areas of endeavor, but merely to suggest a direction for future exploration.

Chapter 15

On the Relation Between Logic and Thinking

The question of whether logic is descriptive of the thinking process, or whether its relation to thinking is normative only, seems to be easily answered. Our reasoning does not, for example, ordinarily follow the syllogistic form; and we do fall into contradictions. On the other hand, logic unquestionably provides criteria by which the validity of reasoning may be evaluated. Logical forms thus do not describe actual thinking, but are concerned with the ideal, with "how we ought to think." And yet a problem seems to be concealed beneath this easy solution.

It is interesting to note that a number of the older writers on logic regarded their discipline as the science of thought. It will not be possible here to survey the vast literature, some of which bears only by implication on our problem, but some examples will illustrate this position. Cohen and Nagel summarize the older view: "An old tradition defines logic as the science of the laws of thought" (1934:18). Kant holds that "logic is a science of the necessary laws of thought, without which no employment of the understanding and the reason takes place" (1885:3). Psychology, on the other hand, supplies only the contingent, not the

This paper was written when I was a Fellow of the John Simon Guggenheim Memorial Foundation.

necessary, rules of thought. John Stuart Mill likewise views logic as comprising the science of reasoning, as well as an art, founded on that science (1872:18). He continues:

Whatever has at any time been concluded justly, whatever knowledge has been acquired otherwise than by immediate intuition, depended on the observance of the laws which it is the province of logic to investigate. If the conclusions are just, and the knowledge real, those laws, whether known or not, have been observed. (1872: Intro., sec. 5)

Boole, as a final instance, regards "the laws of the symbols of Logic" as "deducible from a consideration of the operations of the mind in reasoning" (1854:45–46). Boole deduces the law of contradiction, for example, from a fundamental law of thought (1854:49–51).

More recent writers, on the other hand, have tended to reject the view that the laws of logic are those of the human understanding. Again, only a few illustrations will be given. Cohen remarks:

That the laws of logic are not the universal laws according to which we do actually think is conclusively shown, not only by the most elementary observation or introspection, but by the very existence of fallacies. (1944:2–3)

A similar point is made by Nagel:

Little need be said in refutation of the view that logical principles formulate the "inherent necessities of thought" and are generalized descriptions of the operations of minds. Surely the actual occurrence of beliefs in logically incompatible propositions makes nonsense of the claim that the principle of noncontradiction expresses a universal fact of psychology. (1956:66)

Regarding the work of Boole referred to above (*An Investigation of the Laws of Thought*), Cohen and Nagel comment: "The title is a misnomer" (1934:112). A more extreme statement of this point of view is by Bertrand Russell:

Throughout logic and mathematics, the existence of the human or any other mind is totally irrelevant; mental processes are studied by means of logic, but the subject-matter of logic does not presuppose mental processes and would be equally true if there were no mental processes. (1904:812)

Schiller, too, holds that syllogistic reasoning "has nothing whatever to do with actual reasoning, and can make nothing of it"
(1930:282). He describes the "Laws of Thought" (laws of identity,
contradiction, and excluded middle) as "verbal conventions"
(1930:251).

The changed point of view with regard to the relation between
logical principles and the laws of thought seems to be a function
of an altered intellectual climate rather than of any fundamental
discoveries about the nature of reasoning. It thus seems worth-
while to reopen the question, the more so since it has implications for a number of central issues in the psychology of thinking.
First, however, it may be of interest to examine a few more forms
in which the present question has been raised.

Discussion of the figures of the syllogism has at times centered
on their relevance to actual thinking. J. N. Keynes (1887:230–231)
cites several writers who reject the fourth figure because they
hold that we do not actually reason in it. Kant (1885:84–90),
indeed, finds all but the first figure both useless and false; the
fourth in particular he calls unnatural. Keynes, on the other
hand, argues for the admission of Figure 4 on the same grounds,
namely its relevance to actual thinking. "It is not actually in
frequent use, but reasonings may sometimes not unnaturally fall
into it" (1887:232).

Psychologists investigating reasoning processes have tended to
underemphasize the role of logic in the thinking of their subjects.
To illustrate, Bruner, Goodnow, and Austin suggest that

much of human reasoning is supported by a kind of thematic process
rather than by an abstract logic. The principal feature of this thematic
process is its pragmatic rather than its logical structure. (1956:104)

Individuals, they say, tend to prefer "empirically reasonable propositions" to logical ones (ibid.). Morgan and Morton conclude
that:

A person is likely to accept a conclusion which expresses his convictions
with little regard for the correctness or incorrectness of the inferences
involved. Our evidence will indicate that the only circumstance under
which we can be relatively sure that the inferences of a person will be

logical is when they lead to a conclusion which he has already accepted. (1944:39)

Lefford states that the principles of logical inference "are techniques which are not the common property of the unsophisticated subject" (1946:144). He goes so far as to distinguish from the logical inference

psychological inferences which may be made by the ordinary person. . . . A psychological inference is not valid or invalid except when judged as a logical inference: psychological inference is purely a fact. (1946:145)

Common to all these statements by the psychologists is the assumption that logical principles are irrelevant, if not antithetical, to much actual reasoning.[1] This conclusion is derived from the high incidence of wrong inferences of subjects under test conditions, especially in the case of emotionally relevant material. A different conclusion has been drawn by Von Domarus from observation of errors in the reasoning of schizophrenic patients. This author argues, not that the reasoning of his subjects is unrelated to logic, but rather that it conforms to a logic whose laws are different from those of Aristotelian logic. This is "paralogic," which excludes the law of contradiction and "accepts identity based upon identical predicates" (1944:111). This idea has been elaborated by Arieti (1955), who sees the operation of this logic (which he calls paleologic) not only in schizophrenic and primitive thinking, as Von Domarus does, but also in dreams, in some infantile thinking, and in the transference situation in psychoanalysis.

Again it is of interest to find that the earlier writers mentioned above were equally aware of the problem of error, but viewed it in a way that was entirely compatible with their conception of logic as the science of the laws of the mind. "It is easy to see how truth is possible," writes Kant, "since in it the understanding acts according to its own essential laws" (1885:44). Error, however, is difficult to understand since it constitutes "a form of thought inconsistent with the understanding." Its source is thus not to be sought in the understanding itself, but rather in the "unobserved influence of the sensibility on the understanding," the sensibility

being that faculty which "supplies the material for thought."
Boole likewise considers that "the phaenomena of incorrect reasoning or error . . . are due to the interference of other laws with
those laws of which *right* reasoning is the product" (1854:409). He
reminds us that "the laws of correct inference may be violated,
but they do not the less truly *exist* on this account" (1854:408).
Mill is still more explicit. Discussing the fallacies of ratiocination, he points out that since

the premises are seldom formally set out . . . it is almost always to a
certain degree optional in what manner the suppressed link shall be filled
up. . . . [A person] has it almost always in his power to make his syllogism
good by introducing a false premise; and hence it is scarcely ever possible
decidedly to affirm that any argument involves a bad syllogism. (1872:
Book 5, ch. 6, sec. 3)

In the case of arguments consisting not of a single syllogism but of
a chain of syllogisms, he considers the most common fallacy of
ratiocination to lie in a changing of the premises as the argument
proceeds.

Two clearly contrasting alternatives thus present themselves: is
logic (or Aristotelian logic) largely irrelevant to the thinking
process, or is it concerned with the laws of thinking? Since we will
here be concerned only with deductive reasoning, we may reformulate the question more specifically in these terms. But since, as
has so often been pointed out, the premises from which we reason
are commonly not spelled out, since our inferences so frequently
appear as enthymemes,[2] this fact must be taken into consideration. We may ask: If we know the premises—tacit as well as explicit—from which a person reasons, can we put the process in
syllogistic form? Do the rules of the syllogism describe processes
that the mind follows in deductive reasoning, even when the syllogistic form is not explicitly employed?

It has been shown above that the existence of error has been
used as evidence for the irrelevance of logic to the actual thinking
process. On the other hand, a different interpretation of error has
been suggested. Since the problem of error seems to be a particularly fruitful one in which to join the issues before us, it will be
taken as the context for the present discussion. Once more we

may reformulate our question as follows: Do errors in deductive reasoning mean that the logical process has been violated? As Mill expresses it, does the occurrence of error mean that the syllogism is a bad one? Or can the error be accounted for otherwise? Is it possible that a process that would follow the rules of logic if it were spelled out is discernible even when the reasoning results in error?

The distinction being made here is a familiar one in the psychology of learning and thinking. Thus Koffka (1935: ch. 12) distinguishes between learning as accomplishment and the learning processes responsible for this accomplishment. Köhler's (1925) distinction between "good errors" and stupid ones is likewise relevant. Good errors, he points out, "may, in a certain sense, be absolutely appropriate to the situation" (1925:217), although they solve the problem no more than do stupid ones. Wertheimer, too, distinguishes between solutions obtained by "blind" procedures and "fine, genuine solutions" (1959). Again the difference is one of process, since in both cases the result may be the same. In the same way, in connection with the present problem, we may ask: Given contrasting results—correct solutions and errors in deductive reasoning—what can we say about the thinking processes that account for them? Are the processes necessarily different because their effects are different?

Illustrative data that bear on this issue will be presented. They were obtained from forty-six graduate students of psychology who were asked to evaluate the logical adequacy of deductions presented in the context of everyday problems. Most of the subjects had no training in formal logic.[3] The material was presented under group conditions, the subjects writing out their judgments and their grounds for making them. Instructions included an explicit statement that the logical adequacy of the arguments was to be judged, not the truth of the statements.

Individual interviews were also conducted with a different set of subjects. Although the results agree generally with those obtained under group conditions, they will not be presented because of a problem already mentioned. Mill, it has been seen, pointed to the difficulty of recognizing a bad syllogism because a person can easily introduce into his incompletely stated argument a new premise that will make the inference valid. It was often difficult to decide whether the material elicited by direct questioning consisted of new premises not entering into the original inference, or whether the subject was, as intended, making clear his original understanding of the premises. Although the group data are less rich than the individual interviews, and although the products of written communication are likely to be less spontaneous reflections of the thinking process than interviews, they exclude this possibility of overlooking true fallacies; indeed, if anything, they overestimate the incidence of bad syllogisms, since the reasoning is often incompletely described in the case of apparent errors.

The present data will be used only to illustrate the reasoning processes in cases of error; no quantitative results will be presented. As many authors have shown, the incidence of error in deductive reasoning depends on the form of the syllogism and its contents, as well as on instructions to the subjects. Quantitative results would have relevance only to the particular conditions studied here, whereas an inquiry into the nature of the errors obtained might be of more general interest.

Several processes may be distinguished which led to error in dealing with the presented material:

1. *Failure to accept the logical task.* More specifically, this means failure to distinguish between a conclusion that is logically valid and one that is factually correct or one with which the subject agrees. This source of error has already been reported by Henle and Michael (1956:124).

A sample syllogism follows, along with responses in which errors occur because of failure to grasp or accept the logical task.

Syllogism 6. A group of women were discussing their household problems. Mrs. Shivers broke the ice by saying: "I'm so glad we're talking about these problems. It's so important to talk about things that are in our minds. We spend so much of our time in the kitchen that of course household problems are in our minds. So it is important to talk about them." (Does it follow that it is important to talk about them? Give your reasoning.)

Responses:
"The conclusion does not follow. The women must talk about

household problems because it is important to talk about their problems, not because the problem is in their minds."

"No. It is not important to talk about things that are in our minds unless they worry us, which is not the case."

"No. Just because one spends 'so much time' in the kitchen it does not necessarily follow that household problems are 'in our minds.'"

It should be noted that subjects who failed to accept the logical task frequently gave correct responses that are just as irrelevant to the question of the relation of logic to the thinking process as are the errors just cited. A few examples follow:

"Yes. It could be very important to the individual doing the talking and possibly to some of those listening, because it is important for people to 'get a load off their chest,' but not for any other reason, unless in the process one or the other learns something new and of value."

"Yes. It seems obvious that problems which are in the forefront of one's mind bring more consideration to them and possibly newer aspects when they are discussed with another. Two heads may be better than one."

"Yes it does. By talking household problems, a problem can be solved or worked through."

The errors illustrated here clearly do not demonstrate an inability of the subjects to reason logically, since they have not accepted the logical task. They have evaluated the content of the conclusion, not the logical form of the argument. Richter makes the same distinction, carrying the analysis a step farther. Apart from careless mistakes and those arising from "imperfections in the classifying operation"—i.e., from an inability to make logical deductions, he describes errors arising from "a general failure to grasp the concept of 'logical validity'" and those arising from "the specific inability to differentiate 'logical validity' from another attribute of syllogisms," namely their factual status (1957:341). To apply to the present data, the factual criterion needs to be interpreted to mean what is believed to be true or reasonable as well as what is known to be true. With Richter's distinction in mind, we may note that no subject failed completely to grasp the logical task. Still, one individual judged on the basis of belief rather than logical validity in the case of nine out of ten syllogisms, and several others judged in this manner with at least half of the syllogisms presented.

2. *Restatement of a premise or conclusion so that the intended meaning is changed.* In a number of cases examination of the material from which a subject reasoned showed that it differed from that which was originally presented. In such cases the validity of the argument can, of course, be judged only in relation to the syllogism actually employed, not the one intended.

In the case of syllogisms in which a conclusion from two particular premises was to be evaluated, the premises were occasionally restated as universals, from which the conclusion followed. The following syllogism permitted this kind of change:

Syllogism 8. Mrs. Cooke had studied home economics in college. "Youth is a time of rapid growth and great demands on energy," she said. "Many youngsters don't get enough vitamins in their daily diet. And since some vitamin deficiencies are dangerous to health, it follows that the health of many of our youngsters is being endangered by inadequate diet." (Does it follow that the health of many youngsters is being endangered by inadequate diet? Give your reasoning.)

Responses:
"Yes. Youngsters (A) don't get vitamins (B). Not getting vitamins (B) dangerous to health (C). Youngsters (A) in danger of poor health (C)."

"This follows. . . . Youth doesn't get enough vitamins. Vitamins are necessary or bad health results. Therefore youth are endangered. All of these follow logically, and I believe a correct inference has been made."

Other changes were introduced into the premises by subjects whose reasoning was found to be correct even though their answers to the intended problem were wrong. The same syllogism (syllogism 8) will be used to illustrate.

Responses:
"There is some question about the equivalence of 'don't get enough vitamins' and a vitamin deficiency dangerous to health. If one assumes their equivalence, then the conclusion just about manages to follow."

"Correct if we assume that the youngsters are lacking those vitamins in their diet which endanger health."

"It seems to follow, assuming that the deficient vitamins are also the vital ones."

Everyday discussions permit greater scope for such changes in meaning than does the material employed here. Private meanings of terms or idiosyncratic or unconscious equations of concepts may enter in to prevent two people from drawing the same conclusion even though they start ostensibly from the same material.

3. *Omission of a premise.* Occasionally a subject employed only one of the presented premises. The informal manner in which the premises were set out made possible this treatment of the material. Syllogism 6 (see above) will be used to illustrate.

Responses:
"Not correct logically. (a) A group of women spend much of their time in the kitchen; (b) thus household problems occupy their minds. . . . (c) Therefore it is important to talk about them. Mrs. Shivers' subjective thinking."

"Doesn't follow from the preceding statement. Because she spends a lot of time in the kitchen and household problems are on her mind, it doesn't follow that it is important to talk about them."

In a few cases, indeed, both of the intended premises were omitted by the subject. For example (syllogism 6):

"No it doesn't follow. The fact that she spends much time in the kitchen has nothing to do with whether or not it is important to talk about the problems."

It will be seen that in all these cases in which a premise has been omitted, the subject correctly reports that the conclusion does not follow. If we disregard the intended premises and consider only the material actually used in reasoning, the subjects' deductions are seen to be correct.

4. *Slipping in of additional premises.* Under the present conditions this device was infrequent, but it seems to be more common where premises are stated less completely, and where the issues are of more immediate practical concern, as in everyday discussion. For example, premises may be added that are so commonplace, so much taken for granted, that they escape attention.

Instances of the adding of assumptions to our material follow. Since they are readily understandable, and for the sake of brevity, the responses will be quoted without the presented syllogism.

Responses:
"Without intending sophistry it must be pointed out that the implicit premise is 'crime is bad'. If this is granted, the conclusion follows that if comics contribute to influence the youth along criminal paths, they should be eliminated."

"If comic books are an evil influence, then they should be got rid of." Here the subject is clearly employing an implicit premise that he added to the material presented, namely "Whatever is an evil influence should be got rid of."

Again in these cases, wrong answers are obtained by correct reasoning if we consider the syllogism as the subject understood it rather than the one the investigator hoped to present.

When all the above processes have been taken into account, a considerable number of errors remain. Do these represent true fallacies? It is difficult to say since in these cases either no account of the reasoning process is supplied, or an unclear explanation is given, or else the subject merely sets out the premises and conclusion given to him without comment. It might be that many of these errors would have been found on examination to involve processes similar to the ones described here, so that no error in reasoning is involved. On the other hand, the possibility of true fallacies cannot be excluded.

In connection with the unexplained errors, it is worth noting that almost as many correct responses as errors were unexplained or unclearly explained. The absence of explanation is thus no reason to suspect a reasoning process of being fallacious.

It must also be mentioned that the processes described above as producing apparent errors although the deductive process is correct are by no means viewed as constituting a complete list. They were observed with particular materials and under particular conditions; and it is to be anticipated that further research will expand this list. Chapman and Chapman (1959), for example, have suggested several additional processes by which error is produced in syllogistic reasoning, one of which involves a misunderstanding of the task different from that described here.

Despite the limitations of the present data, they do show clearly that when subjects arrive at apparently invalid conclusions, or when they fail to spot a fallacy, they often do so because they have worked with materials different from those intended or because they have undertaken a task different from the one intended. In such cases, if we consider the materials and task as they were actually understood by individual subjects, we fail to find evidence of faulty reasoning. It must be concluded that the presence of error does not constitute evidence that the laws of logic are irrelevant to actual thinking. The data tend, rather, to support the older conception that these laws are widely discernible in the thinking process.

DISCUSSION

An examination of errors in syllogistic reasoning leads to two conclusions. 1) While the possibility of fallacy often cannot be excluded, it is, in Mill's words, "scarcely ever possible decidedly to affirm that any argument involves a bad syllogism." 2) Where error occurs, it need not involve faulty reasoning, but may be a function of the individual's understanding of the task or the materials presented to him. Spinoza has stated our present conclusion in more general terms:

When men make errors in calculation, the numbers which are in their minds are not those which are upon the paper. As far as their mind is concerned there is no error, although it seems as if there were, because we think that the numbers in their minds are those which are upon the paper. If we did not think so, we should not believe them to be in error. For example, when I lately heard a man complaining that his court had flown into one of his neighbor's fowls, I understood what he meant, and therefore did not imagine him to be in error. This is the source from which so many controversies arise—that men either do not properly explain their own thoughts, or do not properly interpret those of other people; for, in truth, when they most contradict one another, they either think the same things or something different, so that those things which they suppose to be errors and absurdities in another person are not so. (*Ethics*, part 2, prop. 47, Scholium)

Such a conclusion, which the present analysis supports, is of some importance if, as Mill writes, "to draw inferences has been said to be the great business of life" (1872: Intro., sec. 5). Our data suggest that the intelligent adult is not so inept at carrying on this business as several recent accounts have made him out to be.

In considering the place of logical inference in everyday life, it is necessary also to take into account what Aristotle has termed the "practical syllogism," the case in which

the conclusion drawn from the two premises becomes the action. For example, when you conceive that every man ought to walk and you yourself are a man, you immediately walk; or if you conceive that on a particular occasion no man ought to walk, and you yourself are a man, you immediately remain at rest. In both instances action follows unless there is some hindrance or compulsion. . . . Again, I need a covering, and a cloak is a covering, I need a cloak. What I need I ought to make; I need a cloak, I ought to make a cloak. And the conclusion "I ought to make a cloak" is an action. The action results from the beginning of the train of thought. If there is to be a cloak, such and such a thing is necessary, if this thing then something else; and one immediately acts accordingly. That the action is the conclusion is quite clear. (701a)

Aristotle points out that this whole process need not be explicit.

The mind does not stop and consider at all one of the two premises, namely, the obvious one; for example, if walking is good for a man, one does not waste time over the premiss "I am myself a man." Hence such things as we do without calculation, we do quickly. (*Ibid.*)

Again, "My appetite says, I must drink; this is drink, says sensation or imagination or thought, and one immediately drinks."

If we include, as it seems we must, the practical syllogism in the "great business of life," that of drawing inferences, it becomes difficult indeed to accept the conclusion that human beings are unable to reason logically. A couple of contemporary examples will suggest how ubiquitous is the practical syllogism in everyday life. "It is too far to walk to the Public Library; I must take a subway or bus. The Fifth Avenue bus passes the Public Library. I must take the Fifth Avenue bus." "I do not want to wear the same dress two days in succession. I wore this dress yesterday; so I do not want to wear this dress today." It is difficult to see how the individual could cope with the ordinary tasks of life if the practical syllogism embodied techniques which are not, as one author quoted above put it, "the common property of the unsophisticated subject," if, indeed, it were not a natural mode of functioning of the conscious mind.

Furthermore, if people were unable to reason logically, so that each arrived at different conclusions from the same premises, it is difficult to see how they could understand each other, follow one another's thinking, reach common decisions, and work together.

It might be argued that in the case of the practical syllogism we are dealing not with an implicit logical process, but with a learning process in which each response is cued off by the preceding one. But there are cases in which the practical syllogism leads to a solution which is genuinely novel for the individual. This is surely so for some of the examples cited above, at least the first time they occur.

Two further implications of the present data may be mentioned. They suggest an approach to the problem of the influence of needs and attitudes on the reasoning process. For the problem remains: why do motivational influences so often appear to impair thinking? It is a plausible hypothesis that these influences do not distort the reasoning process, as has frequently been stated or implied— indeed that they do not act at all on the reasoning process—but rather that they affect the materials with which thinking works.

That motivational processes may act on reasoning in the manner suggested here receives support from a recent study by Kopp (1960), who subjected to a similar analysis reasoning processes related to the delusions of paranoid schizophrenics. His subjects, like the present ones, made errors which were found to lie more in the premises from which the reasoning proceeded than in the actual drawing of inferences.

In this connection, it would be interesting to analyze Arieti's examples of "paleological" thinking in the terms of the present study. Unfortunately, the published data are too scant to permit such an analysis. The examples presented would be fallacies in terms of Aristotelian logic if one could assume that the premises as understood by the subject are the same as those understood by the examiner. That this is the case may be doubted in a number of instances; and the search for an archaic logic thus seems premature. Some examples will be given which seem to call for an analysis different from Arieti's.

Arieti cites the case of a woman who "needed to identify herself with the Virgin Mary because of the extreme closeness and spiritual kinship she felt for the Virgin Mary" (1955:195). The reasoning process is described as follows: "The Virgin Mary was a virgin; I am a virgin; therefore, I am the Virgin Mary." In the absence of additional material, we may only speculate that the proposition "I am the Virgin Mary" was not a conclusion deduced from the stated premises, but that it belongs rather in the category of revealed truth or intuition, not in that of deductive inference. It seems likely to me that the syllogism quoted above was in the nature of a justification to the examiner of this intuition rather than the grounds for belief in it. The argument itself could be evaluated only in the light of additional information.

Another example of Arieti's illustrates what he considers to be the propensity of young children "to indulge in paleologic thinking":

A girl, three years and nine months old, saw two nuns walking together, and told her mother, "Mommy, look at the twins!" She thought that the nuns were twins because they were dressed alike. The characteristic of being dressed alike, which twins often have, led to the identification with the nuns. (1955:199)

Again a different interpretation suggests itself: rather than viewing it as a deduction, we may take this process more simply as an instance of an inaccurate concept. Arieti also discusses dream symbols as examples of paleologic thinking. It is particularly difficult for me to view such symbols as inferences, as if they were the conclusions of processes of deductive reasoning. They seem, rather, to involve a much more immediate grasping of similarities.

It is amusing to note that Arieti regards some delusions of identification as instances of paleologic, and describes the "formal mechanism" by which they are produced in a way that could easily be restated as a valid hypothetical syllogism:

If A may be identified with B because they have a common quality, it will be sufficient for me to acquire a quality of the person I want to be identified with, in order to become that person. (1955:207)

Further discussion of the problems raised by Arieti must await more complete data.

The present study has implications also for another problem. To label an inference fallacious, as is clear from the analysis of this paper, is to make a statement about the results of reasoning, but not about the process that is responsible for these results. It might be a matter of considerable interest to study systematically and in detail the reasoning involved in various fallacies. It might be found that many fallacies are produced, not by faulty reasoning, but by specific changes in the material as the subject understands it. Some of the syllogisms employed here involved the fallacy of the undistributed middle; here changes of premises from particulars to universals and other changes in the meaning of premises were not uncommon. Two of the arguments presented contained illicit conversions, but no relevant data were obtained since the subjects systematically ignored the conversion and centered their attention on other parts of the material.[4] In connection with illicit conversions, the discussion of Chapman and Chapman (1959) is of interest; these authors suggest implicit assumptions and changes in meaning that may be involved in the acceptance of such conversions. Mill's observation that fallacies frequently involve changing the premises has been cited above. He analyzes several examples of the fallacy *a dicto secundum quid ad dictum simpliciter*[5] in these terms (1872: Book 5, ch. 6, sec. 4). Fallacies of ambiguity seem likewise to lend themselves to the kind of analysis suggested here.[6]

In conclusion, observations have been presented which are consistent with the view that the rules of the syllogism describe processes that the mind follows in deductive reasoning, even when the syllogistic form is not explicitly employed.[7] A word of caution is necessary at this point. The present observations apply to deductive reasoning only. Even within this category, a very limited number of logical forms has been studied; and the study has been concerned only with the evaluation of presented arguments, not with the construction of arguments of one's own. The investigation needs to be extended before the generality of the conclusion can be assessed. It must also be pointed out that there are many types of thinking to which logical analysis does not apply at all, for example many aspects of free association, fantasy, many creative processes. To apply logical analysis to such processes (for example, Arieti's discussion of dream symbols) is as much an error as to ignore the underlying logical structure of incompletely stated arguments.

Chapter 16

Of the Scholler
of Nature

My theme is the Psychologist's Fallacy. This was long ago described by William James as the Psychologist's *"confusion of his own standpoint with that of the mental fact* about which he is making his report" (1890, 1:196). Indeed, one of the contexts in which James illustrates this fallacy is close to that in which it will be considered here: "We have the inveterate habit, whenever we try introspectively to describe one of our thoughts, of dropping the thought as it is in itself and talking of something else" (1890, 1:278).

Perhaps nowhere has the psychologist's fallacy had more serious consequences—nowhere is it more important to describe the data as they are—than in the case of human thinking; for our whole estimate of man is necessarily tied to our view of his ability to reason logically.

In this connection, contemporary psychologists and philosophers have given us little basis for optimism. We hear, in psychology, of paralogic and paleologic, of atmosphere effects, of psychological as opposed to logical inferences, of the preference of individuals for empirically reasonable propositions over logical ones, and so on. All these expressions are used to summarize the overwhelming impression of fallacies and errors which derives from the psychological investigation of reasoning processes. The rules of logic, it is widely held, do not apply to thinking as it is practiced by human beings.

Philosophers, for their part, likewise maintain the strict separation between logic and thinking. As a single example, Nagel remarks: "Little need be said in refutation of the view that logical principles formulate the 'inherent necessities of thought' and are generalized descriptions of the operations of minds" (1956:66).

On the other hand, earlier scholars took the opposite position. At least from the time of Ramus (1555), logic was held to deal with the laws of thinking:

The syllogism is a law of reason, truer and more just than all the laws which Lycurgus and Solon once fashioned. . . . I say, a law of reason, proper to man, not being in any sense shared with the other animals. (Cited by Howell 1961:159–160)

This idea is taken up by the English Ramists and brought to bear on the controversy over publishing scholarly works in the vernacular. Thus Dudley Fenner (*The Artes of Logike and Rethorike*, 1584) says that since it is true that

the common vse and practise of all men in generall, both in reasoning to the purpose, and in speaking with some grace and elegancie, hath sowen the seede of these artes, why should not all reape where all haue sowen? (Cited by Howell 1961:220)

In the same tradition is Abraham Fraunce, author of *The Lawiers Logike:*

Coblers bee men, why therefore not Logicians? and Carters haue reason, why therefore not Logike? (1588:2)

The preceptes of artificiall Logike both first were collected out of, and alwayes must be conformable unto those sparkes of naturall reason, not lurking in the obscure head-pieces of one or two loytering Fryers. . . . So that, Art, which first was but the Scholler of nature, is now become the maystres of nature, and as it were a Glasse wherein shee seeing and viewing herselfe, may washe out those spottes and blemishes of naturall imperfection. (*Ibid.*)

Every common person or silly soule useth Logike in some part and practiseth of himselfe by naturall instinct that which artificiall Logike doth prescribe in her severall rules and constitutions. (1588:5)

The Port-Royalists (1662) agree that the mind's operations "are done quite naturally and sometimes done better by those ignorant of the rules of logic than by persons instructed in these rules" (Arnauld 1964:29). They subtitle their work on logic *The Art of Thinking*. This is very close to Kant's definition of logic (1885) and not far from that of John Stuart Mill (1872).

Thus, for at least three centuries it was taken for granted that logic deals with the laws of thinking; today this position is quite generally rejected. The interesting thing about this change in point of view is that we know no more about the problem today than was known in the sixteenth century. It has never been properly investigated.

The present paper will make use of an empirical investigation of fallacies and other errors in thinking undertaken to reopen the question of whether actual thinking conforms to, or violates, the rules of logic.[1] Is it true, as the Port-Royalists put it (Arnauld 1964:293), that the rules of the syllogism are rarely transgressed? While it may seem to many that this problem has been solved, it will be maintained here that previous studies have committed the psychologist's fallacy, and that investigation cannot be conclusive in the absence of specific understanding of the actual thinking processes of individual subjects.

It is by no means suggested that we think and talk in syllogisms. A fully explicit syllogism is so unusual in ordinary conversation that it is likely to strike us as funny. The question is, rather, whether after the fact, if we try to recast the thinking of a subject in syllogistic form, we will have a good syllogism or a bad one. If the syllogism is descriptive of human thinking, it is a very formal, very generalized description, a paradigm rather than a literal description. But while formal and explicit syllogisms are not to be expected in the thinking of Coblers and Carters, it would not be astonishing to find there the frequent use of enthymemes. Although in common conference, wee neuer name them—to borrow another phrase from Fraunce (1588:120)—yet doo wee secretly practise them.

The investigation of the relation of Aristotelian logic to thinking is, of course, only a beginning, a part of the much larger problem of the relation of logic to thinking; and directions for further research will be indicated below. Still, Aristotelian logic may not be insignificant as far as human thinking is concerned.

METHOD

The study takes as its tools the syllogism and the conversion. It is perhaps necessary to say a few words on behalf of the principal instrument employed here. The syllogism is often said to be tautological and thus of no interest to a psychology of thinking. Here two considerations, at least, suggest that psychologically many syllogistic inferences are not tautological, but may result in a true gain in knowledge. First, we may have both the major and the minor premise, but fail to organize them in relation to each other. This may be the case, for example, when we have too much information at hand, or unordered information, or when the relevant premises exist in different contexts. Then we are unable to draw a conclusion, which hardly suggests a tautology.

The next consideration is more important and here, for a while, I will follow Augustus De Morgan. He points out that to make the objection that the syllogism assumes what it concludes is tacitly to assert that the minor premise is superfluous, since it was already known to be subsumed under the major. In the instance

All men are mortal;
Plato is a man;
Therefore Plato is mortal

the objection tacitly assumes that we know Plato to be a man as soon as we know him to be Plato. But this cannot be assumed in advance. Plato may be a book written by a man of that name, or a dog, or a town in the Midwest. *Plato*, in other words, does not carry the label *man* with it; the major tells us nothing about Plato until we have the minor. To summarize in De Morgan's words:

Grant the minor to be superfluous, and no doubt we grant the necessity of connecting the major and the conclusion to be superfluous also. Grant any degree of necessity to the minor, and the same is granted to the connection of the major and the conclusion. (1847:259)

The question of whether or not the syllogism is a tautology, then, can be seen to be a matter of the importance of the minor premise. An additional example may widen our context and likewise suggest that the minor need by no means be superfluous:

Although we do not usually state problems in this way, a good deal of problem solving may be viewed as a search for the minor premise. Thus when we try to solve the problem presented by a detective story, we start with certain major premises, usually not stated as proper premises, but nevertheless effective: the guilty person is the one with the strongest motive; the criminal is the least likely person, etc. Solution comes with the discovery of the minor.

In short, I will discuss the solving of syllogisms not as a study of tautology, but as a study of reasoning.

Syllogisms and other logical problems were presented to subjects who were asked to evaluate the inferences involved and to explain their answers. Instructions emphasized the necessary character of logical inferences and the distinction between material truth and logical validity; several simple examples were given. After minimal instruction in their use, Venn diagrams were also employed in certain phases of the investigation as an additional source of information about subjects' specific understanding of the material. In the interest of making the material sound natural, the syllogisms were embedded in a story. They were not properly stated syllogisms, but could all be restated as proper syllogisms with subject, predicate, and copula in premises and conclusion. Subjects were sixth, seventh, and eighth grade children.

RESULTS

It might be thought that, whatever else we may say about the syllogism as a tool of investigation, at least it enables us to be sure whether an inference is correct or incorrect, since logical criteria are clear. But it turns out that these criteria are by no means easy to apply to thinking as it naturally occurs. We need to distinguish between the thinking *process* and the *results* it produces. It may not be assumed that, because an answer is wrong, the reasoning process responsible for it is faulty. In order to evaluate a person's inference, we need to know the materials from which he *actually* reasoned—not simply the materials as an experimenter understood them. A judgment about an inference apart from such knowledge of the subject's understanding of the premises and of the task is an instance of the psychologist's fallacy. In what follows, therefore, an inference will be considered fallacious only where there is a failure to draw the correct conclusion *from the premises employed.*[2]

General results of the study will be stated very briefly as background for one particular set of findings which clearly illustrates the present theme. With procedures that made it possible to understand the specific assumptions of the children to a considerable extent, essentially no fallacies were found. In a class of sixth graders, for example, given some 200 problems in all, there was only a single candidate for a fallacy—and this one might well have been a matter of incomplete information about how the premises were understood. This result confirms earlier findings with adult subjects (Henle 1962).

DEDUCTION OR INDUCTION?

While the investigator in this field becomes accustomed to the elusiveness of the fallacy—indeed John Stuart Mill (1872: Book 5, ch. 6, sec. 3) discussed it explicitly—another finding was entirely unexpected. The following problem was given:

Schliemann dug on the hill, and presently he uncovered five rich graves filled with treasure. One grave contained a golden mask portraying a face with thin lips and a pointed beard. "I've got my man," said Schliemann. "This must be Agamemnon. Agamemnon had thin lips and a pointed beard."

Was Schliemann reasoning correctly? Does it follow from what he said that the mask is that of Agamemnon?

Here the middle term is undistributed in both premises, and no conclusion can be drawn. At first sight, the subjects' performance is less than impressive. In a group of seventh graders, over half the children made errors, and an eighth grade group made even more.

Once again, however, we need to ask how the subjects understood the task and the material; and when we do this, it is not at all clear what an error is. Examination of the data suggests that the subjects were not making deductive inferences at all, but rather inductions. These were inductions, to be sure, based on only two characteristics; but the subjects were no more incautious in this regard than Schliemann himself; this part of the story happens to be true. The accounts of a number of subjects suggest that the process is an inductive one:

Yes. The mask fitted the description.

Yes, because he looked like the mask.

Yes, if he knew the way the king looked . . .

The description fits.

Given the two characteristics in common, these subjects infer that the two faces are alike and that, therefore, the mask was Agamemnon's.

The impression that we are dealing with induction, not deduction, is strengthened by the appearance of words expressing probability rather than logical necessity. Thus:

Yes, if Agamemnon had these characteristics, it probably is him.

Yes, if he knew the way the king looked, he had a very good chance it might be the king.

Yes, if both Agamemnon and the mask had thin lips and a pointed beard, it could be him.

These expressions, which are typical, are rather impressive in view of the emphasis on logical necessity in the instructions.

These data suggest a new dimension to our problem: if we are to know whether a subject is making valid inferences, we must know first of all whether these inferences are deductive or inductive—a distinction, it appears, that is not always easy to make. A problem intended to be deductive does not necessarily call forth a deduction.

If this interpretation of the findings is correct, the tendency to make inductive inferences should be strengthened with an increase in the number of characteristics that Agamemnon and the mask have in common. The following problem was given to new subjects:

. . . One grave contained a golden mask portraying a face with thin lips, a pointed beard, curly hair, and shifty eyes. "I've got my man," said Schliemann . . . .

With four characteristics, there is a very strong tendency to infer that the mask is that of Agamemnon. Of twenty-six subjects, twenty-four made the inference, and all but two of these when they were first presented with the problem. Now there is a very considerable tendency to generalize beyond the characteristics given to the identity of mask and face; and in this case the probability words are much reduced in frequency and also weaker. For example:

Yes, he had all the characteristics of what he was looking for. Of course there would be a very slim probability that he was wrong.

Of those subjects who refused to make the inference, all did so on the basis of the undistributed character of the middle term. For these subjects the problem may still be a deductive one, though this is by no means clear. For example:

There are many people who might have had these characteristics, so the mask was possibly not Agamemnon's.

With two characteristics in common, the judgment that the mask is not necessarily Agamemnon's is correct if the inference is regarded as deductive, and better if we consider it inductive. Now, with four characteristics in common, the deduction remains invalid, but the induction is no longer so clearly hazardous. Surely we do worse things in everyday life if not in science.

With seven characteristics in common, the judgment that the mask is Agamemnon's seems reasonable, and in this case the inference is almost irresistible. Eighteen of nineteen subjects concluded that the mask was Agamemnon's, indeed often that it must have been. The one remaining subject sounds like a young scientist:

No, because although it is very likely the grave of Agamemnon, it could be the grave of another man with the same characteristics.

Now a new procedure was introduced, mainly with new subjects. After the first presentation of this problem, new material was offered with the intention of showing the undistributed character of the middle term. It is now clear that, at least for some subjects, it probably acted—when it did—to indicate that the grounds for the induction were inadequate:

"But Henry," said his wife Sophia, "your Uncle Wilhelm had thin lips and a pointed beard." "Nevertheless," said Schliemann, "this is the mask of Agamemnon."

Was Schliemann reasoning correctly? Does it follow from what he said before that the mask is that of Agamemnon?

In the case in which two characteristics were said to be shared by Agamemnon and the mask, five subjects (33 percent of those who had previously accepted the conclusion) changed to what would be a correct judgment if evaluated by deductive standards, or a more cautious one if evaluated by inductive standards. This figure was reduced to three (17 percent) in the group with four characteristics in common, and to a single subject (5 percent) in the group given seven characteristics in common. Other subjects were temporarily shaken by the new material, changed their judgment, but then reverted on the final question to the conclusion that the mask was Agamemnon's. A number of other subjects consistently maintained this opinion in the face of the new evidence; the figure is not far from 50 percent in each group.

How is it possible to maintain the judgment that the mask is Agamemnon's in the face of the disturbing new material? Since the process seems to have been the same for all three groups of subjects, a few examples will suffice. Subjects either bolstered their opinion with additional considerations drawn mainly from other parts of the story, or they endeavored to rule out Uncle Wilhelm as the owner of the mask:

It is doubtful that any other person of that time would match the description. Even if he did, he would probably not be rich enough to have a mask made.

It was found where the grave supposedly was.

People are not buried with riches nowadays.

Agamemnon died and had a mask of himself made before Uncle Wilhelm even lived.

Would his Uncle be buried with the Greeks?

It is interesting to note that in many cases Uncle Wilhelm is seen as playing only the role of a competitor for the ownership of the mask, rather than as illustrating the more general point that other people besides Agamemnon might possess the same characteristics. Probably this is the reason why a number of subjects, at first shaken in their judgment, reverted to their previous inference that the mask was indeed Agamemnon's. Viewed in this restricted manner, Uncle Wilhelm does not present very formidable contradictory evidence.

DISCUSSION

These findings, and others not reported here, reopen the question: Does thinking transgress the rules of the syllogism? No evidence that it does has been obtained. When the subject accepts the task, and when we know what material he uses and how he understands it, evidence for fallacies is essentially lacking. The more closely one understands a given reasoning process, the less likely is one to find a fallacy.

If subjects are able correctly and apparently naturally to use the deductive process, they are equally ready to make inductive inferences. In fact too ready—for, as Thurber puts it, the conclusion you jump to may be your own. Free of the constraints of necessary implication, the inductive process needs to be tamed. It has not yet been sufficiently disciplined in these eleven- to fourteen-year-olds, and probably not in many adults either. Again, however, it would seem plausible that where errors occur, it is not because the thinking process itself is faulty, but because it is rashly employed.

However they may be regarded today, such conclusions would not have surprised the earlier writers on the relation of logic to thinking. The Port-Royalists state:

Most of man's errors derive not from his being misled by wrong inferences but rather from his making inferences from premises based on false judgments. (Arnauld 1964:12)

Or a sentence that Descartes wrote in the *Rules for the Direction of the Mind* might serve as a conclusion for this part of the study:

None of the mistakes which men can make . . . are due to faulty inference; they are caused merely by the fact that we found upon a basis of poorly comprehended experiences, or that propositions are posited which are hasty and groundless. (Rule 2)

If, then, the very large number of errors that individuals make are not errors of ratiocination, new problems arise. Errors will have to be understood in terms of the individual's specific understanding of the material presented. Subjects of this study consistently made assumptions that were not wrong, and not unreasonable, but that were too narrow to do justice to the given premises. Thus new questions present themselves: Why do subjects make these too restricted assumptions? and how can they be overcome? The study of the understanding of premises is likely, at this point, to bring us into the more familiar territory of obstacles and aids to problem solving.

The present rather neutral and impersonal material probably almost entirely excluded influences of nonrational factors on the thinking of the subjects. In everyday life, of course, these are not excluded. But to recognize such influences is merely to raise questions, not to answer them. The present findings suggest, once more, that an examination of the premises—the individual's interpretation of the material as well as his effort to understand it— may lead to a clarification of such effects. Thus the position that we tend not to make deductive errors does not lead to a narrowly rationalistic conception of man. Rather, it makes questions of the nature of nonrational influences more precise and directs the search for them.

Only categorical syllogisms (and conversions not discussed here) have so far been investigated. But the present method of explicating thinking processes is equally relevant to other logical principles and logical forms.

With regard to the law of noncontradiction, for example, Nagel suggests: "Surely the actual occurrence of beliefs in logically incompatible propositions makes nonsense of the claim that the principle of noncontradiction expresses a universal fact of psychology" (1956:66).

The present findings suggest that every apparent violation of the principle of contradiction presents a *problem*. If it appears that a given proposition is, in a particular thinker's mind, considered both true and false, it is necessary to ask: Is it the *same* proposition in both cases? If a given item should be judged true in one context and false in another, there would be no necessary violation of the principle of contradiction. Such a possibility is no more astonishing than the fact that a given gray color looks reddish on one background, greenish on another. Of course this is no more than a hypothesis to be tested by specific cognitive investigation; but once it has been stated, it also becomes clear that the statement that persons believe in logically incompatible propositions is likewise no more than a hypothesis, itself requiring test.

The kind of analysis undertaken here may likewise be extended to hypothetical syllogisms. Suppose, as a single example, that somebody denies an accusation against a friend. We might dismiss this as mere bias, as unwillingness to consider the evidence, etc. And this might indeed be the case. On the other hand, there might be implicit a real thinking process that demands investigation. It might, if spelled out, be something like this:

If this were the case, he would be a dishonest man;
But he is not a dishonest man;
Therefore, this is not the case.

This is a perfectly good hypothetical syllogism (*modus tollendo tollens*). If this is really the implicit reasoning, it is not to be dismissed as bias or delusion. The original proposition might be wrong, but that has nothing to do with the validity of the inference.

Once the possibility of such implicit premises is recognized, a very wide range of problems opens up. For example, the authors of *The Art of Thinking* suggest that some people "judge by a very convenient general rule: I am right, I know the truth. Such a person easily infers that those not of his opinion are wrong—in fact, such a conclusion follows necessarily from the general principle" (Arnauld 1964:268). If we realize that the premise "I am right" is usually implicit, the case becomes relevant to our present problem of the implicit logic of apparently illogical processes.

And this is no isolated instance. Even with the experimental material, subjects sometimes slipped unintended premises (that is, premises unintended by the investigator) into the presented material. In everyday life this probably happens very frequently. The psychologist or logician, for example, is often tempted implicitly to assume that material presented to subjects is understood by them in the same manner as by the psychologist himself: it has been the thesis of this paper that such an unexpressed assumption (and not errors of ratiocination) leads to errors in conception of the thinking process. A most interesting group of these added propositions are assumptions that an individual makes about himself, about other people, about the world he lives in—assumptions only dimly glimpsed or unreportable by the person himself but perhaps subject to clinical investigation. Or into a set of premises we may slip assumptions that go unnoticed because they concern what is taken for granted, what is regarded as too commonplace to mention. In all such cases, the explication of such added assumptions might force us to view as valid a process that seemed to be illogical before they were taken into account.

In the same way, two people, making different assumptions of this kind, might come to different—though valid—conclusions, with each one suspecting the other of an erroneous inference.

One final area in which the present approach is relevant will be mentioned: the analysis of so-called paralogic. In most cases the published material is not full enough to permit specific analysis, but a single example of what Arieti calls paleologic will suggest the possibilities here. This author describes a schizophrenic patient who "was noticed to have the habit of wetting her body with oil. Asked why she would do so, she replied: 'The human body is a machine and has to be lubricated'" (Arieti 1948:332). Here all that is needed is to make explicit the clearly implied major premise: All machines have to be lubricated. It can be seen that the action is a valid conclusion from the premises (practical syllogism).

The apparently successful reduction of a case described as paleological to a valid categorical syllogism raises a serious question. It was pointed out above that paleologic and related systems were invented because of the widely held view that the rules of logic do not apply to human thinking (or to the thinking of psychotics or other selected groups of human beings). These groups are supplied with what is held to be their own logic even if it violates the rules of Aristotelian logic. Indeed, logic now becomes a branch of psychology, referring to the "organization of the cognitive processes which are involved in the act of understanding the world" (Arieti 1963:62). In this manner logic loses its objective character: presumably any thinking process may now be called logical.

It may now be asked: Does not the present approach have precisely the same consequence? If a syllogism appears to be a bad one, the search is instituted for an implicit premise that will make it good. Two considerations are relevant here. First, since the approach is an empirical one, only those premises actually supplied by subjects may be introduced into the reasoning process. Every syllogism thus permits the judgment: valid, invalid, or uncertain (by virtue of insufficient information). Second, the present discussion is by no means a form of psychologism. It does not, like paralogic and paleologic, attempt to make logic coextensive with thinking by making it illogical. Rather than denying logical requiredness, denying the demands of necessary implication, it seeks to show that such requiredness is central in actual human thinking.[3]

In summary, this paper has attempted to bring the problem of the relation of logic to thinking back to the clear-sighted analysis it received in the sixteenth to nineteenth centuries. This is, of course, only a first step. If we are able to extricate ourselves from the two blind alleys of psychologism and of the radical separation of logic from the study of thinking, we may be able to proceed in new directions, unforeseen or only adumbrated by our forebears. A few such directions have been suggested here.

Part VI

People

Chapter 17

One Man Against the Nazis— Wolfgang Köhler

In the 1920s and early 1930s, psychology was flourishing at the Psychological Institute of Berlin University under the direction of Wolfgang Köhler. There was truly an all-star cast of characters. In addition to the director, Max Wertheimer had been there from about 1916 until 1929, when he left to accept the chair at Frankfurt. Kurt Lewin, too, came to Berlin after World War I and remained until his resignation in 1933. Köhler's last assistants in Berlin are still known, although all of them died young: Karl Duncker, whose studies of problem solving and of induced move-

Acknowledgement is gratefully made to the Harvard University Archives for permission to publish the three letters from Köhler to Ralph Barton Perry; to the Archives of the History of American Psychology for permission to use Köhler's letter to Donald K. Adams; and to the Library of the American Philosophical Society for permission to publish all the other documents and letters here included. I would like to express warm thanks for cooperation to Whitfield J. Bell, Jr. and Murphy D. Smith of the American Philosophical Society and to John A. Popplestone and Marion White McPherson of the Archives of the History of American Psychology.

I am grateful to Margaret Speicher, who translated some of the documents and who checked all of my translations.

This article is the story neither of the destruction of German psychology by Hitler nor of the fate of the Gestalt psychologists after the Nazis' rise to power. (For a good account of the latter, see Mandler and Mandler 1968.) It is, rather, a chapter in the life of Wolfgang Köhler.

ment remain classics; von Lauenstein, who is known mainly for his theory and investigation of time errors—an important problem, since time errors offer a good opportunity to study the behavior of young memory traces; von Restorff, whom we know for her work with Köhler on the isolation effect (sometimes called the Restorff effect) and on theory of recall. The chief *Assistent* at the institute, Hans Rupp, chief by virtue of seniority, will hardly figure in our story.[1]

Berlin, with Köhler and Wertheimer, was the seat of Gestalt psychology in those days, along with another highly productive seat at Giessen under Koffka until 1924, when Koffka came to America. Berlin had seen the publication of major theoretical and experimental contributions to Gestalt psychology. Wertheimer published, among others, major papers on Gestalt theory, including the paper on perceptual grouping. Köhler's *Die physischen Gestalten in Ruhe und im stationären Zustand* appeared in 1920. His work on chimpanzees was still appearing, and there were numerous papers, both theoretical and experimental, many of them in perception but also in other fields. His translation of his book *Gestalt Psychology*, into German was published in 1933. Lewin's early papers on perception and on association appeared, and then the long and influential series, published with his students, on *Handlungs- und Affektpsychologie*.

Among the students at the institute, I will mention only a few, mainly names we know today. Rudolf Arnheim and later Werner Wolff worked in the field of expression; Metzger's work on visual perception was under way, including the work on the *Ganzfeld*. Gottschaldt's studies on the influence of past experience on visual form perception came out of the institute; his figures are still in use in the Embedded Figures Test. Hans Wallach did his first work there. Kopfermann's beautiful experiments on depth perception, Ternus' on phenomenal identity, von Schiller's on stroboscopic movement, and much, much more excellent work were all products of the Psychological Institute. A number of young American Ph.D.s came to study and work at the institute, for example, Robert B. MacLeod, Donald K. Adams, Karl Zener, Carroll Pratt, Leonard Carmichael, and others.

On January 30, 1933, the Nazis came to power. The first effects on German universities were dismissals of Jewish professors and others considered to be hostile to the new regime. The story is well known. The dismissals ranged from Nobel laureates (including Einstein, Haber, Franck, Hertz) to *Assistenten*. Hartshorne relates an anecdote which he says was widely believed—that Max Planck, the great physicist, petitioned Hitler to stop the dismissal of scientists for political reasons; he stressed the importance of science for the country. Hitler is said to have replied, "Our national policies will not be revoked or modified, even for scientists. If the dismissal of Jewish scientists means the annihilation of contemporary German science, then we shall do without science for a few years!" (1937:111–112).

About the dismissed scholars, their university colleagues kept silent. As Köhler remarked years later, "Nothing astonished the Nazis so much as the cowardice of whole university faculties, which did not consist of Nazis. Naturally this corroborated the Nazis' contempt for the intellectual life" (n.d.).

The future of an independent professor was, of course, uncertain. As early as April 1, 1933, Köhler, briefly outside of Germany, wrote to Ralph Barton Perry:

Nobody in Germany with any decency in his bones . . . knows very much about his near future. If nothing happens, I shall be in Chicago for the meeting of the American Association. . . .
As to myself, my patriotism expects the Germans to behave better than any other people. This seems to me a sound form of patriotism. Unfortunately it is very different from current nationalism which presupposes that the own people are right and do right whatever they are and do. However, there will still be some fight during the next weeks. Don't judge the Germans before it is over.

With the dismissal of James Franck, the great experimental physicist, Köhler made public his stand. The fight had begun. On April 28, 1933, he wrote, for the *Deutsche Allgemeine Zeitung*, the last anti-Nazi article to be published openly in Germany under the Nazi regime, "Gespräche in Deutschland" (Conversations in Germany). The courage of such an act may be indicated by the fact that everybody expected Köhler to be arrested for it.

Why, ask the powerful men who rule Germany, have many valuable people not joined the Nazi party? Of them Köhler comments, "Never have I seen finer patriotism than theirs." Regarding the wholesale dismissal of Jews from universities and other positions, he continues:

During our conversation, one of my friends reached for the Psalms and read: "The Lord is my shepherd, I shall not want. . . ." He read the 90th Psalm and said, "It is hard to think of a German who has been able to move human hearts more deeply and so to console those who suffer. And these words we have received from the Jews."
Another reminded me that never had a man struggled more nobly for a clarification of his vision of the world than the Jew Spinoza, whose wisdom Goethe admired. My friend did not hesitate to show respect, as Goethe did. Lessing, too, would not have written his *Nathan the Wise* unless human nobility existed among the Jews. . . . It seems that nobody can think of the great work of Heinrich Hertz without an almost affectionate admiration for him. And Hertz had Jewish blood.
One of my friends told me: "The greatest German experimental physicist of the present time is Franck; many believe that he is the greatest experimental physicist of our age. Franck is a Jew, an unusually kind human being. Until a few days ago, he was professor at Göttingen, an honor to Germany and the envy of the international scientific community."

Perhaps the episode of Franck's dismissal

shows the deepest reason why all these people are not joining [the Party]: they feel a moral imposition. They believe that only the quality of a human being should determine his worth, that intellectual achievement, character, and obvious contributions to German culture retain their significance whether a person is Jewish or not.

Expecting arrest, the Köhlers and members of the institute spent the night of April 28 playing chamber music. But the Nazis did not come.

Four months later, reprints of this article were still being circulated. Letters poured in, for the most part from strangers, occasionally critical, but the overwhelming majority was full of admiration for Köhler's courageous stand. Warm thanks were expressed by Jew and non-Jew alike. The following letter, as a single example, was signed only "A German Jew":

Today I read your article, "Conversations in Germany." I am not ashamed to admit that, despite my 65 years, I was deeply moved by it and tears came to my eyes. I asked myself: Are there really Germans in Germany who can still muster such courage?

I am a Jew, born in Germany as were my father and grandfather. I am a simple merchant, not a politician, who formerly for many years employed hundreds of Christian workers of all parties and religions and who enjoyed the greatest respect and recognition from them.

These lines are simply intended to express to you my respect for your straightforward, fearless way of thinking.

I omit my name since it is not relevant. I feel that in spirit I want to shake your hand, since I have children who now may no longer look upon Germany as their homeland.

On November 3, 1933, the government decreed that professors must open their lectures with the Nazi salute. Köhler flipped his hand in a caricature of the salute and said:

Ladies and gentlemen, I have just saluted you in a manner that the government has decreed. I could not see how to avoid it.

Still, I must say something about it. I am professor of philosophy in this university, and this circumstance obligates me to be candid with you, my students. A professor who wished to disguise his views by word or by action would have no place here. You could no longer respect him; he could no longer have anything to say to you about philosophy or important human affairs.

Therefore I say: the form of my salute was until recently the sign of very particular ideas in politics and elsewhere. If I want to be honest, and if I am to be respected by you, I must explain that, although I am prepared to give that salute, I do not share the ideology which it usually signifies or used to signify.

The National Socialists among you will particularly welcome this explanation. Nobility and purity of purpose among the Germans are goals for which the National Socialists are working hard. I am no National Socialist. But out of the same need to act nobly and purely, I have told you what the German salute means in my case and what it does not mean. I know you will respect my motives.

A witness reports that the audience of 200 greeted these remarks with thunderous applause, despite the presence of numerous brownshirts and many Nazi sympathizers (Crannell 1970).

There was no real interference with the work of the institute until one evening in the beginning of December 1933, when Köhler gave the psychological colloquium. The doors to the colloquium room were guarded by troops, some in uniform, others in civilian clothes. When the students and assistants wanted to leave after the colloquium, they were stopped and their student cards examined.

Köhler did not then interfere with the inspection. When it was over, he telephoned the rector of the university, Eugen Fischer, protesting the unannounced raid. A discussion was arranged: the rector, who admitted that the procedure had been incorrect, agreed to exempt the Psychological Institute from further inspections of this kind. He had no objection to Köhler's informing the psychological colloquium of this agreement, and Köhler did so.

In the rector's absence, on February 26, 1934, Deputy Rector Bieberbach ordered another inspection of the institute. In accordance with his agreement with the rector, Köhler refused permission, and the inspection was not carried out. The rector was informed and offered no objection.

But trouble was ahead. A trip to Norway the next month gave Köhler another opportunity to write freely to Perry:

I am trying to build up a special position for myself in which I might stay with honour. As yet it seems to work, but the end may come [any] day. Quite exciting sometimes, not a life of leisure, occasionally great fun. The art is not to act in passion, but to make at once use of any occasion when the others make a mistake; then it is time to push a foot forward or to hit without serious danger for oneself. You will say that such is the method of cowards. But think of the difference in strength! . . .

Good work is being done in Berlin, as though we had to do what the emigrants are no longer able to do in Germany. Unfortunately my assistants have been in serious danger several times because of political denunciations—a denunciation a month is more or less our current rate; as yet, however, it has always been possible to save them.

Again the rector left town, and on April 12, 1934, Bieberbach ordered a new inspection "despite the agreement between Rector Fischer and Professor Köhler." The search of the institute was carried out under the leadership of a law student named Hennig, who submitted a report full of suspicions, innuendos, and accusations but no more hard evidence than the discovery of a couple of foreign newspapers in an office (newspapers not banned by the regime) and the smell of cigarette smoke in an unoccupied room.

His impertinent report insulted Professor Köhler and ended with the recommendation that two assistants, Drs. Duncker and von Lauenstein, as well as three employees, be dismissed. He recommended that the institute be moved to new quarters which would be easier to supervise and even suggested the need for another structure of the institute "which corresponds better to our time and our spirit."

Köhler angrily informed the rector on April 13 that he was, for the time being, unable to continue to direct the institute and that he had therefore transferred the directorship to his chief assistant, Professor Rupp. He reminded Rector Fischer that the agreement between them had been violated and that his authority as director had been seriously undermined; only when the situation was rectified would he resume his duties as director.

Bieberbach, the deputy rector, replied (April 14), reaffirming his "self-evident right" to inspect every part of the university. Köhler telephoned the minister of science, art, and education, Dr. Achelis, and on April 18 sent him a copy of the whole correspondence, including Hennig's report along with his own detailed reply. He requested an immediate end to a situation which he could not regard "as compatible with the dignity of the University of Berlin."

On the same date, Rector Fischer replied to Köhler's letter of April 13, denying that there had ever been any agreement that the Psychological Institute be exempted from inspections. He expressed the desire to settle the disagreement without the intervention of the ministry and requested an oral reply from Köhler.

Köhler's reply was *written* (April 20, 1934). In his letter he assures the rector that he welcomes an oral discussion when clarification has been achieved on the earlier one in which the agreement had been made, but he makes it altogether clear that the rector's account does not correspond with the facts:

With the greatest astonishment I read in your letter the sentence: "Of an agreement between us that there would be no inspection of students in your Institute there was obviously never any question," as well as the further one: "I have only said to you that the inspecting student had to announce himself to the Director of the Institute on his appearance." . . . Something of value is to be expected from an oral discussion with you only when you recall how we came to this agreement and how, until a short time ago, it was taken for granted by both of us.

Köhler concludes that as soon as the rector and he agree again about that earlier agreement, he will welcome an oral discussion.

Two weeks later, May 3, Fischer expresses his disagreeable surprise that Köhler attaches a condition to an oral discussion to try to settle the issues between them. He asserts that it is "a matter of one opinion against another."

Köhler's reply on May 8, even less than the others in this series, hardly corresponds to the kind of communication normally expected from a professor to the rector of his university.

I can give the following explanation: If another person, in a discussion with me, makes a detailed and completely unmistakable agreement with me, if for months afterward this agreement is carried out on both sides, but one day the other declares that the agreement was never made, then prudence forbids me to have another discussion with this person before he has corrected his mistake in a manner that produces confidence again. For who would protect me from a mistake of the same kind which could result from a further discussion? This holds for discussions with the Rector Magnificus exactly as for anyone else.

He points out that the rector has simply continued to renounce his agreement without giving any thought to the actual facts of the case.

This cannot continue. . . . It is . . . extremely important, even if it has until now been taken for granted, that the administration make no error in memory which concerns matters of morals. I therefore ask you to communicate with me in writing by May 19 whether you have, in the meantime, recalled our agreement. I assume that in the meantime you will also find words of reproach and regret about the behavior of Hennig as authorized by the Rectorate and about his incredible report.

Thus Köhler is again in effect calling the Rector Magnificus of his university a liar, he makes clear that a matter of morals is involved, and he delivers what can only be called an ultimatum.[2] A copy of this letter and of Fischer's letter of May 3 was sent to the minister with the following remark:

It is unusual for a professor to behave in this way toward the Rector. But the behavior of the Rector which leads me to do so is much more unusual. The dilatory handling of the matter I can no longer permit, and I must therefore insist that an untenable situation come to an end in a reasonable time.

Apparently no reply was received, either from the rector or from Dr. Achelis. On May 21, after the expiration of the ultimatum, Köhler (now in Scotland on a brief lecturing tour) sent to the ministry and to the dean of the philosophical faculty a request for retirement.

On the same day he wrote to Perry:

My resignation is most likely to be final. Since most of the serious workers in psychology had to leave before, and since my excellent assistants would not stay without me, this means the abolition of German psychology for many years. I do not regard myself as responsible. If only 20 professors had fought the same battle, it would never have come so far with regard to German universities.

The reply to Köhler's request for retirement was a letter from an official of the ministry to the effect that the transfer of civil service personnel to retirement status cannot simply be done upon request. Köhler is asked to discuss the matter with Dr. Achelis.

Meanwhile, the situation was deteriorating at the institute. A handyman, one Herr Schmidt, whose denunciation was apparently responsible for the dismissal of von Lauenstein, refused to carry out instructions, claiming the protection of the rector. Representatives of the German Student Organization (Nazis, of course) interfered in the administration of the institute, and the rector did nothing about it. In June 1934, a torchlight procession planned by students at the institute to honor Professor Köhler was forbidden. Students were called to the Department for Political Education and threatened when they tried to defend the institute. Two students, in an interview with the leader of the German Student Organization, heard Köhler attacked as a man who does not "stand on the ground of National Socialism" and who "identifies with the Jew Wertheimer." They learned that Duncker's habilitation would be prevented and that the attack on Köhler and his assistants was just the beginning.

In July 1934, matters had temporarily improved: the ministry had intervened. On July 21, after a morning meeting, Köhler wrote to thank the *Ministerialdirektor* for his "intervention and benevolent justice." He assured him that he would withdraw his resignation as soon as the following conditions were met: the reinstatement of von Lauenstein, the granting of leave and subsequent transfer of the handyman Schmidt, the dismissal of the leader of psychology students of the German Student Organization, and a public statement from the ministry.

It was not until September 24, 1934, that the ministry, represented by Vahlen, wrote to the rector of the University of Berlin the conclusions of his investigation of the Psychological Institute. Vahlen expresses his conviction that the personal attacks on Professor Köhler were unjustified, nor can he approve of the measures taken, with the rector's permission, by the student organization. No action was taken against Hennig, the student leader of the raid on the institute, only because he had been removed from his position for other reasons. The ministry considered justified Köhler's objections to the methods used by the leader of the student group.

On the other hand, Vahlen finds reason to criticize Köhler's refusal to discuss matters with the rector, as well as the tone of his letters. He disapproves in particular of Köhler's interruption of his duties as director of the institute and of his activities there. He assures the rector that Professor Köhler has his confidence, and he expects all measures aimed at discrediting the institute to stop immediately.

The public statement made by the ministry is the following:

Accusations which have been raised against the Psychological Institute force me to point out that Professor Köhler has the confidence of the Minister. I expect from the Student Organization that no more cases of hostile behavior take place against Professor Köhler, his Institute, and his students.

A copy of this letter was sent to Köhler, along with a repetition of criticisms of Köhler's behavior toward the rector, with whom Vahlen asks him to cooperate in the future.

A month later, Köhler was in the United States, delivering the

William James Lectures at Harvard. Here he received a letter from Bieberbach, the deputy rector, asking him to sign an oath of loyalty to Adolf Hitler. The letter went unanswered until February. In the meantime, on January 7, 1935, Vahlen wrote to Köhler that the vacancy created by the departure of Professor Kurt Lewin had been filled. Dr. Keller of Rostock had been appointed in December, although Köhler had not been consulted. Vahlen assumes that Köhler will give his consent retroactively, and he is reassured by the opinion of the acting director, Rupp, that Köhler would have no objection. The minister asks for Köhler's opinion and wants to know whether, under these circumstances, Köhler's request to resign still holds.

On February 2, Köhler wrote that the law requiring a loyalty oath does not apply to him, since he has submitted his resignation to the ministry. On the next day he replied to Vahlen's communication of January 7. He refers to the minister's earlier criticisms of the intrusions into the administration of the institute, for which he is grateful. But that same letter had contained reference to the "peculiar composition" of the circle close to Professor Köhler and had criticized the manner in which he had defended himself against the rector. He takes exception to both points, and on the basis of them had been considering for some time whether to renew his request to resign. Then he received the news of Dr. Keller's appointment. He can only see this as a continuation of the measures that first led him to request retirement: it is totally impossible for him to direct the institute when, time after time, important decisions are made without even consulting him. He can therefore not withdraw his request for resignation. For this, as he writes to the minister, he would need a most dramatic and binding assurance that he could be director of the Psychological Institute of the University of Berlin "without repeatedly being subjected to the kind of treatment that only a weakling with no sense of honor could tolerate."

Apparently Köhler again requested reinstatement of his assistants, and this request was denied. Accordingly, a new request to resign was addressed to the minister on August 22, 1935, when Köhler was again in Germany. In it he points out that it is impossible for him to continue his work without these assistants, who represent new points of view now beginning to spread to all countries.

And so ended the great days of the Psychological Institute of the University of Berlin. Even before his final resignation, Köhler wrote an obituary notice to an American friend, Donald K. Adams:

I feel obliged to announce to all those who have taken a friendly interest in the Psychological Institute at Berlin that this institute does not exist any more—though the rooms and the apparatus and Mr. Rupp are still there. The government has decided in May to dismiss all the assistants who were trained by me and in June, during the term, they were suddenly forbidden to continue their work and their teaching: Duncker, von Lauenstein and von Restorff. Since, at my last visit in Berlin, I had expressly stated orally and in official documents that I could not possibly remain as director without the help of my young friends and since this is a clear case of their modern brutality (another man uses this method in order to push *me* out), the measure is morally equivalent to my own dismissal too. I shall have a last interview with the Nazi authorities in August. But there is not one chance in a hundred for my staying on in Germany. . . . We were depressed for some days but have come back to the fighting spirit once more. Personally, I shall be glad when I have no contact with the official Germany of today, and I have so many good friends in this country, more indeed than over there. My deepest anxiety refers to the assistants. I am not yet sure whether I shall be able to place them somewhere.

The new Nazi director of the institute would not allow Köhler's students to remain;[3] and of course his assistants were gone. A few went to other universities, some emigrated, some died. The young generation of Gestalt psychologists was effectively wiped out.

It is difficult to guess what would have been the effect on psychology in Germany, and indeed in the world, if the Psychological Institute had been allowed a few more productive years. It was perhaps the outstanding psychological institute of its time. Max Planck, in a letter to Köhler in the midst of the struggle, speaks of the importance of its preservation "in its unique significance for science and for our university." The institute attracted students from many countries; and the ideas of Gestalt psychology were respected and were spreading in Germany and in other countries.

It is possible that our science would be different today if that institute had been able to continue its work.

The courageous struggle of Wolfgang Köhler against the Nazis could not save the Psychological Institute. Was that struggle in vain? I think not. For as we look back on it, it shows us once more what a human being can be.

Chapter 18

An American
Adventure

In 1925, Wolfgang Köhler, the great Gestalt psychologist, was professor of philosophy and director of the Psychological Institute at the University of Berlin. An invitation to Clark University, as visiting professor, gave him his first glimpse of America.

At that time, not long after the end of World War I, a German professor in the United States was a rarity. Köhler was much interviewed, and he learned much about this country. He was soon impressed by the friendliness of Americans; even the dogs, he is reported to have said, are friendly. He enjoyed the varied beauties of the country, its freshness, its enormous possibilities, the sometimes naive belief in "a distinguished entity called progress."

Not long before, Köhler had spent six years observing the intelligent behavior of chimpanzees at the anthropoid station which the Prussian Academy of Sciences had established on the island of Tenerife in the Canary Islands. His book on this work, translated as *The Mentality of Apes*, was widely known in America, and he was frequently invited to lecture on the problem solving of apes. But not in the South. After all, 1925 was the year of the Scopes

This material is taken from an informal talk by Wolfgang Köhler, "A Strange Experience in 1925." It is used with the permission of the American Philosophical Society, in whose library the original manuscript is deposited.

trial in Tennessee, the famous "monkey trial," in which a young high-school teacher was convicted of teaching evolution. Köhler subsequently learned that one of the best Southern universities would not invite him to speak on his work with the chimpanzees because it would "arouse a storm of indignation all over the state."

During the summer, Köhler was invited to teach at the University of California at Berkeley. One lecture in his course on comparative psychology concerned the communication of crickets which, in line with the then-fashionable negativistic views about the abilities of animals, were widely believed to have no sense of hearing. How, then, explain the chirping in alternation of males and females? This was thought to be a matter of crude vibrations propagated in the ground and picked up by tactile receptors. And the sense of smell surely sufficed to account for the sexual behavior of these creatures.

Such statements raised doubts in the mind of a high-school teacher in Vienna who made such elegant tests, with so light a touch, that Köhler remarked that he was "sometimes tempted to call him the Mozart among . . . experimental zoologists." One experiment, which Köhler described to his students, tested the thesis that crickets merely feel the vibrations caused by chirping, rather than hear them. The Viennese instructor used two little balloons and attached to each a small gondola. In one gondola sat a male cricket, a female in the other. A spacious hall permitted the balloons to be released far from each other. Presently one cricket began to chirp, the other answered, and the alternation continued, even though there was now no possibility of propagation of vibrations in the ground.

Another experiment took up again the relation of chirping to the feeling of vibrations and added a test of the thesis that it was merely the sense of smell that was responsible for the "interesting personal relations" between crickets. A male cricket was placed in a house in one part of Vienna, a female in another at the other end of town. Thus all the smells and all the vibrations of the city separated the two creatures. The two houses were connected by phone. Soon one cricket began to chirp. An answering chirp came from the phone, to which the first cricket immediately moved. Whenever the chirping was heard—by the observer and by the cricket—the partner at the other end of the connection moved to the telephone, wherever it was placed.

The issue of hearing in crickets was finally settled. But this story is only incidentally concerned with the sensory capacities of insects. Two days after the lecture, Köhler's students brought him a San Francisco newspaper's report of it: "German Scientist Observes Ants Flirting by Telephone." "The experiments," Köhler commented in astonishment, "had become my experiments and the crickets had become ants. You can imagine the more specific sweet content of the article."

After a good laugh, the incident was forgotten—forgotten, that is, until, after several weeks, Köhler returned to New England. Leaving his train, he was immediately accosted by reporters eager for more juicy details. Köhler tried to correct the report and was once more able to forget the incident.

On the way home, early in 1926, he spend a week in Paris and happened to buy a copy of the Paris edition of a New York newspaper. This time the story was on page 1: "Noted German Scientist Studies Love Life of Ants." Could he now be finished with the matter? Only until he returned to Berlin. On his desk was a hand-written letter from England: "Any further information you will be kind enough to send us would be welcomed with real enthusiasm."

This is the story, as Köhler put it, of how he once "almost became famous by mistake."

Chapter 19

A Tribute to Max Wertheimer:
Three Stories of Three Days

In 1940, a few years before his death, Max Wertheimer published a marvelous little essay entitled "A Story of Three Days." It is a story of a man whose contemplation of the world situation led him to a passionate search for clarification of the nature of freedom. The world was at war, under the shadow of Nazism, brutality, and repression; it was a time when "freedom in the humane meaning of the word was proclaimed false, outworn, useless." In this situation, the man had to know: What, fundamentally, is freedom? "What does it require? Why is it so dear to me?" I hardly need add that this was a good man, a humble empiric, open-minded, thirsting for understanding.

I would like to relate this story briefly, drawing considerably on Wertheimer's own words. I do so because the story—itself a fable—may be taken also as a fable for Wertheimer's own search for clarification of fundamental problems. Wertheimer's story is a story of more than thirty years, but so, too, I suspect, was that of the man of our tale. I will treat both as stories of three days.

The man of Wertheimer's story first went to a sociologist and

This paper was presented as a Centennial Lecture at the 1980 convention of the American Psychological Association in Montreal. It was part of APA's observance of the Centennial of experimental psychology and was also presented in observance of the Centennial of Max Wertheimer's birth, April 15, 1880.

was fascinated to hear how different were the ideas of freedom in different societies and how different the ways of realizing them. "But why is freedom so dear to you?" he asked. "What is it essentially?" The sociologist's answer was that an individual's standards, his values and goals, are conditioned by his social group, that ethical standards are relative.

"Is that all?" asked the man. "Is it just that society has taught you to value freedom? Are there no requirements of freedom? No requirements for men as they should be? For society? Is no decision possible among the various systems?" The sociologist was sympathetic, but he could not help. Pushed, he defined freedom as absence of hindrances from doing what one wants to do. The man went away bewildered and saddened.

He continued his search in his own library. Now he read about people's slavery to institutions and their struggles for freedom from them. He read a book by a famous psychoanalyst who held that culture is based on coercion and instinctual renunciation, which may in some individuals become internalized. Freedom would then mean removal of all restraints on instinctual wishes.

Is that all that freedom is? asked the man. I must see a philosopher.

This he did the next day. The philosopher explained determinism to him: every action is causally determined; the belief in freedom of action and of choice is an illusion. The philosopher showed him that modern ideas of determinism were basic to all he had heard and read the previous day. The man went away more bewildered than ever.

On the third day he reviewed what he had learned. There is no freedom because everything is determined. Or else freedom means absence of restraints, external or internal, so that one can follow whatever impulse comes to mind. It all seemed utterly strange and superficial to the man; it seemed blind to the real problems of freedom. He had to restate the issues for himself, and now he did it by consulting his own experience: "Have I not seen in my experience strong and indeed very characteristic cases of men, of children, who were free, [others] who were unfree? What were the essentials?" (Wertheimer 1940/1961:59). Then he thought of those who had fought for freedom in former times. Certainly they were not fighting in order to be able to do just anything they might wish to do. Did they not demand justice for everybody? He thought back to his discussions with the scholars, to his reading. "The real question," he realized, "was, what kind of attitude, what rules, what institutions make for the free, what for the unfree?" (1940/1961:61–62). The problem is not that all determinants are factors against freedom, but which ones? "If a man is blind . . . and you open his eyes, give him knowledge, make him see, you may thereby strongly influence him, change him, determine him, but are you thereby limiting his freedom?" (1940/1961:62). And he continued: "Is it not sheer piecemeal thinking to say 'restraint is restraint', if a kidnapper restrains . . . a child in order to extort ransom, and if another restrains the gangster from doing it in order to help the child?" (ibid.). And likewise with institutions: which ones limit freedom? "Is limiting freedom the essence of institutions for true education?"

Now he began to see the basic issues of freedom. And he understood more clearly why freedom was so dear to him. I will not follow him in his further thinking, except to say that he realized that he had only taken the first steps in grasping what was fundamental in freedom. He had begun to see the problems, and he was looking forward to the next steps. Marvelous tasks for investigation! The task, he knew, was to face each problem "with the attitude of the free man, productively, sincerely" (1940/1961:64).

Now I come to the Story of Wertheimer's Three Days—remember that they cover a period of more than thirty years, starting around 1910 and continuing to the end of his life in 1943. The story concerns a major preoccupation of Wertheimer's—productive thinking. Like the man in our other story, he was a good man, open-minded, passionately seeking to understand. He believed in the old "conception of *homo sapiens*" which

implies that . . . some abilities are important for man (although not always actually realized). Among these are the ability and tendency to understand, to gain insight; a feeling for truth, for justice, for good and evil, for sincerity. Connected with the realization of these abilities is the old conception of human dignity as an inner task of man. (1935:353)

"What occurs," asked our man, "when, now and then, thinking

really works productively? What happens when, now and then, thinking forges ahead? What is really going on in such a process?" (1959:1).

First he went to see an anthropologist. "I think I can help you," said that scholar. "In the thinking of indigenous peoples you can see in vague and rudimentary form the forerunners of our own thought processes." (I remind you that this part of the story comes from around 1910.)

But even if these people show rudimentary thought processes, said our man to himself, what are the specific characteristics of this stage? It is no solution to call the process rudimentary; it merely opens up problems for investigation.[1]

"Indigenous peoples for the most part lack number concepts," continued the anthropologist. "They lack the precise, abstract numerical system of which we are so justly proud."

What thought processes do such people employ where we use numbers? wondered our man. What problems do they address? That is the question. I must consider their actual behavior when they count, trade, build, and so on. I will see how quantities are expressed in their languages. I will not start from the preconception that their thinking is rudimentary as compared with ours.

When a tribesman wants to build a hut, does he count the number of posts needed and fetch them? Or does the idea of a hut simply include the required posts? There seem to be structures which are less abstract than our numbers that may serve a similar function; they seem to be intermediate between Gestalt qualities and concepts. Nor are they exclusive to indigenous peoples. A large family sits down to dinner and somebody, without counting, remarks that one person is missing. We recognize a rectangle or other polygon by its shape, not by counting sides and angles. We distinguish natural pairs which depend on their belonging together: two eyes, two shoes, a married couple.

Like the natives, we, too, use nonquantitative concepts or group structures in everyday life: a pinch of salt, a herd of cattle, a load of hay, and so on. Or we may say: He is a man in his twenties. When we refer to a dozen people, we do not necessarily mean exactly twelve, but a range, say from eleven to fourteen.

Such concepts are neither inadequate nor vague, thought our

man. There are many occasions on which numerical precision is meaningless. It is often senseless to carry one's calculations to an exactness which the material itself does not permit. In business, for example, it makes no sense to continue with decimal places beyond any possibility of dividing a product; who wants to buy 38.793 percent of a refrigerator?

No, thought our man, there is nothing rudimentary about these number analogues—neither ours nor those of indigenous peoples. It is simply that there is a point beyond which precision makes no sense. Are there differences between us and indigenous peoples in our use of numerical operations such as division, multiplication, addition? Our number system permits any arbitrary division, whereas tribal peoples respect the natural parts of an object itself. Thus they can divide four arrows into four arrow heads and four shafts, but not into three and five. If we make the latter division, which our numerical system permits, it is scarcely sensible. And nobody is interested in half a pot or a fifth of a goose.

Likewise, although our number system asserts it, a x b is not always equivalent to b x a. A huge amount occurring a few times need not be the same as a small amount occurring many times. A hurricane with winds of 100 miles an hour is by no means equivalent to 100 breezes of 1 mile an hour.

And so, too, in addition. It is only rarely that three boats belonging to one village and two to another equal five. But this may be the case in a common war expedition.

I will not continue with the many examples our man considered. There are differences between our number system and the number analogues of tribal peoples, he realized. Our numbers possess universal transferability. We are able to carry out operations with numbers and apply them to any material whatsoever. Indigenous peoples, on the other hand, may have different systems for counting people, animals, money, fruit. Again, there are tribes who possess as many as three kinds of money that are not interchangeable.

Their thinking, in other words, is more tied to concrete situations, more rooted in actuality than ours. Our thinking, as illustrated in our use of numbers, may indeed be remote from reality. They refuse to perform numerical operations where there is no natural relation among the things concerned. Our attitude toward numbers is obviously an advantage so far as technological progress is concerned. But it may not be so in coping with the concrete situations of everyday life.

These natural groups and quantity-structures of indigenous peoples—and of ourselves—are interesting, thought our man. It may be that they, rather than counting, are the origin of numerical concepts.

And how many problems opened up before him! I will have to refer you to Wertheimer's text for these specific problems. To begin research, observation, along with occasional testing, will suffice. In all cases, the problem must make sense to the people tested. If indigenous peoples—or anyone else who has not learned in Western schools to accept the absurd—are given endless tasks that seem to them to be nonsensical, they will not only fail, but may even purposely mislead the investigator. (Remember that Wertheimer said this in 1912.)

That evening the man continued his search in his own library. He took up a book by an associationist, the most prominent representative of that approach, whose influence on education was very great. He read: "Reasoning . . . is only an extreme case of what goes on in associative learning" (Wertheimer 1959:9 n. 6). "The mind is ruled by habit throughout," continued the noted associationist (1959:152). The man thought of solutions to problems which he had admired, solutions by adults or by children; and he remembered conversations with other psychologists who saw them simply as a matter of recall of past experience. Sensible learning, one of his friends had said, is nothing but the work of a mass of previous associations (1959:68).

Of course, said our man, past experience plays a role in productive thinking. Who could deny it? But what *kind* of past experience? Is it a matter of blind connections learned by rote? or of structural grasp of something previously learned? And how does such past experience enter? Does it occur blindly, perhaps by chance? or is it a matter of fitting the functional requirements of the task? Even if the solution were entirely a matter of past experience, all problems of productive thinking would remain, for how was the solution achieved the first time? how was it brought to bear on the present situation?

Besides, he thought, doesn't past experience sometimes obstruct problem solving? Sometimes, in order to solve a problem, we must overcome old ways of seeing the situation; this is often the most difficult part of the process. He thought of the years that Einstein had spent in working out his theory; before he could make real progress, he had to overcome the resistance of a very strong structure, the traditional structure of physics. He thought of more modest cases in which thinking could not progress until a previous view had been overcome. No, he said, past experience, although necessary to thinking, will not clarify the problems of productive thinking.

I must see a logician, said our man.

And so, on the second day, he went to see a logician. "I need to know," he said, "what happens when thinking works productively. Can you help me?"

"No," said the logician. "We know nothing about your problem. If logic teaches us anything about thinking, it 'teaches us how thinking *should* proceed and not how it *does* proceed'" (Reichenbach 1966:1).

"But I am interested in thinking at its best," said the man.

"The actual process of thinking evades distinct analysis," said the logician. "As far as there are any laws observable they are formulated in psychology; they include laws both of correct and of incorrect thinking, since the tendency to commit certain fallacies must be considered a psychological law in the same sense as the more fortunate habits of correct thinking" (*ibid.*).[2]

"But does not even the syllogism yield discoveries?" asked our man. "Cannot the discovery of the planet Neptune in a first approach be regarded as a syllogism?" (cf. Wertheimer 1959:5–6).

"Some of my colleagues regard the syllogism as a petitio principii, a begging of the question, a taking for granted what is to be proved," said the logician. "In any case, you would be surprised what a small part of logic the syllogism occupies (see Langer 1953:340) and how rarely it is found in common speech."

Again our man was bewildered. As he left the logician, he

thought: I must clarify for myself when a syllogism is a productive process, when a petitio.[3] He considered:

All men are mortal;
Socrates is a man;
Socrates is mortal.

Am I merely recapitulating what I know when I conclude that Socrates is mortal? If the conclusion is to be something new, neither the major premise nor the minor may assume knowledge of the conclusion. One might say that Socrates' mortality is implied in the premise that all men are mortal.[4] I will therefore take another case where this possibility does not exist. Suppose our friend Socrates has to pay his taxes. He goes to the main tax office and is asked to which tax district he belongs. He does not know—he has received no forms. "But surely you know where you live? Good—you live on X Street. X Street belongs to tax district 426." Socrates, through syllogistic reasoning, has learned where he must pay his taxes. This is a modest discovery, to be sure, but still a discovery. Whatever we knew about Socrates before the process, we did not know where he must pay his taxes.

Next our man considered another example. This Socrates, together with his good friend Alcibiades, has for years been a member of the board of directors of a certain organization. They were in the habit of attending the annual business meeting, where the budget of the organization was discussed. One day Socrates returns from a trip to find a letter informing him of a unanimous decision by the board concerning the budget. He is outraged. I must call Alcibiades, he thinks. But first he reads on: the budget, which had to be settled early this year, was approved after a long speech by Mr. Alcibiades.

If Socrates had been thinking in syllogisms, the reasoning might have gone something like this:

All men of good will would vote against the resolution;
Alcibiades is a man of good will;
Therefore . . .

But Alcibiades had voted for the resolution. The Alcibiades who made the speech is not the same as the Alcibiades of the syllogism. Something has happened to the material of the syllogism; the minor term, the subject of the conclusion, has undergone a change, a recentering.

This is no mere fiction, thought our man. How often it has occurred in the writing of history. When new facts are discovered, or properly taken into account for the first time, a change occurs in the way a historical figure is viewed. It is a recentering of the material. The concept has been enlarged, often improved or deepened.

Our man began to see that even the simple syllogism might be productive. Sometimes, it is true, the middle term may stand as a mere bridge mediating between the major and minor terms. There may, in such empty and meaningless cases, be no more than a relation of coexistence between the terms. But there are other cases where the bridge is required meaningfully. Further, there are cases in which the terms cannot simply be brought together; first we must ask: How must I conceive of the minor term to relate it to the major? Must I transform it in accordance with the viewpoint of the major? In such a case a productive process is needed to solve the syllogism.

On the third day, our man reviewed what he had learned. From the anthropologist nothing, it is true, about primitive stages of thinking. But he had viewed innumerable instances of number analogues or Gestalt qualities or nonquantitative concepts that serve well in coping with life situations—modes of thinking we ourselves employ. Some of these—Gestalt qualities, natural groups—are present in perception as well as in thought, and the prospect of exploring thinking from the point of view of the knowledge gained in perception opened up before our man.

The logician, he realized, had not been much interested in productive thinking. But had he not himself seen that the syllogism might lead to genuine discovery or might require a reconstituting of one term in order that it be seen under the aspect of the other?

He began to think of other problems. The idea of recentering makes much problem solving clear, not only the solving of syllogisms. Take the simplest geometrical example. Given an isosceles triangle, its top angle ninety degrees and given the length of its side, what is the area? One has only to recenter, to see the triangle as a tilted half square, and the answer is obvious. A new centering clarifies the structure of the material. Our man thought of problem after problem.

But I am not interested merely in correct solutions, said our man. I have watched children turn out answers to questions by procedures in which they have been drilled. They may find the right answer without understanding it. Or a person may solve a problem by blind trial and error. What is the difference? Real thinking, he said, involves grasping the requirements of the problem, acting in accordance with them. Solving the problem means changing the situation in the direction of structural improvement (cf. Wertheimer 1959 passim).

Nor am I interested only in solutions, he continued. Often the posing of a fruitful question is the most vital part of the achievement (1920/1925:181n). Many times the first task of thinking is to realize that there is a problem (1959:242). Or the task may be to go deeper into a given problem, to expand the problem that has been set (1959: e.g., 141). The goal of the thinking process may itself be a foolish one, and then the first task of thinking is to evaluate the problem (1959:77).

I wish I could go on to tell you more about how our man observed in detail, and in many variations, actual problem solving. Sometimes his problems were very modest ones, solved by young children, in other cases important problems with which great thinkers grappled. From these careful observations, he set about working out concepts which would begin to do justice to productive thinking.

Since I have another story to tell you, instead of continuing, I will refer you to Wertheimer's *Productive Thinking*, a book that, in any case, is more exciting in the reading than in the retelling. This is a book that opens up problem after problem to the reader as it did to our man.

My next story is again a story of three days. Only three days remained before the APA convention, and I wanted to know what progress had been made in conceptualizing productive thinking.

On the first day I went to see a famous behaviorist and I put my question to him. "Thinking," of course, "is behaving" (Skinner

1974:104). I suppose you mean creative behavior, said the behaviorist kindly. Contemporary science sees such behavior in terms of operant conditioning.

Operant conditioning solves the problem more or less as natural selection solved a similar problem in evolutionary theory. As accidental traits, arising from mutations, are selected by their contribution to survival, so accidental variations in behavior are selected by their reinforcing consequences. (Skinner 1974:114)

"Do you mean that chance accounts for every discovery, every work of art, every new solution?" I asked in astonishment. Happy accident and selection by reinforcement, said the behaviorist. "And creative thinking is largely concerned with the production of 'mutations'" (*ibid.*). Of course, the behaviorist continued, artists and scientists have ways of increasing the probability of such mutations (cf. Skinner 1972:340). And remember that the artist or scientist is simply the locus of original behavior. If his "personal and genetic histories had been different," his contribution would also have been different (Skinner 1972:355).

"But is the solution unrelated to the requirements of the problem?" I asked. "How do you know, in any given case, when you have the right solution?" Oh, said the behaviorist, we need to take the mystery out of problem solving. "A person has a problem when some condition will be reinforcing but he lacks a response that will produce it. He will solve the problem when he emits such a response" (Skinner 1974:111).

I left in bewilderment. Is a solution correct because it is reinforcing—and reinforcing because it is correct? Or are there no right and wrong solutions, only reinforcing and nonreinforcing ones?

And is chance all there is to productive and to creative thinking? Of course, happy accidents sometimes occur, but they must be recognized as relevant and must be utilized if they are to contribute to the solution.

Are problems solved, as the behaviorist also seemed to say, because all their ingredients have been learned in the past? (Skinner 1974:113) How were the ingredients brought together? How brought to bear on this present situation? Are not all the problems thrown into the past, as Wertheimer had suggested in connection with similar explanations? A problem is not solved by being relocated, Köhler once remarked (1938:39).

Perhaps I need to see a cognitive behaviorist, I thought.

So on the second day I found a famous cognitive behaviorist. In spite of the imminence of APA, he was very kindly willing to spend some time with me.

I am sorry that I do not have time to tell you what he told me. When I left, I asked myself: Have I learned anything new? This is the old conception of trial and error, with chance successes selected, only it is implicit trial and error. Nothing is solved by calling the process covert. Is there not much productive thinking in which there is no evidence of trial and error, either overt or covert? I recognized other familiar difficulties in his account.

I went home to read contemporary association theory. I admired its new sophistication, its subtlety, and its readiness to tackle problems that earlier associationists had ignored. But I felt that if I wanted to learn something new about productive thinking, I would do well to spend my third day, the last before the convention, with a cognitivist.

Once more I was fortunate. A noted cognitive scientist agreed to see me. Indeed, when I had explained my mission, he seemed glad that I had come, so that he could set me straight on issues that had come up on the two previous days. "The view that cognition can be understood as computation is ubiquitous in modern cognitive theorizing," he said, "even among those who do not use computer programs to express models of cognitive processes." He continued: "The computational view of mind rests on certain intuitions regarding the fundamental similarity between computation and cognition" (Pylyshyn 1980:111).

Again I can only give you high points of the conversation. He saw cognitive processes "in terms of formal operations carried out on symbol structures" (ibid.). "The process is . . . carried out," he explained, "by the fixed functional capacities provided by the biological substrate" of the system (1980:121), what he called the functional architecture. This architecture, he stressed, is functional, not a matter of anatomical constraints. It may possibly include "extremely primitive elementary symbol processing operations," as well as "extremely abstract constraints," such as linguistic universals (1980:132).

Again I left with a head full of questions. I remembered those intuitions about which the cognitivist spoke, for example scientists' intuitions about the similarities between computation and cognition. I thought of questions—as well as stages of thinking that precede questions, like wonder and puzzlement. Are all these—intuitions, questions, wonder—matters of computation? What are the primitive operations which in part constitute the functional architecture of the system? His only example seemed to me to constitute a fascinating problem, not a function to be dropped unanalyzed into the system. What are the other primitive operations? Tasks for the future, my cognitivist had implied.

No, I said to myself as I was packing my bag for Montreal. The tasks are tasks for the present. I have no objection if anybody wants to construct a virtual machine that could account for cognitive processes, provided that it is indeed functional and not a machine in the ordinary sense of the word, in which direction of processes is determined by built-in anatomical constraints. But does not the virtual machine constrain processes in much the same way as a real machine? If it is a matter of the specifications, "of the sorts of things that are contained in the language user's manual"—e.g., available operations, restrictions on how they can be put together, etc. (Pylyshyn 1980:123)—to what extent does it allow the free play of natural dynamics? And to what extent is the programmer's manual, the virtual machine, itself constrained by the properties of the real machine?

Besides, I asked myself, what cognitive processes are being considered? I tried to remember the examples the cognitivist had used. The ability to rotate images, to solve a transitivity problem, the cognition that one must find one's way out of a burning building—these are not productive processes. Are all the interesting problems to be thrown into the future? That is as bad as consigning them to the past.

And so I come to the moral of my fable—indeed of my three fables: Max Wertheimer's problems are still with us.

Chapter 20

Robert M. Ogden and Gestalt Psychology in America

Gestalt psychology arose in Germany around 1910 and was officially launched in 1912 by the publication of Max Wertheimer's paper on perceived movement. By 1935, all the major Gestalt psychologists were in America.

How this migration came about is a complicated story. In the early years of the century, it was by no means unusual for American students and young American Ph.D.s to study in Europe. As a result, the major Gestalt figures, Wertheimer, Wolfgang Köhler, Kurt Koffka, and Kurt Lewin, were known personally to quite a number of American psychologists. Except for Wertheimer, they were also known in the United States from their previous visits here. In addition, their work preceded them to America. There-

I am grateful to Dr. Frank S. Freeman for calling my attention to Ogden's role in bringing Gestalt psychology to America and thus for inspiring this research. My thanks go to the Department of Manuscripts and University Archives, Cornell University Libraries, for use of the following collections: Robert M. Ogden Papers, Accession #14/23/467, Edward Bradford Titchener Papers, Accession #14/23/545, and Papers of the Emergency Committee in Aid of Displaced German Scholars, Accession #3/5/123. I wish to thank the Archives of the History of American Psychology at the University of Akron for much of the Ogden-Koffka correspondence. Finally, I wish to express my gratitude to Mrs. Helen O. Brown for permission to use the Ogden letters and to Dr. Molly Harrower for permission to use the Koffka letters.

fore, when political events in Germany made it necessary for many intellectuals to emigrate, America was quite naturally the place for these psychologists to come.

Robert Morris Ogden played an important and little-known role in bringing the Gestalt psychologists to this country. The literature on Ogden's relation to Gestalt psychology is easy to summarize. E. G. Boring gave it two sentences, describing Ogden as "one of the early men to welcome Gestalt psychology" (1950:599). Karl Dallenbach called Ogden "the first and principal proponent of Gestalt psychology in America" and mentioned his bringing Gestalt psychologists to his faculty as visiting professors (1959:475). Jean and George Mandler (1968) referred briefly to Ogden's influence on Koffka's American career, and Mitchell Ash (1980) likewise noted it. The only more-than-casual discussion is Frank Freeman's (1977) brief account of Ogden's role in introducing Gestalt psychology to America.

Robert M. Ogden (1877–1959) graduated from Cornell University in 1901. It was E. B. Titchener, therefore, who introduced him to psychology and subsequently played a role in the background of this story. Ogden continued his studies with Oswald Külpe at Würzburg, taking the Ph.D. in 1903. In the present connection, however, his important visit to Würzburg was in 1909, when he spent the better part of the summer again in Külpe's laboratory, where he met Koffka, then Külpe's assistant.

The details of Ogden's distinguished career need not concern us here. After two years as an assistant in the psychology department at the University of Missouri, he joined the Department of Philosophy and Psychology at the University of Tennessee; next he became professor of psychology at the University of Kansas until 1916, when he was called to Cornell as professor of education and chairman of the department. One notable action in this capacity was his invitation to Sergeant Seth Wakeman, in 1919, to become an instructor in the education department. Ogden moved over to the psychology department in 1939. He became dean of the College of Arts and Sciences at Cornell in 1923 and remained in that position until his retirement in 1945.

Between 1911 and 1921 there were a few exchanges between Ogden and Koffka, mostly Christmas greetings, and occasional mention of Koffka in Ogden's other correspondence. For example, Ogden wrote to H. S. Langfeld in 1915: "I have not had any recent news from Germany. I wish I could learn something of some of my friends. Koffka, for instance, may be fighting, or killed."[1]

Koffka was not dead, however, and in 1921 he and Ogden again exchanged Christmas greetings.[2] From that time on, their correspondence continued with no more than normal interruptions for the next twenty years, until Koffka's death. A letter from Ogden dated January 19, 1922, contains two important items: "I have on my desk your recent book on Mental Development given me by Titchener for review in his American Journal of Psychology." It should be noted, then, that Titchener gave Ogden this fateful assignment. Ogden continued:

I wonder if you would not find it somehow to your interest to help me out with a general critical review (Sammelreferat) on Perception for publication in the *Psychological Bulletin?* I have been one of the cooperating editors of the *Bulletin* for a good many years. . . . I have accepted editorial responsibility for the topic Sensation and Perception. . . . There has been nothing published on the recent work in perception, the bulk of which has been done in Germany.[3]

The first introduction to Gestalt psychology in English was Koffka's article on perception in the *Psychological Bulletin* of 1922, and here Ogden was inviting him to write it. Why Koffka? Ogden explained it in part in this same letter: "The main point is the reestablishment of international comity in our science." But Titchener was playing a role in the background, which can be seen in the selection of Koffka. In a letter the next day to Eleanor Gamble of Wellesley, Ogden remarked:

I had hoped that one of Titchener's men here at Cornell would assume responsibility for the review on Perception but find "T" opposed to their doing any work other than for the [American] Journal [of Psychology]. I have, therefore, written to Koffka in Germany to see if he would not undertake this topic for me.[4]

Koffka accepted on the condition that he could do it from the point of view of Gestalt psychology, and Ogden gladly agreed. As Koffka wrote:

I want to do all I can, to retie the strings broken by this pernicious war, particularly I shall try my best to reestablish the international solidarity of Science. . . . I want to show to American colleagues the work, our small circle, Wertheimer, Köhler, myself & some others are doing. This seems to me the rise of a new scientific epoch, reaching far beyond the scope of Psychology.[5]

Koffka wanted to write in English, because he wanted to do the wording of the new theories himself, but he asked for Ogden's help in finding translations for some technical terms, for example "Gestalt." In Germany, he remarked, "*Struktur*" was used almost synonymously, but this would not do for America, where structural psychology—Titchener's psychology—was something altogether different. Ogden relayed Titchener's suggestions: for "Gestalt," Koffka should use "configuration" or "*morphe*." (Why Titchener did not use "*morphe*" for his own structural psychology was not explained, nor was it made clear why Titchener found a German but not a Greek word too formidable.)[6]

Koffka went to work on his article. In the meantime, Ogden completed his review of Koffka's book, which we know as *The Growth of the Mind* (1924) and sent a copy to Koffka, inviting his comments. Ogden remarked:

I find the book very sympathetic to me. Many of the points which you make are ones which I have also used in my teaching. . . . I wish your book could be translated and put on sale in this country to supply the needed corrective for the loose and unscientific point of view which underlies most of our educational psychology.[7]

Koffka, who doubted that German reviewers would be as sympathetic as Ogden, found that Ogden had "grasped the structure-principle most thoroughly."[8]

Meanwhile, Koffka worked at his task. He found his review article getting terribly long, and then he had to copy the whole thing himself, presumably by hand, for the editor of the *Psychological Bulletin*, Shepard Ivory Franz, wrote to Ogden that he was sorry to learn that Koffka's manuscript would have to be typed.[9] (I remind the reader that economic conditions in Germany were terribly bad after World War I. For example, Koffka had to ask for five dollars to cover the expense of his article.[10] Again, about a year later, he wrote to Ogden that butter cost 1,600,000,000 marks a pound.)

Ogden wrote to Franz of Koffka's article: "I regard it as a first rate piece of work and a real contribution, inasmuch as no such general review of the new position has yet been published, even in Germany."[11]

During the correspondence that dealt with the manuscript, Koffka was free with his criticism of Titchener's position, the traditional structural psychology. This is the position that Ogden defended, though, to his credit, he added: "My mind is by no means closed on this subject."[12] To what extent it was open will become clear.

Ogden's letter to Koffka of October 11, 1922, contained important news:

I am now engaged with two other members of my Department in translating your book on Mental Development. We have undertaken it as an exercise in German especially in the interest of our Assistant who desires to perfect himself in the use of the language. If we are able to complete the task this term as we have planned I should like to get it published.[13]

Koffka was, of course, delighted: "The prospect of an American edition is a great thing to me."[14]

What started as an exercise in German was to occupy many hours of Ogden's time during the next several years, hours of translation and of new translations of Koffka's revisions.

By the end of 1922, Ogden found it necessary to explain to Titchener his attraction to Gestalt psychology. Titchener was ready with his criticism of it:

If I have been otherwise somewhat enthusiastic in my acceptance of the Gestalt-theorie, it is because the problems of "Educational Psychology" seem to lend themselves so much more readily to the type of solution proposed by Koffka, than they do to the incomplete, and, as it has long seemed to me, impossible system of Thorndike.[15]

But Ogden was still sending Titchener his manuscripts to criticize. One of these was his 1924 book *Hearing*, which was thoroughly criticized by Titchener in manuscript form and later dedicated to him, surprising and pleasing Titchener. How far and how fast Ogden moved theoretically may be seen in the fact that his next book, *Psychology and Education* (1926), was published in 1926 and dedicated to Koffka.

Indeed, Ogden may have felt torn between the two kinds of psychology during this period. Thus he sent a paper on meaning to Titchener for criticism. Titchener commented critically, adding: "I don't follow you all the way—naturally—with regard to the inclusion of perceptive meaning within the existential sphere."[16] Ogden seemed to gloss over any difference between them; his letter of thanks included the remark:

I am gratified to know that you find a "systematic" approximation between us; because this reassures me that I am not misreading altogether the experimental data over which you have so large a command.[17]

Of this same paper, which he read in published form, Koffka wrote:

I was extremely pleased to see you take up the colors of the Gestalt theorie so vigorously. You, and this cannot be said of many others, have fully grasped the wide purport of our principles.[18]

And he, too, added his own point of criticism.

That there could be a systematic approximation between Titchener and a paper that Koffka saw as taking up the colors of Gestalt psychology is so altogether out of the question as to require no discussion.

For months, the main content of the Ogden-Koffka correspondence was progress on the translation and arrangements with the publisher, with occasional comments on psychology and psychologists. Then, in February 1924, when Ogden could announce that the manuscript was nearing completion, a new direction came into his letters: "I hope before long we shall be able to bring you to this country."[19] Koffka responded enthusiastically to what he called the best passage in Ogden's letter. After a frank criticism of Ogden's book on hearing (which I mention to show the openness of the relation: flattery did not get Koffka to America), he says:

Of course I should love to come to your country & I think it would be much the best to have me stay there for more than a very short visit. A theory can only be grasped & fully appreciated, if one sees it working. Gestalt-theorie can make its way only through the laboratories & this needs time. So if you want me over there & are able to arrange it, I should be most willing to do my best.[20]

In May 1924, Ogden took formal steps to arrange an invitation to Koffka to spend a year at Cornell. But before doing so, he felt the need to discuss the matter with Titchener. Titchener responded:

I have not the very slightest objection to your inviting Koffka over here for a year; on the contrary, I think that he would be an asset to the university community. It was extremely decent of you to ask whether I had any objection; . . . I feel, nevertheless, that it would be impertinent for me to raise an objection, even if I entertained one; but I do not.
. . . I am rather definitely concerned that the invitation shall be issued and known to be issued by the department of education, without involvement of the department of psychology. My only reason is that I do not want Koffka's visit to be charged even partially to the account of my own department; that would undoubtedly prejudice any chances that I might myself have of getting somebody from Europe in the future.[21]

Thus when Ogden wrote to Koffka that he had been laying plans to bring him to Cornell for the next academic year, he made it clear that "education is a department separate from Psychology and Philosophy. I am sure Professor Titchener and his staff will extend you a cordial welcome, but the responsibility for your appointment and for the details of your work falls solely upon me."[22] Ogden added:

Köhler's visit to this country as a non-resident lecturer at Clark University during the second term of next year has been announced and it will be a fine thing to have you both in this country at the same time.

On June 17, 1924, the formal invitation was sent to a delighted Koffka:

I shall be only too glad to accept it, & I do hope that I shall be able to fulfil your expectations in a field that is not quite my own.

In his letter of acceptance, Koffka also indicated that he was most willing to deliver a series of public lectures, the Schiff Lectures, and was looking forward to his courses and seminars. In addition, he discussed a number of practical details, for example:

Shall I bring a frock coat, & that suit that in Germany is called a "cutaway" & in England a morning coat? From my inquiries I presume that your answer will be yes for the frockcoat & no for the other thing. But I want to know for certain.

He concluded the long letter:

In a little over two months we shall shake hands after how many years! It has been awfully good of you to exert yourself so strongly in order to bring this about. And be sure, I am very grateful for your great friendliness.[23]

Thus Ogden gave Koffka the first three opportunities to introduce Gestalt psychology to America: the invitation to write his article on perception for the *Psychological Bulletin*, the translation of *The Growth of the Mind* into English, and the first visit of a Gestalt psychologist to this country.

What did Titchener—the lion in his lair, as Koffka once described him[24]—think of all this? Before answering I must emphasize that in this period Titchener was still perhaps the foremost experimental psychologist in America. For example, when the president of Harvard wanted advice about a major appointment,[25] he consulted Titchener, even though Titchener had, a decade before, turned down what was then the major post in American psychology, the professorship at Harvard. Titchener's *Text-book of Psychology* was the first experimental work since Wundt's *Physiological Psychology* to be published in all three of the major languages.[26] When jobs were available, Titchener moved his men around like pieces on a chessboard. For example, when Langfeld got the position at Princeton, Titchener wrote to Boring:

I suppose that the path is now open for Pratt to stay with you at Cambridge. I think at the moment—though I may possibly change my mind—that I shall let Kimball Young get the Smith place and put Bishop into Pittsburgh.[27]

And Titchener never had enough new Ph.D.s to fill the demand for them in other universities.

How, then, did Titchener take the beginnings of Gestalt psychology in America, beginnings that centered so largely in Cornell? First of all, of course, he did not like Gestalt psychology. For example, he wrote to Gamble, who was on her way to Europe:

Please remember me to G. E. M. [G. E. Müller], and congratulate him for me on the timeliness and vigour of his criticism of the Gestalt-people. He can do that sort of work as nobody else in the world can, and it is delightful to find that he has the old vim in criticizing.[28]

To Harry Helson he wrote:

The more I consider the general standpoint of the Gestalt people, the less tenable their position seems. They are making precisely the same mistake as the Freudians, erecting a whole system of psychology on a single dictum in the form of an inverted pyramid.[29]

And to H. C. Warren of Princeton a few months later he remarked: "My summer was too busy for anything like construction work, but I went over the whole of the Gestalt literature and spied the weakness of that land."[30]

Titchener seems to have gotten along personally very well with Koffka. In a letter to Boring he commented:

I see a certain amount of Koffka intimately at my seminar, and I have come to like him very well. He is quick witted, and he has the sort of fundamental knowledge that all Germans get as a matter of course, and that our people not only don't have but oftentimes don't see the need of.[31]

Still, Titchener seemed to be uneasy about having "all these strangers," as he called them,[32] both at Cornell and at Clark; and even more, it must have rankled to have psychology taught in a department other than his own. When, for example, the *Alumni News* erroneously referred to Koffka as a visiting professor of psychology, Titchener demanded a correction in the next number of that periodical.[33] The same issue arose when Titchener was asked to introduce Köhler at a public lecture at Cornell that same spring. He wrote to Ogden:

I have been thinking things over; and I think that international courtesy should weigh more heavily on the positive side than putting the department in a false position should weigh upon the negative. So I will undertake to introduce Koehler on the evening of Thursday-week. I need not say that personally I am very glad indeed to do him this little friendly service; my only scruple was the scruple that I have felt all the year about the relation of psychology in the university to the university department of psychology.[34]

At the same time, Titchener seemed miffed that Koffka was not doing any work in his laboratory. He renewed his invitation via Ogden, adding:

He has told me himself once or twice, rather apologetically, that he has been running about the country a good deal during this first term; and I have taken this to mean that he felt himself unable to settle down to any piece of experimental work.[35]

Ogden was summoned to Titchener's seminar, along with Wakeman and Koffka if they cared to come;[36] and Ogden accepted for all of them.[37]

Titchener clearly wanted any psychological work at Cornell to be done under his aegis. Despite the continued friendly exchange of letters between Titchener and Koffka, and Koffka's affection for Titchener (he expressed real grief at the news of Titchener's death in 1927), Titchener was probably not sorry to see Koffka leave Cornell for summer teaching at the University of Chicago and then sail home to Giessen.

Koffka's visit to America was a great success. Ogden's correspondence shows wide appreciation of the article in the *Psychological Bulletin*, which prepared the way; of *The Growth of the Mind*, which had appeared in Ogden's translation before the visit and was being revised during it; and of Koffka's lectures both at Cornell and during his "running about the country." It was this visit that led to his subsequent invitations to the University of Wisconsin, where he spent the academic year 1926–27, and then to Smith College, where he remained from 1927 until his death in 1941. Ogden had a large share in the responsibility for all this, and Koffka was warmly appreciative:

I feel that for myself my visit to America has been a great gain. I have profited more in general experience than I have in any other year. And I had an awfully good time, coming in contact with people of the highest type of mind & exchanging views with them. All this I owe to you. And therefore my last letter must go to your address.[38]

In the fall of 1925, Wakeman left Cornell to accept a position in the Department of Education at Smith College. Before the end of his first term there, together with the psychologists, he invited Köhler, who was still in the country, to give public lectures and round tables at Smith.[39] Wakeman, who must have been a very energetic person, looked at the psychology department and found it wanting—it was too applied for him. He wrote to Ogden that he and the dean were "at work upon the Department of Psychology,"[40] that they hoped to make room in it for "some one familiar with Gestalt." Ogden responded, "If you can secure either Köhler or Koffka, you will, in my opinion, be doing extraordinarily well."[41] Wakeman went to work to raise money for a research chair and began negotiations with Köhler, who in the meantime had received offers from several other American universities. Negotiations dragged on until Wakeman, afraid of losing both his top candidates, finally wrote to Koffka not to commit himself to anything until he heard from him. The details are incomplete, but Köhler decided against Smith. In April 1927, Koffka wrote to Ogden that he had accepted the position at Smith despite a very tempting offer from Wisconsin.[42] Before he went to Northampton, he and a friend bought a little Chevrolet with a rumble seat and drove to California to teach summer school.[43]

During this same summer of 1927, Ogden met Wertheimer in Berlin. As he wrote to Boring, he "was especially impressed by Wertheimer who is very likeable and very stimulating."[44]

Meanwhile, preparations were being made to hold an International Congress of Psychology at Yale in 1929. Years earlier, an abortive attempt had been made to hold such a congress in America, with Titchener and James McKeen Cattell as vice presidents. These preparations were given up, however, apparently because Europeans could not be counted upon to attend. Every effort was made to insure the participation of Europeans at the 1929 congress, and to this end lecture tours, summer teaching, and other invitations to Europeans were arranged.

Koffka and Ogden had apparently already been talking about bringing Wertheimer to Cornell so that he could attend the congress. Ogden worked on it behind the scenes and by February 1928 was able to write, not a definitive invitation, but a personal inquiry to Wertheimer which could help him in making plans to bring him over for the year 1929–1930.[45] Wertheimer responded in a friendly albeit noncommittal way: he did not want to come without his family, and he did not know whether the salary Ogden suggested would therefore be sufficient.[46] Ogden replied, remarking on the difficulties on both sides in putting his suggestions into effect.[47]

The Ogden-Koffka correspondence reveals that Wertheimer remained in doubt about coming and that Ogden was unable to raise the money for an appointment.[48] The matter was settled in April 1929, when Wertheimer received a call to Frankfurt. A visit to Cornell was therefore no longer feasible.[49]

Having failed in his efforts to bring Wertheimer to Cornell, Ogden was all the more eager to arrange a visit by Köhler. He arranged what was called a "nonresident lectureship," which was actually a resident lectureship for a period of no less than four weeks but which Ogden hoped would extend for the rest of the spring term.[50] Köhler's lectures began on April 22, 1929,[51] and we know from a letter that Köhler wrote to Helson that he was still at Cornell on May 16.[52] Thus Ogden brought a second major Gestalt psychologist to Cornell.

Finally, Ogden was also instrumental in bringing yet another prominent Gestalt psychologist, Kurt Lewin, to Cornell. Lewin had been in America in 1932, as a visiting professor for half a year at Stanford. On his way west, he stopped at Smith College, and Ogden met him there, possibly for the first time. He was, however, long familiar with Lewin's work.

Lewin left California by way of the Pacific so that he could lecture in Japan and the Soviet Union before returning to Berlin. This was in January 1933—and at the end of that month, the disaster of Hitler occurred. In April 1933, Ogden wrote to Koffka: "Do you know anything of [Lewin's] plight, or of Wertheimer's?"[53] Koffka replied: "I am terribly afraid about my friends." Lewin, in particular, was in a vulnerable position because his "official salaried position is that of an assistant who can be dismissed any time. On the other hand he has fought in the world war & may for that reason keep his place."[54]

In June 1933, Ogden wrote to Koffka that he had learned of a movement

to procure a fund which will enable a number of American universities to invite some of the ousted German professors to accept two-year appointments. President Farrand [of Cornell] is to be chairman of the organizing committee [the Emergency Committee in Aid of Displaced German Scholars]; so if the fund is raised, I presume we shall invite one or more of the men to Cornell.[55]

Ogden asked for Lewin's address and continued:

Of course, I have no assurance that we would invite Lewin even if the scheme works out; but I should like to have his address when the time comes.[56]

A week later, Koffka had important news for Ogden:

Köhler is here. . . . You can imagine how much we have learned from him about Germany. . . . Katz' case seems particularly bad, & Wertheimer's also rather unfavourable. Lewin, on the other hand, could stay on if he liked. He is on leave of absence now, although he might have resumed his lectures in May. Of course he has no chance of ever getting a chair in Germany, but Köhler has still the hope that he can persuade him to stay in Berlin.[57]

Ogden replied:

I am glad to know that Lewin is not altogether out. I have placed his name on our list of persons who would be welcome at Cornell. I don't know that he will be invited, or if he would care to accept, but the prospects for satisfactory work, and perhaps even a future appointment in the Nursery School research, are rather better than those in any other department at Cornell—so far as I see.[58]

How did Ogden manage to place Lewin on this list? Frank Freeman recalls: "Ogden came into my office early in 1933 to discuss with me the advisability of inviting Lewin to Cornell."[59] There was obviously also discussion with Dr. Ethel Waring of the Nursery School, who, Alfred Marrow tells us, became acquainted with Lewin and his work in Berlin in 1929 (1969:74); and others were doubtless also informally consulted. The scant formal record is in the files that contain the correspondence of President Livingston Farrand with the Emergency Committee in Aid of Displaced German Scholars. Here we find a memorandum in which the deans of the College of Agriculture, the College of Arts and Sciences (this was Ogden), and the Graduate School present to President Farrand a list of German professors whom they would be glad to have for a time at Cornell.[60] A subsequent memorandum placed Lewin at the head of the list:

The Deans feel that, if Dr. Lewin will come, he can probably contribute more toward strengthening a field of growing interest than would be true of other persons in the list.[61]

And so, largely through the good offices of Robert M. Ogden, Lewin spent the academic years 1933–35 at Cornell. At the beginning of the second year, Farrand reported to the Emergency Committee: "I am very glad to say that Dr. Lewin has been a great success here and we are very glad indeed to have him for this second year."[62] There was, nevertheless, no prospect of a permanent appointment at Cornell, so Lewin left in 1935 for the Iowa Child Welfare Research Station at the University of Iowa.

Ogden thus succeeded in bringing to Cornell three of the four leading figures in Gestalt psychology. His role in introducing Gestalt psychology to America cannot be called that of a catalyst, however, since Ogden himself did not remain unchanged by the reaction. All his writings, from the middle 1920s, were in the spirit of Gestalt psychology. And this is the man who could write: "Titchener was responsible for my career as a psychologist."[63]

Notes

INTRODUCTION

1. Note to nontechnical reader or beginning student: If you do not understand these uses of the term "stimulus," you are far ahead of your more advanced contemporaries who think that they do.

2. An expanded treatment of criticisms and misunderstandings of the concept of psychophysical isomorphism is to be found in Henle (1984).

3. I am grateful to Professor Skinner for permission to publish his letter (see appendix to essay 13).

4. Köhler, in 1930, similarly showed the parallel between trial and error theories of learning and Darwinian theory. See W. Köhler (1930/1971).

5. Problem finding has been shown to be an important predictor of success in visual art by Getzels and Csikszentmihalyi (1976). More recently, Owen (1982) has studied artists at work and has emphasized problem finding as an ever-present part of the process.

4. ON PLACES, LABELS, AND PROBLEMS

1. I am here adopting the terminology of these authors. I myself would express matters differently in order to avoid certain implicit assumptions.

2. The term "projection" has acquired a variety of meanings, particularly in the experimental literature, when results did not yield "classical" projection. Freud himself uses the term in several ways. Cf. Halpern (1977).

3. As long ago as 1932, Franz Alexander, in *The Medical Value of Psychoanalysis*, mentioned these two "psychic mechanisms" as "so generally accepted and employed not only in psychiatry, but even in general thought and conversation, that the young student of medicine often does not even know their origin in the psychodynamic system of Sigmund Freud" (1932: 31). Actually, Freud attributes the term and the concept of rationalization to Ernest Jones. See Freud (1929/1953–1974, 21:249).

4. Attention should be called to Lewin's analysis of the psychoanalytic

concept of regression, which he finds encompasses two kinds of problem. See Barker, Dembo, and Lewin (1941).

It may be added that Freud himself seems at times to have been aware of the undeveloped character of some of his own theories. In connection with a discussion of his speculations on the life and death instincts, he writes: "We need not feel greatly disturbed in judging our speculation upon the life and death instincts by the fact that so many bewildering and obscure processes occur in it. . . . This is merely due to our being obliged to operate with the scientific terms, that is to say with the figurative language, peculiar to psychology (or, more precisely, to depth psychology). We could not otherwise describe the processes in question at all, and indeed we could not have become aware of them. The deficiencies in our description would probably vanish if we were already in a position to replace the psychological terms by physiological or chemical ones" (1920, 18:60).

Freud is probably wrong in suggesting that we go from psychological prototheory (to borrow a term from Jerome Bruner [1956:466]) to physiological or chemical theory. The important step is from prototheory to theory in psychology. If the functional problems are worked out, at least to some extent, in psychological terms, then we may be able to consider the problem of their relations to physiology and, indeed, to carry them farther from the physiological side.

5. Unless, of course, a question is begged as a deliberate device in disputation and is not a fallacy.

5. FREUD'S SECRET COGNITIVE THEORIES

1. References to Freud will be to the *Standard Edition of the Complete Psychological Works of Sigmund Freud*, James Strachey, editor. Only volume and page numbers will be given in the text.

2. This is a statement that would be hard for anybody who accepted Freud's theories to credit.

3. Nor is Helmholtz mentioned in Freud's published correspondence with Wilhelm Fliess (M. Bonaparte, A. Freud, and E. Kris 1954).

4. One popular variety of these theories gives past experience the task of integrating sense data into phenomenal objects; an example is the theory that Rorschach adopted, quoted below. Freud might have rejected the theory in this form. In an entirely parallel connection, speaking of acquired prestige (apropos of Le Bon), he remarks: "Since in every case it harks back to the past, it cannot be of much help to us in understanding this puzzling influence" (18:81).

5. Helmholtz tells us that in the first edition of the *Physiological Optics* (1866) he used the term *unconscious inference*, the major premise being formed from a series of experiences of sense impressions, the minor being some fresh sense impression. "Recently," he adds in 1878, "I have refrained

from using the phrase *unconscious inference* in order to avoid confusion with what seems to me a completely obscure and unjustified idea which Schopenhauer and his followers have designated by the same name" (1878/ 1971:381). But as late as 1894 he still found this earlier employed expression "at least to a certain extent . . . admissible and appropriate" (1878/ 1971:508).

6. Freud's confusion of physical and phenomenal terms must be considered characteristic of his time. It is still found today, but there is less excuse for it after Koffka's incisive clarification of the meaning of the stimulus (1935:e.g., 80) and after the many discussions, by Gestalt psychologists and by others, of the difference between the physical and phenomenal worlds. Here is another example of this confusion in Freud: "We might add, perhaps, that the ego wears a 'cap of hearing'—on one side only, as we learn from cerebral anatomy. It might be said to wear it awry" (*S.E.* 19:25). The ego, in this context, is a phenomenal datum or at least a psychological one, and cerebral anatomy, while it may say something about the ego's correlates (in this case about the correlates of its functions), tells us nothing about the ego itself.

7. Since I will not return to this issue, I will add that sense impressions neither lay down nor evoke memory traces; only organized perceptions do.

8. Freud knew, however, that naive realism is wrong. See, for example, 14:171.

9. The same idea is to be found in the *New Introductory Lectures*, 22:70. For another expression of it, see 14:169.

10. It must be noted that identification presupposes the perception of the other person and his qualities. As a result of identification, Freud says, "the first ego behaves like the second in certain respects" (22:63). One must perceive these "respects" in order to assimilate and imitate them. Identification, Freud adds, "is a very important form of attachment to someone else, probably the very first, and not the same thing as the choice of an object" (*ibid.*). He does not tell us whether identification occurs before the child has acquired the experience and before he may be expected to be capable of the inferences and empathy necessary for his theory of the understanding of others. But if "a path leads from identification by way of imitation to empathy" (18:110 n. 2), then a problem seems to exist.

11. Freud's little essay on the "mystic" writing pad (19:227–232) is not to be construed as a theory of memory. He is there concerned with pointing out an analogy to his conception that memory, with its permanent traces, occupies a different place from the perceptual system, which is always ready to receive new impressions. He is interested in the *locus* of memory, not in its *processes*. Cf. also *The Ego and the Id:* "[The ego] starts out . . . from the system *Pcpt.*, which is its nucleus, and begins by embracing the *Pcs.*, which is adjacent to the mnemic residues" (19:23).

12. The "well-known passage" in question is the following: "To avoid

misunderstanding, I must add that I am making no attempt to proclaim that the cells and nerve fibres, or the systems of neurones which are taking their place to-day, are these psychical paths [of association]" (8:148).

13. Freud's associationism even leads him to a remark that seems to suggest the law of effect or the principle of reinforcement: "We cannot escape a suspicion that association with what is recent is rewarded, and so facilitated, by a peculiar bonus of pleasure" (8:124).

14. The following rather far-reaching observation of Freud's may be noted: "If you recall the tricks of mnemotechnics, you will realize with some surprise that the same chains of association which are deliberately laid down in order to *prevent* names from being forgotten can also *lead* to our forgetting them" (15:75). Surprisingly, we may compare this remark with one of Köhler's: "The present theory assumes that it is essentially the same basic principle which is responsible both for recall and for those disturbances [of recall]" (1940:156). The differences outweigh the similarity, however. Freud is thinking in terms of associations, whereas for Köhler, "Recall is here interpreted as an interaction which presupposes a field relation between a particular process and a particular trace" (*ibid.*). Here is another instance of the fact that Freud's cognitive observations do not necessarily demand the interpretation he gives them.

15. He appears to equate these with scientists.

16. A considerable literature on this problem has now grown up.

17. This passage and the one below dated 1907 are to be found in footnotes later added to the *Psychopathology of Everyday Life*.

7. SOME PROBLEMS OF ECLECTICISM

1. A number of the examples to be considered will be taken from Woodworth's writings because I regard him as one of the clearest of the eclectics and one of those whose theories are to be taken most seriously.

2. Since the earlier formulation is the more explicit, and since the later seems not to differ from it in principle, the former will be drawn upon here.

3. Not all of these discussions are eclectic, at least in the meaning used here. Some attempt to understand the contributions of one psychology by translating them into the terms of another, rather than to resolve differences between them. Such work, for example *Personality and Psychotherapy* by Dollard and Miller (1950), will not be considered here. It presents interesting problems of its own which deserve separate treatment.

4. For example: "It is to a certain degree arbitrary where one draws the boundary between the motor-perceptual system and the inner regions, whether for instance one considers the understanding of speech as an event within the boundary zone or within the inner-personal systems" (Lewin 1936:178).

5. In this connection Bronfenbrenner comments on Lewin's neglect of

the content of psychical systems: "This is indeed an unfortunate over-sight" (1951:214). The thesis will be developed elsewhere that this is no oversight, but that Lewin undertook a different task.

6. These remarks in no way detract from the excellence or the signifi-cance of these authors' study.

7. If a theory of common factors were correct, there should never be more than 100 percent transfer, since two activities cannot have more than 100 percent of their factors in common. Yet, as Katona (1940) has shown, cases exist in which performance on the test activity is superior to that on the training task.

It is of interest to note also that Woodworth's theory, while it succeeds in reconciling the differences, appears to lump together cases that do not belong together. There is evidence that transfer of specific data is dif-ferent, in process as well as in the magnitude of the effect, from the ap-plication of principles derived from one set of data to new material. (Cf. Katona 1940.)

8. For example: "As to connections, several may be established before the conditioning is complete, but the primary one connects the condi-tioned stimulus with the meaningful character it acquires as the first event in a regular sequence" (1947:121–122). Also, "In experiments that offer alternatives and demand a choice, what has to be learned is a dis-tinction between stimulus-objects and not between motor responses. . . . What has to be learned is the difference between the two alleys" (1947:122).

9. "When a new percept is in the making—when an obscure stimulus-complex is being deciphered, or when the meaning of a cue or sign is being discovered—an elementary two-phase process is observable. It is a trial-and-check, trial-and-check process. The trial phase is a tentative reading of the sign, a tentative decipherment of the puzzle, a tentative character-ization of the object; and the check phase is an acceptance or rejection, a positive or negative reenforcement of the tentative perception" (1947:124).

Among the implicit assumptions seems to be the view that organization is not primary in perception, nor prior to the effects of learning; as well as the idea that there is no fruitful distinction to be made between percep-tion and interpretation.

10. As a final illustration, Welch states: "This distinction between ele-mentary and higher forms of learning involves the distinction between a situation where the new elements are simple in nature, or simple in char-acter and are simply integrated, and a situation where the new elements are complex and integrated in a complex manner" (1948:188). This state-ment implies an elementaristic view of the learning process—learning being envisaged as the integration of elements—which would be far from acceptable to all the psychologists Welch is trying to reconcile.

11. It is interesting to note that eclecticism seems to have presented similar problems in other fields of knowledge in their comparative youth. I quote an observation on the medical science of a century ago:

"And as the rules derived from fundamental truths seemed to come into unsolvable contradiction with the experiences and the sanctioned standards of practice, there sprang up under the name Eclectic the representatives of sober elucidation, of the *juste milieu*, of the medium of the extremes. The breach between theory and practice, which they feared, was avoided or postponed if theory gave up the pretension to penetrate into particulars and if practice agreed that, because of its youthful immaturity, it should be excluded from counsel, and progress in silence and in hope. The conflict was settled and peace was achieved, not by the reconciliation of the parties, but by separating them. The so-called impartial examination of the facts should lead only to a middle road between them. [The eclectics] thought they had principles and avoided their application; they proclaimed themselves free and in practice clung to the consequences of old dogmas. They practiced tolerance not because they included the truth of each dogma, but because a chasm existed between theory and life, beyond which theory didn't matter" (Henle 1846:9).

8. ON CONTROVERSY AND ITS RESOLUTION

1. Since this point will become relevant in a more specific connection below, further discussion is postponed.

2. Reference will also be made to a discussion of the instinct controversy by Krantz and Allen (1967) and one of the Baldwin-Titchener controversy by Krantz (1969).

3. Persevering in efforts to solve a problem is not, of course, necessarily a matter of continuing in the same line of thinking. But it must be remembered that the perceived problem itself contains directions for its solution.

4. Enlightening, of course, for future generations of psychologists who were saved from Titchener's errors by his very thoroughness in working out his approach.

5. Polanyi points to evidence by D. C. Miller that appeared to contradict the theory of relativity, and he comments: "Little attention was paid to the experiments, the evidence being set aside in the hope that it would one day turn out to be wrong" (1958:13).

6. I am unable, however, to confirm Krantz's finding (1969) that some 40 percent of Titchener's final article (1896) in this exchange was devoted to "implicit or explicit attack upon the professional or personal character" of his opponent. Only if no distinction is made between criticism—which is the function and the value of a polemical article—and invective, can I approximate this figure. To blur this distinction seems to me to be a serious error.

7. These problems need, of course, to be dealt with much more specifically. For one such attempt, see Henle (1955).

8. Cf. Titchener: "I almost wonder whether Professor Baldwin and my-

self are not using the term 'reaction experiment' in two totally different senses" (1896:237).

9. Some eclectic failures to resolve controversies have been analyzed from a different point of view by Henle (1957, 1965). The method here under discussion is not eclectic in the sense used in those papers. There, eclectics in psychology were shown to attempt to resolve differences by ignoring them. Calkins' resolution is offered in full awareness of the differences in the points of view to be subsumed under a more comprehensive theory.

9. A WHISPER FROM A GHOST

1. I have taken up this problem elsewhere (Henle 1974), so the present discussion can be brief.

2. Titchener continued to be concerned with the question of the relation of these "affective pressures" to pleasure or displeasure "in the ordinary empirical sense." As he wrote to L. B. Hoisington: "A localized pressure is still a pressure and not a feeling" (Titchener Papers, March 9, 1927).

3. Titchener wrote to Boring: "It is precisely the beauty of Rand that he keeps his dates fluid, always in the neighborhood of the exact year, and so leaves the final choice to the erudition or sagacity of the reader. You make your dates rigid, and therefore always run the risk of error" (Titchener Papers, October 17, 1923). I doubt, however, that Titchener meant to encourage dating as fluid as that of the present example.

4. To his credit, Boring remarks of his paper on the stimulus error, published in 1921: "The reader must be warned that Titchener expressly repudiated this interpretation of the stimulus-error, although not in print" (1950:436).

5. A similar letter was written to Philip W. Hausmann, November 18, 1924 (Titchener Papers).

6. I have seen this same quotation, likewise taken out of context, in another article on Watson: "In 1956 Bergmann paid Watson the following compliment on the pages of the *Psychological Review:* 'Second only to Freud, though at a rather great distance, John B. Watson is, in my judgment, the most important figure in the history of psychological thought during the first half of the century. Nor is his impact limited to the science of psychology.'"

12. E. B. TITCHENER AND THE CASE OF THE MISSING ELEMENT

1. Boring's contribution to the history of psychology has been so great that it is not necessary to deny his errors. To do so would be to treat him less seriously than he deserves.

2. It must be added that, if Boring had seen the problem, he would have

seen the solution. Given Titchener's view that feelings lack clearness, he says, and his view that observation depends on attention: "How then could we ever know about these feelings?" (Boring 1933:225–226). But since Boring's chronology was confused, he did not see the solution as an answer to the present problem.

3. This figure includes Young's investigation of 1921, which did not come from the Cornell laboratory; but it does not include his more polemical paper of 1922. The papers in question are: Roese and Foster (1916), Young (1918a, 1918b, 1921), Corwin (1921).

Incidentally, there are no more than four empirical studies of affection edited by Titchener before 1910: Major (1895), Hayes (1906), Nakashima (1909a, 1909b).

14. THE SNAIL BENEATH THE SHELL

1. The "tip of the tongue" phenomenon has been investigated by Brown and McNeill (1966).

2. Polanyi speaks of the obstacle to be overcome in problem solving as a "logical gap"; he views the "width of the logical gap as the measure of the ingenuity required for solving the problem" (1958:123). "Gap" is used here in the much more specific sense of an emptiness-with-shape, and the width of the gap in the present meaning has no necessary relation to difficulty. It refers, rather, to the size of the emptiness.

3. In order to show that a problem exists, it is sometimes necessary to illustrate it in an unfamiliar context before showing it in connection with familiar phenomena. Thus Wertheimer (1923) studied grouping factors first in connection with constructed dot patterns before he applied them to the familiar forms of our perceptual world.

4. Polanyi (1958:291) offers further examples of phenomena too far from the individual's thinking to arouse curiosity.

5. Other phantom problems rest on an erroneous premise (Planck 1949:56).

6. I have relied largely on Brewster Ghiselin's valuable collection, *The Creative Process* (1955).

15. ON THE RELATION BETWEEN LOGIC AND THINKING

1. A different, but related, position is that represented by Dollard and Miller (1950), who hold that being logical is a learned drive. The child, it is argued, is punished for logical contradictions and absurdities, for illogical and contradictory plans. The result for most people is "a learned drive to make their explanations and plans seem logical" (1950:120). The implication is, of course, that without this specific training the individual's thinking would not be (or seem) logical.

2. "A syllogism that is incompletely stated, in which one of the prem-

ises or the conclusion is tacitly present but not expressed, is called an enthymeme" (Cohen and Nagel 1934:78).

3. It must be recognized, of course, that the lack of formal training in logic is insufficient guarantee of the naiveté of subjects. It can only be pleaded that we have no better criterion at the present time. Whatever the informal self-education of subjects in this respect, the results to be presented cannot be regarded as the product of formal instruction in logic.

4. This unexpected finding cannot be attributed to an insensitivity of the subjects to logical processes. Rather, the fault lies with the investigator who, in the effort to make the problems sound natural, included irrelevancies that were taken by many subjects as the material for evaluation.

5. "This is committed when, in the premises, a proposition is asserted with a qualification, and the qualification lost sight of in the conclusion; or oftener, when a limitation or condition, though not asserted, is necessary to the truth of the proposition, but is forgotten when that proposition comes to be employed as a premise" (Mill 1872: Book 5, ch. 6, sec. 4).

6. It is interesting to note that Mill's view comes close to the hypothesis offered here. It is true that he describes fallacies of ratiocination as: "those which have their seat in the ratiocinative or deductive part of the investigation of truth" (1872: Book 5, ch. 6, sec. 1).

However, he adds that it is by the rules of the syllogism "that a reasoner is compelled distinctly to make his election what premises he is prepared to maintain. The election made, there is generally so little difficulty in seeing whether the conclusion follows from the premises set out, that we might without much logical impropriety have merged this fourth class of fallacies in the fifth, or Fallacies of Confusion" (1872: Book 5, ch. 6, sec. 3).

The latter class includes: "all those fallacies in which the source of error is not so much a false estimate of the probative force of known evidence, as an indistinct, indefinite, and fluctuating conception of what the evidence is" (1872: Book 5, ch. 7, sec. 1). (This class includes errors involving ambiguity of terms, begging the question, and fallacies of irrelevance.)

7. If it could be established generally that the laws of logic are those of the human mind, this would not be to give the former the status of "mere facts" or to make them relative to particular conditions; rather, it would be to recognize the requiredness in thinking (cf. Köhler 1938: especially 45, 52).

16. OF THE SCHOLLER OF NATURE

1. The data to be reported here were collected when I was a Fellow at the Center for Cognitive Studies, Harvard University. See also Henle 1962.

2. It will be noted that the psychologist's fallacy is not a fallacy in the present sense but, strictly speaking, a methodological error.

3. Cf. Köhler 1938: especially 45, 52. Also Köhler 1971:189–193.

17. ONE MAN AGAINST THE NAZIS—WOLFGANG KÖHLER

1. It should be mentioned that at that time an *Assistent* in a German university already had the Ph.D. but was not yet *habilitiert*, that is, had not yet the so-called right to teach, which was conferred after a second dissertation.

2. The letters lose something in translation. For example, the form of address to the rector was not simply "you," but "your Magnificence."

3. Hans Wallach. Personal communication, September 10, 1973.

19. A TRIBUTE TO MAX WERTHEIMER: THREE STORIES OF THREE DAYS

1. This part of the story is based on Wertheimer's article "Über das Denken der Naturvölker" (1912/1925). Most of the examples used here are his own.

2. Of course Wertheimer could not have read the particular logical sources cited here. But the logician's views expressed here are common among logicians and have been for more than a century.

3. This section of the paper draws on Wertheimer's article "Über Schluss-prozesse im produktiven Denken" (1920/1925). I have relied in part on an unpublished translation of this paper by Richard Skurdall, whose help is gratefully acknowledged.

4. It is likely that our man's analysis of this syllogism is too cautious. It is the minor premise that tells us that Socrates is a man, and only then is his mortality implied in the major. Without the minor, Socrates might be the name of a town, of a dog, or of any number of other things.

20. ROBERT M. OGDEN AND GESTALT PSYCHOLOGY IN AMERICA

1. Ogden Papers. R. M. Ogden to H. S. Langfeld, October 12, 1915.
2. Ogden Papers. K. Koffka to Ogden, December 17, 1921.
3. Ogden Papers. Ogden to Koffka, January 19, 1922.
4. Ogden Papers. Ogden to E. Gamble, January 20, 1922.
5. Ogden Papers. Koffka to Ogden, February 14, 1922.
6. Ogden Papers. Ogden to Koffka, March 9, 1922.
7. Ogden Papers. Ogden to Koffka, April 11, 1922.
8. Ogden Papers. Koffka to Ogden, April 23, 1922.
9. Ogden Papers. S. I. Franz to Ogden, July 31, 1922.
10. Ogden Papers. Koffka to Ogden, February 14, 1922.
11. Ogden Papers. Ogden to Franz, August 2, 1922.
12. Ogden Papers. Ogden to Koffka, August 3, 1922.
13. Ogden Papers. Ogden to Koffka, October 11, 1922.
14. Ogden Papers. Koffka to Ogden, October 28, 1922.
15. Ogden Papers. Ogden to E. B. Titchener, December 12, 1922.

16. Ogden Papers. Titchener to Ogden, December 14, 1922.
17. Ogden Papers. Ogden to Titchener, December 22, 1922.
18. Ogden Papers. Koffka to Ogden, June 2, 1923.
19. Ogden Papers. Ogden to Koffka, February 29, 1924.
20. Ogden Papers. Koffka to Ogden, March 22, 1924.
21. Titchener Papers. Titchener to Ogden, May 13, 1924.
22. Ogden Papers. Ogden to Koffka, May 31, 1923.
23. Ogden Papers. Koffka to Ogden, July 2, 1924.
24. Ogden Papers. Koffka to Ogden, December 5, 1925.
25. Titchener Papers. Titchener to President Lowell, April 19, 1926.
26. Titchener Papers. Titchener to G. S. Hall, October 13, 1922.
27. Titchener Papers. Titchener to E. G. Boring, May 7, 1924.
28. Titchener Papers. Titchener to Gamble, February 26, 1924.
29. Titchener Papers. Titchener to H. Helson, July 8, 1925.
30. Titchener Papers. Titchener to H. C. Warren, October 7, 1925.
31. Titchener Papers. Titchener to Boring, March 4, 1925.
32. Titchener Papers. For example, Titchener to L. N. Wilson, May 16, 1924.
33. Titchener Papers. Titchener to R. W. Sailor, June 8, 1925.
34. Ogden Papers. Titchener to Ogden, May 12, 1925.
35. Ogden Papers. Titchener to Ogden, January 22, 1925.
36. Ogden Papers. Titchener to Ogden, February 13, 1925.
37. Ogden Papers. Ogden to Titchener, February 14, 1925.
38. Ogden Papers. Koffka to Ogden, July 27, 1925.
39. Ogden Papers. S. Wakeman to Ogden, December 15, 1925.
40. Ogden Papers. Wakeman to Ogden, January 12, 1926.
41. Ogden Papers. Ogden to Wakeman, January 26, 1926.
42. Ogden Papers. Koffka to Ogden, April 1, 1927.
43. Ogden Papers. Koffka to Ogden, May 24, 1927.
44. Ogden Papers. Ogden to Boring, September 12, 1927.
45. Ogden Papers. Ogden to M. Wertheimer, February 16, 1928.
46. Ogden Papers. Wertheimer to Ogden, March 18, 1928.
47. Ogden Papers. Ogden to Wertheimer, April 9, 1928.
48. Koffka Papers. Ogden to Koffka, October 15, 1928; November 11, 1928.
49. Koffka Papers. Ogden to Koffka, April 26, 1929.
50. Koffka Papers. Ogden to Koffka, October 15, 1928; November 11, 1928.
51. Ogden Papers. W. Köhler to Ogden, April 16, 1929.
52. Helson Papers. Köhler to Helson, May 16, 1929. Archives of the History of American Psychology, University of Akron.
53. Koffka Papers. Ogden to Koffka, April 13, 1933.
54. Ogden Papers. Koffka to Ogden, April 17, 1933.
55. Koffka Papers. Ogden to Koffka, June 8, 1933.

56. Ibid.
57. Ogden Papers. Koffka to Ogden, June 14, 1933.
58. Koffka Papers. Ogden to Koffka, June 21, 1933.
59. Frank S. Freeman, personal communication, November 17, 1981.
60. Emergency Committee. Deans to President Farrand, June 20, 1933.
61. Emergency Committee. A. R. Mann (provost) to Farrand, July 15, 1933.
62. Emergency Committee. Farrand to Stein (treasurer of the Emergency Committee), September 18, 1934.
63. Ogden Papers. Ogden to S. S. Visher, July 5, 1939.

References

Abt, L. E. 1950. A theory of projective psychology. In L. E. Abt and L. Bellak, eds., *Projective Psychology*. New York: Knopf.

Adrian, E. D. 1962. Creativity in science. *Perspectives in Biology and Medicine* 5:269–274.

Alexander, F. 1932. *The Medical Value of Psychoanalysis*. New York: Norton.

Allport, G. W. 1937. *Personality*. New York: Holt.

Arieti, S. 1948. Special logic of schizophrenic and other types of autistic thought. *Psychiatry* 11:325–338.

Arieti, S. 1955. *Interpretation of Schizophrenia*. New York: Brunner.

Arieti, S. 1963. Studies of thought processes in contemporary psychiatry. *American Journal of Psychiatry* 120:58–64.

Aristotle. *The Basic Works of Aristotle*, R. McKeon, ed. New York: Random House, 1941.

Aristotle. *Movement of Animals*. E. S. Forster, trans. Cambridge, Mass.: Harvard University Press, 1945.

Arnheim, R. 1949. The Gestalt theory of expression. *Psychological Review* 56:156–171.

Arnheim, R. 1969. *Visual Thinking*. Berkeley and Los Angeles: University of California Press.

Arnheim, R. 1974. "Gestalt" misapplied. *Contemporary Psychology* 19:570.

Arnauld, A. 1662. *The Art of Thinking: Port-Royal Logic*. J. Dickoff and P. James, trans. Indianapolis: Bobbs-Merrill (Library of Liberal Arts), 1964.

Asch, S. E. 1948. The doctrine of suggestion, prestige and imitation in social psychology. *Psychological Review* 55:250–276.

Asch, S. E. 1952. *Social Psychology*. New York: Prentice-Hall.

Asch, S. E., J. Ceraso, and W. Heimer. 1960. Perceptual conditions of association. *Psychological Monographs*, vol. 57, no. 3.

Ash, M. G. 1980. Fragments of the whole: Documents of the history of

Gestalt psychology in the United States, the Federal Republic of Germany, and the German Democratic Republic. In J. Brozek and L. J. Pongratz, eds., *Historiography of Modern Psychology.* Toronto: Hogrefe.

Ayer, A. J. 1956. *The Problem of Knowledge.* Harmondsworth: Penguin.

Bandura, A. 1977. *Social Learning Theory.* Englewood Cliffs, N.J.: Prentice-Hall.

Bandura, A. 1982. The psychology of chance encounters and life paths. *American Psychologist* 37:747–755.

Barker, R., T. Dembo, and K. Lewin. 1941. *Frustration and Regression: An Experiment with Young Children.* Iowa City: University of Iowa Press.

Bartlett, F. 1958. *Thinking: An Experimental and Social Study.* London: Allen and Unwin.

Bernard, C. 1927. *An Introduction to the Study of Experimental Medicine.* H. C. Greene, trans. New York: Macmillan.

Berg, J. H. Van den. 1955. *The Phenomenological Approach to Psychiatry.* Springfield, Ill.: Thomas.

Bergmann, G. 1956. The contribution of John B. Watson. *Psychological Review* 63:265–276.

Bonaparte, M., A. Freud, and E. Kris, eds. 1954. *The Origins of Psycho-Analysis. Letters to Wilhelm Fliess, Drafts and Notes: 1887–1902 by Sigmund Freud.* New York: Basic Books.

Boole, G. 1854. *An Investigation of the Laws of Thought.* London: Macmillan.

Boring, E. G. 1929. The psychology of controversy. *Psychological Review* 36:97–121.

Boring, E. G. 1933. *The Physical Dimensions of Consciousness.* New York and London: Century.

Boring, E. G. 1937. Titchener and the existential. *American Journal of Psychology* 50:470–483.

Boring, E. G. 1942. *Sensation and Perception in the History of Experimental Psychology.* New York: Appleton-Century.

Boring, E. G. 1948. The nature of psychology. In E. G. Boring, H. S. Langfeld, and H. P. Weld, eds., *Foundations of Psychology.* New York: Wiley.

Boring, E. G. 1950. *A History of Experimental Psychology.* 2d ed. New York: Appleton-Century-Crofts.

Boring, E. G. 1954. Psychological factors in the scientific process. *American Scientist* 42:639–645.

Boring, E. G. 1955. Dual role of the *Zeitgeist* in scientific creativity. *Scientific Monthly* 80:101–106.

Boring, E. G. 1963. *History, Psychology, and Science: Selected Papers.* R. I. Watson and D. T. Campbell, eds. New York: Wiley.

Boring, E. G. 1969. Titchener, meaning and behaviorism. In D. L. Krantz, ed., *Schools of Psychology: A Symposium.* New York: Appleton-Century-Crofts.

Bowers, K. S. 1973. Situationism in psychology: An analysis and a critique. *Psychological Review* 80:307–336.

Brody, N. and P. Oppenheim. 1967. Methodological differences between behaviorism and phenomenology in psychology. *Psychological Review* 74:330–334.

Bronfenbrenner, U. 1951. Toward an integrated theory of personality. In R. R. Blake and G. V. Ramsey, eds., *Perception: An Approach to Personality*. New York: Ronald Press.

Brown, R. and D. McNeill, 1966. The "tip of the tongue" phenomenon. *Journal of Verbal Learning and Verbal Behavior* 5:325–337.

Bruner, J. S. 1956. Freud and the image of man. *American Psychologist* 11:463–466.

Bruner, J. S., J. J. Goodnow, and G. A. Austin. 1956. *A Study of Thinking*. New York: Wiley.

Calkins, M. W. 1906. A reconciliation between structural and functional psychology. *Psychological Review* 13:61–81.

Calkins, M. W. 1930. Autobiography. In C. Murchison, ed., *A History of Psychology in Autobiography*, 1:31–62. Worcester, Mass.: Clark University Press.

Chapman, L. J. and J. P. Chapman. 1959. Atmosphere effect re-examined. *Journal of Experimental Psychology* 58:220–226.

Cohen, M. R. 1944. *A Preface to Logic*. New York: Holt.

Cohen, M. R. and E. Nagel. 1934. *An Introduction to Logic and Scientific Method*. New York: Harcourt, Brace.

Corwin, G. H. 1921. The involuntary response to pleasantness. *American Journal of Psychology* 32:563–570.

Crannell, C. W. 1970. Wolfgang Köhler. *Journal of the History of the Behavioral Sciences* 6:267–268.

Curtius, L. 1964. *Goethe: Wisdom and Experience*. H. J. Weigand, trans. New York: Ungar.

Dallenbach, K. M. 1959. Robert Morris Ogden: 1877–1959. *American Journal of Psychology* 72:472–477.

De Morgan, A. 1847. *Formal Logic*. London: Taylor and Walton.

Dickstein, L. B. 1981. Conversion and possibility in syllogistic reasoning. *Bulletin of the Psychonomic Society* 18:229–232.

Dollard, J. and N. E. Miller. 1950. *Personality and Psychotherapy*. New York, Toronto, and London: McGraw-Hill.

Duncker, K. 1945. On problem-solving. L. S. Lees, trans. *Psychological Monographs*, vol. 58, no. 5, whole no. 270.

Ekehammar, B. 1974. Interactionism in personality from a historical perspective. *Psychological Bulletin* 81:1026–1048.

Emergency Committee. Papers of the Emergency Committee in Aid of Displaced German Scholars, Accession #3/5/123. Department of Manuscripts and University Archives, Cornell University Libraries.

Eng, E. 1978. Looking back on Kurt Lewin: From field theory to action research. *Journal of the History of the Behavioral Sciences* 14:228–232.

Epstein, W. 1967. *Varieties of Perceptual Experience*. New York: McGraw-Hill.

Fenichel, O. 1945. *The Psychoanalytic Theory of Neurosis*. New York: Norton.

Fraunce, A. 1588. *The Lawiers Logike*. London: William How.

Freeman, F. S. 1977. The beginnings of Gestalt psychology in the United States. *Journal of the History of the Behavioral Sciences* 13:352–353.

Freud, S. *Standard Edition of the Complete Psychological Works of Sigmund Freud*. 24 vols. James Strachey, trans. and ed. London: Hogarth Press, 1953–1974.

    1893. Charcot. *S.E.* 3.

    1895. Project for a Scientific Psychology. *S.E.* 1.

    1893–1895. (Breuer and Freud). *Studies on Hysteria*. *S.E.* 2.

    1900. *The Interpretation of Dreams*. *S.E.* 4–5.

    1901. *The Psychopathology of Everyday Life*. *S.E.* 6.

    1905. Fragment of an analysis of a case of hysteria. *S.E.* 7.

    1905. *Three Essays on the Theory of Sexuality*. *S.E.* 7.

    1905. *Jokes and their Relation to the Unconscious*. *S.E.* 8.

    1911. *Psycho-Analytic Notes on an Autobiographical Account of a Case of Paranoia (Dementia Paranoides)*. *S.E.* 12.

    1911. Formulations on the two principles of mental functioning. *S.E.* 12.

    1913. *Totem and Taboo*. *S.E.* 13.

    1914. The Moses of Michelangelo. *S.E.* 13.

    1915. Repression. *S.E.* 14.

    1915. The unconscious. *S.E.* 14.

    1916–1917. *Introductory Lectures on Psycho-Analysis*. *S.E.* 15–16.

    1920. *Beyond the Pleasure Principle*. *S.E.* 18.

    1920. The psychogenesis of a case of homosexuality in a woman. *S.E.* 18.

    1921. *Group Psychology and the Analysis of the Ego*. *S.E.* 18.

    1922. Some neurotic mechanisms in jealousy, paranoia and homosexuality. *S.E.* 18.

    1923. *The Ego and the Id*. *S.E.* 19.

    1925. A note upon the 'mystic writing pad'. *S.E.* 19.

    1925. Negation. *S.E.* 19.

    1925. *An Autobiographical Study*. *S.E.* 20.

    1926. *Inhibitions, Symptoms and Anxiety*. *S.E.* 20.

    1926. *The Question of Lay Analysis*. *S.E.* 20.

    1929. Dr. Ernest Jones (On his 50th birthday). *S.E.* 21.

    1930. *Civilization and its Discontents*. *S.E.* 21.

    1933. *New Introductory Lectures on Psycho-Analysis*. *S.E.* 22.

    1939. *Moses and Monotheism: Three Essays*. *S.E.* 23.

    1940. *An Outline of Psycho-Analysis*. *S.E.* 23.

    1941. Psycho-analysis and telepathy. *S.E.* 18.

    1941. Findings, ideas, problems. *S.E.* 23.

Getzels, J. and M. Csikszentmihalyi. 1976. *The Creative Vision*. New York: Wiley.

Ghiselin, B., ed. 1955. *The Creative Process*. New York: New American Library. (Originally published Berkeley and Los Angeles: University of California Press, 1952.)

Gibson, J. J. 1967. New reasons for realism. *Synthèse* 17:162–172.

Gibson, J. J. 1967. Autobiography. In E. G. Boring and G. Lindzey, eds., *A History of Psychology in Autobiography*. New York: Appleton-Century-Crofts.

Gibson, J. J. 1971. The legacies of Koffka's *Principles*. *Journal of the History of the Behavioral Sciences* 7:3–9.

Gregory, R. L. 1966. *Eye and Brain*. New York: World University Library, McGraw-Hill.

Gregory, R. L. 1970. *The Intelligent Eye*. New York: McGraw-Hill.

Gregory, R. L. 1973. The confounded eye. In R. L. Gregory and E. H. Gombrich, eds., *Illusion in Nature and Art*. London: Duckworth.

Hall, C. S. and G. Lindzey. 1970. *Theories of Personality*. 2d ed. New York, London, Sydney, and Toronto: Wiley. 3d ed. New York, Santa Barbara, Chichester, Brisbane, and Toronto: Wiley, 1978.

Halpern, J. 1977. Projection: A test of the psychoanalytic hypothesis. *Journal of Abnormal Psychology* 86:536–542.

Hartmann, H. 1964. *Essays on Ego Psychology*. New York: International Universities Press.

Hartshorne, E. Y. 1937. *The German Universities and National Socialism*. Cambridge, Mass.: Harvard University Press.

Harvey, W. 1649. *A Second Disquisition to John Riolan*. R. Willis, trans. In R. M. Hutchins, ed., *Great Books of the Western World*, vol. 28. Chicago, London, and Toronto: Encyclopaedia Britannica, 1952.

Hayes, S. P. 1906. A study of the affective qualities. *American Journal of Psychology* 17:358–393.

Heidbreder, E. 1933. *Seven Psychologies*. New York: Century.

Helmholtz, H. von. 1866. *Treatise on Physiological Optics*. 3 vols. J. P. C. Southall, ed. New York: Dover, 1962. (Originally published 1856–1866; trans. from the 3d German ed, 1909–1911.)

Helmholtz, H. von. 1878. *Selected Writings*. R. Kahl, ed. Middletown, Conn: Wesleyan University Press, 1971.

Henle, J. 1846. *Handbuch der rationellen Pathologie*. Vol. 1. 2d ed. Braunschweig: F. Vieweg.

Henle, M. 1955. Some effects of motivational processes on cognition. *Psychological Review* 62:423–432.

Henle, M. 1957. On field forces. *Journal of Psychology* 43:239–249.

Henle, M. 1957. Some problems of eclecticism. *Psychological Review* 64:296–305. [Ch. 7 of this volume.]

Henle, M., ed. *Documents of Gestalt Psychology*. Berkeley and Los Angeles: University of California Press, 1961.

Henle, M. 1962. On the relation between logic and thinking. *Psychological Review* 69:366–378. [Ch. 15 of this volume.]

Henle, M. 1965. On Gestalt psychology. In B. B. Wolman, ed., *Scientific Psychology*, pp. 276–292. New York: Basic Books.

Henle, M., ed. *The Selected Papers of Wolfgang Köhler*. New York: Liveright, 1971.

Henle, M. 1974. E. B. Titchener and the case of the missing element. *Journal of the History of the Behavioral Sciences* 10:227–237. [Ch. 12 of this volume.]

Henle, M. 1975. Fishing for ideas. *American Psychologist* 30:795–799. [Ch. 13 of this volume.]

Henle, M. 1977. The influence of Gestalt psychology in America. *Annals of the New York Academy of Sciences* 291:3–12. [Ch. 10 of this volume.]

Henle, M. 1978. Gestalt psychology and gestalt therapy. *Journal of the History of the Behavioral Sciences* 14:23–32. [Ch. 3 of this volume.]

Henle, M. 1978. Kurt Lewin as metatheorist. *Journal of the History of the Behavioral Sciences* 14:233–237. [Ch. 6 of this volume.]

Henle, M. 1978. Foreword. In R. Revlin and R. E. Mayer, eds., *Human Reasoning*. New York: Wiley.

Henle, M. 1984. Isomorphism: Setting the record straight. *Psychological Research* 46:317–327.

Henle, M. and M. Michael. 1956. The influence of attitudes on syllogistic reasoning. *Journal of Social Psychology* 44:115–127.

Heywood, R. B., ed. 1947. *The Works of the Mind*. Chicago: University of Chicago Press.

Hilgard, E. R. 1956. *Theories of Learning*. 2d ed. New York: Appleton-Century-Crofts.

Hochberg, J. 1971. Perception. I. Color and shape. In R. S. Woodworth and H. Schlosberg, *Experimental Psychology*. J. W. Kling and L. A. Riggs, eds. 3d ed. New York: Holt, Rinehart and Winston.

Howell, W. S. 1961. *Logic and Rhetoric in England, 1500–1700*. New York: Russell and Russell.

Humphrey, G. 1948. *Directed Thinking*. New York: Dodd, Mead.

Isaacs, N. 1930. Children's "why" questions. In S. Isaacs, *Intellectual Growth in Young Children*. London: Routledge and Kegan Paul.

James, W. 1890. *The Principles of Psychology*. 2 vols. New York: Holt.

Jenkins, J. J. 1974. Remember that old theory of memory? Well, forget it! *American Psychologist* 29:785–795.

Jones, E. 1953–1957. *The Life and Work of Sigmund Freud*. 3 vols. New York: Basic Books.

Jung, C. G. 1938. *Psychology and Religion*. New Haven: Yale University Press. (Reprinted in H. Read et al., eds., *The Collected Works of C. G. Jung*. 20 vols. New York: Pantheon Books, 1953–1979.)

Kant, I. 1885. *Introduction to Logic and Essay on the Mistaken Subtilty of the Four Figures*. T. K. Abbott, trans. London: Longman Green.

Katona, G. 1940. *Organizing and Memorizing*. New York: Columbia University Press.

Kaufman, L. 1974. *Sight and Mind: An Introduction to Visual Perception*. New York: Oxford University Press.

Keynes, J. N. 1887. *Studies and Exercises in Formal Logic*. 2d ed. London: Macmillan.

Koch, S. 1971. Reflections on the state of psychology. *Social Research* 38:669–709.

Koffka, K. 1922. Perception: An introduction to the Gestalt-Theorie. *Psychological Bulletin* 19:531–585.

Koffka, K. 1924. *The Growth of the Mind*. R. W. Ogden, trans. London: Kegan Paul, Trench, Trubner.

Koffka, K. 1935. *Principles of Gestalt Psychology*. New York: Harcourt, Brace.

Koffka, K. 1938. Purpose and Gestalt: A reply to Professor McDougall. *Character and Personality* 6:218–238.

Koffka, K. 1940. Problems in the psychology of art. In R. Bernheimer, R. Carpenter, K. Koffka, and M. C. Nahm, *Art: A Bryn Mawr Symposium*. Bryn Mawr Notes and Monographs, no. 9. Bryn Mawr, Pa.: Bryn Mawr College.

Koffka Papers. Archives of the History of American Psychology, University of Akron.

Köhler, W. 1913. On unnoticed sensations and errors of judgment. In M. Henle, ed., *The Selected Papers of Wolfgang Köhler*, 1971. (Translated and reprinted from *Zeitschrift für Psychologie* 66:51–80.)

Köhler, W. 1920. *Die physischen Gestalten in Ruhe und im stationären Zustand*. Braunschweig: F. Vieweg.

Köhler, W. 1921. Methods of psychological research with apes. In M. Henle, ed., *The Selected Papers of Wolfgang Köhler*, 1971. (Translated and reprinted from E. Abderhalden, ed., *Handbuch der biologischen Arbeitsmethoden*, sec. 6, part D, pp. 69–120.)

Köhler, W. 1925. *The Mentality of Apes*. E. Winter, trans. New York: Harcourt, Brace. (Originally published 1917.)

Köhler, W. 1929. An old pseudoproblem. In M. Henle, ed., *The Selected Papers of Wolfgang Köhler*, 1971. (Translated and reprinted from *Die Naturwissenschaften* 17:395–401.)

Köhler, W. 1929. *Gestalt Psychology*. New York: Liveright.

Köhler, W. 1930. The nature of intelligence. In M. Henle, ed., *The Selected Papers of Wolfgang Köhler*, 1971. (Translated and reprinted from A. Keller, ed., *Kind und Umwelt, Anlage und Erziehung*, pp. 132–146. Leipzig und Wien: Deuticke.)

Köhler, W. 1930. The new psychology and physics. *Yale Review* 19:560–576. (Reprinted in M. Henle, ed., *The Selected Papers of Wolfgang Köhler*, 1971.)

Köhler, W. 1937. Psychological remarks on some questions of anthropology. *American Journal of Psychology* 50:271–288.

Köhler, W. 1938. *The Place of Value in a World of Facts.* New York: Liveright.

Köhler, W. 1940. *Dynamics in Psychology.* New York: Liveright.

Köhler, W. 1941. On the nature of associations. *Proceedings of the American Philosophical Society* 84:489–502.

Köhler, W. 1943. A perspective on American psychology. *Psychological Review* 50:77–79.

Köhler, W. 1947. *Gestalt Psychology.* Rev. ed. New York: Liveright.

Köhler, W. 1950. Psychology and evolution. *Acta Psychologica* 7:288–297.

Köhler, W. 1953. The scientists from Europe and their new environment. In W. R. Crawford, ed., *The Cultural Migration.* Philadelphia: University of Pennsylvania Press.

Köhler, W. 1958. The present situation in brain physiology. *American Psychologist* 13:150–154.

Köhler, W. 1959. Psychology and natural science. In M. Henle, ed., *The Selected Papers of Wolfgang Köhler,* 1971. (Translated and reprinted from *Proceedings of the 15th International Congress of Psychology, Brussels, 1957,* pp. 37–50. Amsterdam: North-Holland.)

Köhler, W. 1965. Unsolved problems in the field of figural aftereffects. *Psychological Record* 15:63–83.

Köhler, W. 1966. A task for philosophers. In P. K. Feyerabend and G. Maxwell, eds., *Mind, Matter, and Method: Essays in Philosophy and Science in Honor of Herbert Feigl,* pp. 70–91. Minneapolis: University of Minnesota Press.

Köhler, W. 1969. *The Task of Gestalt Psychology.* Princeton, N.J.: Princeton University Press.

Köhler, W. n.d. Peace and education. Lecture given during World War II. In the Library of the American Philosophical Society, Philadelphia.

Kopp, S. 1960. "Deductive Reasoning in Paranoid Schizophrenics." Ph.D. dissertation, New School for Social Research.

Krantz, D. L. 1969. The Baldwin-Titchener controversy. In D. L. Krantz, ed., *Schools of Psychology,* pp. 1–19. New York: Appleton-Century-Crofts.

Krantz, D. L. and D. Allen. 1967. The rise and fall of McDougall's instinct doctrine. *Journal of the History of the Behavioral Sciences* 3:326–338.

Kuhn, T. S. 1962. *The Structure of Scientific Revolutions.* Chicago: University of Chicago Press.

Langer, S. K. 1953. *An Introduction to Symbolic Logic.* 2d rev. ed. New York: Dover. (Originally published 1937.)

Larson, C. A. and J. J. Sullivan. 1965. Watson's relation to Titchener. *Journal of the History of the Behavioral Sciences* 1:338–354.

Leeper, R. W. 1943. *Lewin's Topological and Vector Psychology: A Digest and a Critique.* Eugene: University of Oregon.

Lefford, A. 1946. The influence of emotional subject matter on logical reasoning. *Journal of General Psychology* 34:127–151.

Leithäuser, J. G. 1955. *Worlds Beyond the Horizon*. H. Merrick, trans. New York: Knopf.

Lewin, K. 1935. *A Dynamic Theory of Personality*. D. K. Adams and K. E. Zener, trans. New York: McGraw-Hill.

Lewin, K. 1936. *Principles of Topological Psychology*. F. Heider and G. M. Heider, trans. New York: McGraw-Hill.

Lewin, K. 1938. *The Conceptual Representation and the Measurement of Psychological Forces*. Durham, N.C.: Duke University Press.

Lewin, K. 1943. Foreword. In R. W. Leeper, *Lewin's Topological and Vector Psychology: A Digest and a Critique*. Eugene: University of Oregon.

Lewin, K. 1951. *Field Theory in Social Science*. D. Cartwright, ed. New York: Harper.

Major, D. R. 1895. On the affective tone of simple sense impressions. *American Journal of Psychology* 7:57–77.

Mandler, J. M. and G. Mandler. 1968. The diaspora of experimental psychology: The Gestaltists and others. *Perspectives in American History* 2:371–419.

Marrow, A. J. 1969. *The Practical Theorist: The Life and Work of Kurt Lewin*. New York: Basic Books.

Meyer, D. E. 1980. "Some/Is: An Investigation of Logical Thinking." Ph.D. dissertation, New School for Social Research.

Mill, J. S. 1872. *A System of Logic*. 8th ed. London: Longman's.

Morgan, J. J. B. and J. T. Morton. 1944. The distortion of syllogistic reasoning produced by personal convictions. *Journal of Social Psychology* 20:39–59.

Nafe, J. P. 1924. An experimental study of the affective qualities. *American Journal of Psychology* 35:507–544.

Nafe, J. P. 1927. The psychology of felt experience. *American Journal of Psychology* 39:367–389.

Nagel, E. 1956. *Logic Without Metaphysics*. Glencoe, Ill.: Free Press.

Nakashima, T. 1909. Contributions to the study of the affective processes. *American Journal of Psychology* 20:157–193.

Nakashima, T. 1909. Time-relations of the affective processes. *Psychological Review* 16:303–339.

Ogden, R. M. 1924. *Hearing*. New York: Harcourt, Brace.

Ogden, R. M. 1926. *Psychology and Education*. New York: Harcourt, Brace.

Ogden Papers. Robert Morris Ogden Papers, Accession #14/23/467. Department of Manuscripts and University Archives, Cornell University Libraries.

Owen, R. M. 1982. "An Inquiry Into the Creative Process: Visual Artists Speak." Ph.D. dissertation, New School for Social Research.

Perls, F. S. 1947/1969. *Ego, Hunger and Aggression*. New York: Vintage Books.

Perls, F. S. 1969/1971. *Gestalt Therapy Verbatim*. Toronto, New York, and London: Bantam Books.

Perls, F. S. 1969/1972. *In and Out the Garbage Pail*. Toronto, New York, and London: Bantam Books.

Perls, F. S. 1970/1973. Four lectures. In J. Fagan and I. L. Shepherd, eds., *What Is Gestalt Therapy?* New York: Perennial Books.

Perls, F. S. 1973. *The Gestalt Approach and Eye Witness to Therapy*. Ben Lomond, Calif.: Science and Behavior Books.

Perls, F. S., R. E. Hefferline, and P. Goodman. 1951/n.d. *Gestalt Therapy*. New York: Dell.

Planck, M. 1949. *Scientific Autobiography and Other Papers*. F. Gaynor, trans. New York: Philosophical Library.

Plato. *Plato's Theaetetus*. F. M. Cornford, ed. New York: Liberal Arts Press, 1959.

Poincaré, H. 1952. *Science and Method*. F. Maitland, trans. New York: Dover.

Polanyi, M. 1958. *Personal Knowledge*. Chicago: University of Chicago Press.

Pylyshyn, Z. W. 1980. Computation and cognition: Issues in the foundation of cognitive science. *The Behavioral and Brain Sciences* 3:111–132.

Rapoport, A. 1967. Escape from paradox. *Scientific American* 217:50–56.

Reichenbach, H. 1966. *Elements of Symbolic Logic*. New York: Free Press. (Originally published 1947.)

Revlin, R. and V. O. Leirer. 1980. Understanding quantified categorical expressions. *Memory and Cognition* 8:447–458.

Richter, M. N., Jr. 1957. The theoretical interpretation of errors in syllogistic reasoning. *Journal of Psychology* 43:341–344.

Rock, I. 1975. *An Introduction to Perception*. New York: Macmillan.

Roese, K. and W. S. Foster. 1916. The tridimensional theory of feeling from the standpoint of typical experiences. *American Journal of Psychology* 27:157–170.

Rorschach, H. 1942. *Psychodiagnostics*. Berne: Hans Huber.

Russell, B. 1904. The axiom of infinity. *Hibbert Journal* 2:809–812.

Russell, B. 1940. *An Inquiry Into Meaning and Truth*. New York: Norton.

Schiller, F. C. S. 1930. *Logic for Use*. New York: Harcourt, Brace.

Schwartz, G. and P. W. Bishop, eds. 1958. *Moments of Discovery*. 2 vols. New York: Basic Books.

Shepard, M. 1975. *Fritz*. New York: Saturday Review Press.

Skinner, B. F. 1972. *Cumulative Record: A Selection of Papers*. 3d ed. New York: Appleton-Century-Crofts.

Skinner, B. F. 1974. *About Behaviorism*. New York: Knopf.

Spinoza, B. *Spinoza: Selections*. J. Wild, ed. New York: Scribner's, 1930.

Stephens, J. 1920. *Irish Fairy Tales*. New York: Macmillan.

Summerfield, J. D. and L. Thatcher, eds. 1964. *The Creative Mind and Method*. New York: Russell and Russell.

Szent-Györgyi, A. 1962. On scientific creativity. *Perspectives in Biology and Medicine* 5:173–178.

Taylor, C. R. 1969. The eland and the oryx. *Scientific American* 220:88–95.

Titchener, E. B. 1895. Simple reactions. *Mind* 4:74–81.

Titchener, E. B. 1896. The "type-theory" of the simple reaction. *Mind* 5:236–241.

Titchener, E. B. 1896. *An Outline of Psychology*. New York: Macmillan. (2d ed. 1898.)

Titchener, E. B. 1898. The postulates of a structural psychology. *Philosophical Review* 7:449–465.

Titchener, E. B. 1901. *Experimental Psychology*. Vol. 1. New York: Macmillan.

Titchener, E. B. 1908. *Lectures on the Elementary Psychology of Feeling and Attention*. New York: Macmillan.

Titchener, E. B. 1910. *A Text-book of Psychology*. New York: Macmillan.

Titchener, E. B. 1914. On "Psychology as the Behaviorist Views It." *Proceedings of the American Philosophical Society* 53:1–17.

Titchener, E. B. 1915. *A Beginner's Psychology*. New York: Macmillan.

Titchener, E. B. 1917. The psychological concept of clearness. *Psychological Review* 24:43–61.

Titchener, E. B. 1917. Professor Stumpf's affective psychology. *American Journal of Psychology* 28:263–277.

Titchener, E. B. 1923. The expression of simple feeling. *American Journal of Psychology* 34:149.

Titchener, E. B. 1924. The term 'attensity.' *American Journal of Psychology* 35:156.

Titchener, E. B. 1929. *Systematic Psychology: Prolegomena*. New York: Macmillan.

Titchener Papers. Edward Bradford Titchener Papers, Accession #14/23/545. Department of Manuscripts and University Archives, Cornell University Libraries.

Von Domarus, E. 1944. The specific laws of logic in schizophrenia. In J. S. Kasanin, ed., *Language and Thought in Schizophrenia*, pp. 104–113. Berkeley and Los Angeles: University of California Press.

Welch, L. 1948. An integration of some fundamental principles of modern behaviorism and Gestalt psychology. *Journal of General Psychology* 39:175–190.

Wertheimer, M. 1912. Über das Denken der Naturvölker. I. Zahlen und Zahlgebilde. *Zeitschrift für Psychologie* 60:321–378. (Translation in D. N. Robinson, ed., *Significant Contributions to the History of Psychology. Series A. Orientations*, vol. 11. Washington, D.C.: University Publications of America, 1977.)

Wertheimer, M. 1912. Experimentelle Studien über das Sehen von Bewegung. *Zeitschrift für Psychologie* 61:161–265. (Translation in T. Shipley, ed., *Classics in Psychology*. New York: Philosophical Library, 1961.)

Wertheimer, M. 1923. Untersuchungen zur Lehre von der Gestalt: II. *Psychologische Forschung* 4:301–350. (Abridged translation in W. D.

Ellis, ed., *A Source Book of Gestalt Psychology*, pp. 71–88. London: Kegan Paul, Trench, Trubner.)

Wertheimer, M. Über Schlussprozesse im produktiven Denken. In M. Wertheimer, ed., *Drei Abhandlungen zur Gestalttheorie*. Erlangen: Philosophische Akademie. Originally published as a separate. Berlin: DeGruyter, 1920. (Abridged translation in W. D. Ellis, ed., *A Source Book of Gestalt Psychology*, pp. 274–282.)

Wertheimer, M. 1934. On truth. *Social Research*, 1:135–146. (Reprinted in M. Henle, ed., *Documents of Gestalt Psychology*, 1961.)

Wertheimer, M. 1935. Some problems in the theory of ethics. *Social Research* 2:353–367. (Reprinted in M. Henle, ed., *Documents of Gestalt Psychology*, 1961.)

Wertheimer, M. 1940. A story of three days. In R. N. Anshen, ed., *Freedom: Its Meaning*. New York: Harcourt, Brace. (Reprinted in M. Henle, ed., *Documents of Gestalt Psychology*, 1961.)

Wertheimer, M. 1959. *Productive Thinking*. Enl. ed. Michael Wertheimer, ed. New York: Harper. (Originally published 1945.)

Witkin, H. A., H. B. Lewis, M. Hertzman, K. Machover, P. B. Meissner, and S. Wapner. 1954. *Personality Through Perception*. New York: Harper.

Woodworth, R. S. 1938. *Experimental Psychology*. New York: Holt.

Woodworth, R. S. 1947. Reenforcement of perception. *American Journal of Psychology* 60:119–124.

Woodworth, R. S. 1948. *Contemporary Schools of Psychology*. Rev. ed. New York: Ronald Press.

Woodworth, R. S. and D. G. Marquis. 1947. *Psychology*. 5th ed. New York: Holt.

Woodworth, R. S. and H. Schlosberg. 1954. *Experimental Psychology*. Rev. ed. New York: Holt.

Young, P. T. 1918. An experimental study of mixed feelings. *American Journal of Psychology* 29:237–271.

Young, P. T. 1918. The localization of feeling. *American Journal of Psychology* 29:420–430.

Young, P. T. 1921. Pleasantness and unpleasantness in relation to organic response. *American Journal of Psychology* 32:38–53.

Young, P. T. 1922. Movements of pursuit and avoidance as expressions of simple feeling. *American Journal of Psychology* 33:511–525.

Index

Mary Henle's many years of research have earned her a loyal following and a reputation as an original and significant contributor to concepts of modern psychology. In her latest book she analyzes theories of psychology, rather than simply presenting them, and invites her readers—psychologists and students alike—to read these accepted ideas more closely and critically.

1879 and All That argues that psychologists should think more clearly about the concepts, assumptions, and even the words they use. Largely from the vantage point of Gestalt psychology, her own specialty, Henle analyzes examples both from the recent history of psychology and from contemporary developments. She addresses a number of themes, including the need to recognize that labeling a problem is not the same as solving it; the need to analyze an author's assumptions in order to understand the author; and the need to consult primary sources instead of relying on secondary materials.

The goal throughout is to take the student and psychologist beyond the passive reading of psychology history and theory, in which one simply learns what significant figures have said, and to start them on a much more adventurous and exciting path of problem solving and analysis.